Fire Stories

Fire Stories

Paul Hashagen

Fire Books New York 2024

© 2024 by Paul Hashagen

Published by Fire Books New York
70 Division Ave.
Massapequa, NY 11758

First Edition

Softcover: 978-1-938394-87-4

Library of Congress Control Number: 2024903722

Printed in the United States of America

Cover photo: December 20, 1909, A high-pressure hose wagon and water tower battle a stubborn fire in a 7-story loft building on West 14th Street in Manhattan. The blaze required 2 alarms and 3 hours to extinguish. Photo from author's collection.

*To my wonderful daughters
Jessica and Elizabeth*

Also by Paul Hashagen

Historical Fiction
The Twelfth Hour
2008

The Fire of God
2010

Young Heroes
2020

Non-Fiction
100 Years of Valor Rescue Company 1 NYC Fire Dept.
MT Publishing Company 2015

A Distant Fire
DMC Associates 1995

Stories of Fire
Fire Books New York 2017

Fire Rescue — The History of Rescue 1 FDNY
Fire Apparatus Journal 1989

The Firehouses of the Fire Department of the City of New York
MT Publishing Company 2014 (with Larry Woodcock)

The Bravest — The Official History of the FDNY
Turner Publishing 2000 & 2002

Cartoon Books
Hot Flashes
Firehouse Books 1987

Rescue Crew
Fire Books New York 2018

The Big Book of Firefighting Dinosaurs
Fire Books New York 2020

More Hot Flashes Vol. 1 & 2
Fire Books New York 2021

Contents

Introduction	ix
Foreword	xiv
Part 1	1
Samuel Banta	3
Andrew B. Sweet	10
Thomas Lally	13
Henry W. McAdam	25
George L. Ross	31
Every Picture Tells a Story, or Two – Thomas Kain	38
John Francis O'Hara	40
Thomas J. Ahearn	47
George J. Fox	55
Charles E. Field	58
Luke Flanagan	61
Lines & Lions	67
Part 2	69
Steamers & Engineers	71
Chief's Drivers & Aides	85
John Rush	91
Charles W. Rankin	99
Luke E. Henry	108
Daniel Healy	112
Part 3	161
The Parker Building Fire	163
The High Pressure Hydrant System	170
Three Corner Night	181
First Motorized FDNY Apparatus	187
Going Electric	189
1911	192
James D. Halloran	201
The Millionaire Buff	204
Edward J. Worth	217
David J. Oliver	226
Frank C. Clark	235
James Smith	243
Louis Tischler	249

John C. Conners	253
John Kistenberger	261
William A. Dorritie	268
Richard J. Donovan	276
Three Tough Months	280
Fireground Medical Care	290
Acknowledgments	305
Glossary	307
About the Author	311

Introduction

The sun was just climbing over the skyscrapers, early on the morning of December 5, 1991. It was the tail end of a night tour, and we were returning from a run to the East side just off 42nd Street. As we arrived at the scene, we heard reports on our portable radios that the "odor of smoke" was a minor rubbish fire in the base of the elevator. The chief released us, and the second due units. I swung the big rescue rig around and started back toward quarters with Lt. Patty Brown in the seat next to me. Man, I loved working with Patty Brown. We always seemed to get work when Patty was around, and not just work, but challenging work. In our job, the guys that always seemed to miss the tough fires were known as "White Clouds." For me, Patty was a "Black Cloud," heck sometimes it seemed like a tornado!

So, we are heading back to our firehouse on 43rd Street between Tenth and Eleventh avenues when the dispatcher tells us to respond to 251 West 42nd Street. That was only a few short blocks ahead of our present location. We'd be first in by a long shot! Approaching the address I slowed, scanning the buildings to my right, the north side of the street, for any sign of a fire. Nothing was showing.

One unusual thing did strike me though: nobody was moving on the double-wide sidewalk. We slowed to a roll and looked closely at the various stores. One man seemed to understand our plight and made a very simple move: he stepped over and opened the front door of one of the stores. Thick, dirty brown smoke pumped out for a second, then stopped as the door swung closed. We nodded at him; fire located! Patty calmly picked up the radio and transmitted a 10-75 signal for a working fire.

I gave the guys a few moments to climb out the rear doors with their tools before I parked the rig up the block a bit to clear the front of the building. It must be noted this was 42nd Street as it was before the Mouse moved in, before Disney arrived and the block changed. This was the old version of the street: dirty movies, "live sex shows, co-ed models working their way through college" (or so the signs claimed), and all sorts of seedy enterprises. The members of Rescue 1 ducked into the front door of the fire store, an X-Rated video store. They searched for the seat of the fire as Engine 1 pulled up and took a hydrant. Two more engines, two ladder companies, and the chief of the Ninth Battalion were also racing to the scene.

I moved inside and located Patty Brown, who with Kevin Shea had just found the stairs to the basement. We started down the rickety wooden stairs as heavy smoke pumped upwards around us like a freight train's smokestack. Reaching the bottom of the stairs we were beneath the smoke level and visibility was good. We could clearly see we were in a very dangerous position. The basement had an advanced fire roaring in the rear, and the entire cellar around us was packed with cardboard boxes from floor to ceiling. A few boxes had already fallen into the narrow aisles. As the last man down the tight stairs, I said I'd go get the engine and lead them down to the fire.

At the street level, I located the nozzle team and as I was directing them toward the stairs, the crew from the basement came tumbling back up the steps. They reassembled near the door. "It's getting bad down there," Patty said, slightly understated, as we then tried several times, unsuccessfully, to get the line into the raging basement. I crawled to the sidewalk

Introduction xi

and started trying to break the front wall just below the store windows. I knew this area was usually left wide open during construction and would give the cellar a good vent. It worked a little, but this fire was off to the races. Flames were filling the basement and creeping upwards through every pipe chase and void inside the large six-story commercial building.

Pushed back to the street we reported to the chief and explained the situation. The chief and Patty conferred briefly before I was sent to get the pavement breaker. Wow! I thought — real rescue work. We set up the generator on the sidewalk and plunged into the basement of Exposure 4. We spent the next half hour or so chipping away at the mortar and bricks of this building's cellar wall and the adjoining wall of the fire building. It was hard work, the heavy tool dangled from a small portable ladder we'd angled against the wall, the mortar chipping away slowly. The smoke was horrible even in this building, but we believed we were making progress.

Finally, the last couple of bricks dropped away and we could see fire. It was like looking into a furnace. Deep red and orange flames swirled just beyond the opening. A hose was brought in and just as the nozzle was opened, our radios gave us the order to leave the building. "What the f—" I thought. We'd busted our butts for a half hour and NOW we're getting pulled out?

Damn!

I heaved the hammer up onto my shoulder and trudged back toward the front of the cellar and climbed the stairs to the ground floor. On the ground floor, the smoke inside the exposure building was so thick I almost stopped to mask up. The cloud of smoke remained as I walked out the front door, across the double-wide sidewalk, past a parking meter, stepped off the curb and walked out to the middle of 42nd Street (one of the 15 major crosstown streets that are 100 feet wide!). Right at the double yellow line in the middle of the street, I finally stepped into clear air and turned around.

"Holy shit!" I mumbled looking back at the blazing six-story building, now being attacked by several tower ladders, as thick, nasty smoke pumped from every window. My mind switched from: Why are you pulling us out? To: Why did you leave us in there so long?

It was a tough fight, but one that we'd lose.

I watched in exhausted fascination as tower ladders did their modern hydraulic dance. Huge telescoping booms lifted a basket with two firefighters operating a large high caliber nozzle called a *Stang*. The operator could direct this strong stream of water with pinpoint accuracy into the blazing building. Being a student of fire history, I knew this was a classic New York City multiple alarm. Back in the old days these tower ladders would have been water towers, huge erector set-like metal masts that resembled oil well rigs to some degree. They delivered a large amount of water but were somewhat limited compared to our modern equipment, but the tactic was old—surround and drown.

And so, it goes…

As I was writing this book something in the news caught my attention. On the morning of January 9, 2022, a deadly fire broke out in a high-rise residential building in the Bronx. This deadly blaze took the lives of 17 people. It also left more than 30 with life-threatening smoke-related injuries. As news reports from the fire scene unfolded live on television, I heard a reporter say that many of the smoke inhalation victims were receiving specialized medical treatment including an antidote. My ears perked up. An antidote for smoke inhalation? I'd never heard of such a thing. My research shifted from fire horses and high-pressure hydrants to something much more modern. I've added the results of this research to the last section of this book, Fire Ground Medical Care. It's not often you get to write about fire history as it happens.

    Paul Hashagen
    Massapequa, NY

Foreword

My interest in fire history has only grown since my earliest days in the fire service. Starting as a young volunteer in Freeport and continuing as a probationary fireman in the New York City Fire Department, I wondered about the men and the equipment they used in my grandfather's era. He worked at the turn of the twentieth century, when fire departments across the country were changing from horse-drawn to motorized apparatus. They were battling fires in rubber coats and leather helmets. Gloves were rarely if ever used, and breathing protection was limited to a few smoke helmets that were also rarely used.

I wondered about the earliest motorized rigs: some were battery powered, others were gasoline powered. How did they work? How fast did they go? How fast did the horses they were replacing go? It's like a huge puzzle and finding the correct pieces is often difficult. But that is the "fun" of historical research. Back in the late 1980s when I began my writing career, I would travel to my local library and go through old newspapers that were stored on microfilm. Now I can surf the internet and find old newspapers, magazines and books readily available. It's gotten a bit easier if you know where to look.

This book, like *A Distant Fire* before it, is filled with stories of courage, daring and invention, of firefighters trying to keep up with the constantly changing and ever more dangerous buildings they were sworn to protect. Structural steel allowed buildings to soar to dizzying heights, while the wooden aerial ladders still struggled to reach the eighth floor. The storing of new and exotic chemicals and the recent reliance on gasoline as automobile and truck fuel, posed serious problems that had to be dealt with, often with dangerous and deadly results.

While it's fun to find out about the first chief's cars, my real interest is the people who drove them. The chiefs and their drivers, the company officers, the salty senior men and the new recruits. The new tools and new ideas. The solutions to difficult fire and rescue problems. The daily grind of firemen who worked ridiculously long hours with limited equipment and somehow accomplished their missions.

The Roll of Merit is often mentioned in this book. This method of recording and rewarding lifesaving acts of valor, like all human endeavors, was and is imperfect. But it's really the only written legacy that we have left. Those who struggled pulling hoses, breaking windows, pumping engines, and throwing ladders did so with little or no specific mention in fire reports or newspaper stories. Even though they too risked their lives frequently, the average fireman got little or no fanfare. What they did get and cherished dearly was the respect of their peers. Then and now the greatest testament was to be known as "a good fireman." Nice guys are a dime a dozen, but most of them can't make it down a smoky hallway.

I use the term "fireman" in this book. That was the term they used, the name they called themselves. In modern times we changed it to be more inclusive. Fireman and Firefighter—I was proud to be both.

I hope you enjoy these stories of heroic battles, amazing careers, and new-fangled apparatus. Stories of men and machines, and a world of fighting fires—a world that is constantly changing. Sit back and enjoy smoke and flames from the past.

— Part 1 —

Samuel Banta

On January 22, 1883, Samuel Banta joined the New York City Fire Department. Prior to his appointment, the New Jersey-born Banta, who was said to be endowed with Herculean strength, spent his early life traveling the world. His gift with languages helped him in his various roles as he worked as a Russian spy and courier in Afghanistan, where he travelled about the country, dressed as a native while bearing dispatches and other information. He was also in the Russo-Turkish war, in the Zulu war, and in the Transvaal war. He spoke all the Eastern and many of the African languages. It was said his services were also sought to lead one of the recent African exploring expeditions.

After 24 years of travelling, he settled down in New York City to care for his aged mother. He started his fire career working in the new three-story iron, stone, and red brick firehouse built for Hook & Ladder 9 at 209 Elizabeth Street in lower Manhattan. This new building, designed by Napoleon LeBrun & Son, the famous FDNY architects, featured a new fire service innovation—brass sliding poles—the first in the city.

At about 1:45 a.m. on April 24, 1884, fire companies rolled to a reported fire on Pell Street in Manhattan. They were faced with a very dense smoke condition that made fighting the fire extremely difficult. Things were dangerous even outside the fire building. Shortly after starting operations, Assistant Foreman John McDermott of Engine Company 17 was moving through dense smoke, and accidentally walked off the roof of a one-story building in the rear of number 20. He broke his thigh and was taken to New York Hospital. A few minutes later, Foreman Isaac Fisher of Engine 11 had a similar accident, but escaped with only a sprained ankle.

Meanwhile, companies were operating in the adjacent building, the location of the fire, at No. 22 Pell Street. The main body of fire was burning up through the center of the building. Two members of Engine Company 11, Firemen David Soden and W.B. Kirchner, were working on the third floor directing their nozzle toward the blaze. Kirchner had just steadied himself near a windowsill when the floor gave way. David Soden immediately went down with the collapse. Kirchner was dangling from the sill, as Soden plummeted headfirst. He landed hard and was pinned down across his left shoulder and legs by an iron steam pipe, burning timbers and debris.

A hose stream was immediately directed onto the trapped firefighter. Chiefs Wilhelm and Gicquel rallied their men. Soden's position was desperate; all about him loose timbers threatened to tumble down on him. The trapped man was not visible beneath the fiery debris, but his cries could be clearly heard.

Despite only being a second-grade fireman, Sam Banta of Hook & Ladder 9 took action. He grabbed a saw, a crowbar and some rope and despite warnings from other firefighters, Banta moved down into the collapse. He stopped to tie ropes around various beams, then handed the ropes up so men could stabilize the weight as he cut away other timber and removed pieces of debris.

Assistant Foreman John Murphy of Ladder 6 moved down as close as he could with his lantern to provide light for Banta. Working as quickly as safety would allow, Banta uncovered Soden's head. The imprisoned man's pleas were heartrending. "Hurry up boys, I'm dying! Get me out, for God's sake," he uttered in a smoke-choked voice.

Banta continued cutting and clearing. A doctor was brought close. He soaked some brandy into a sponge, then directed Banta to give it to Soden. The delicate cutting continued. From time-to-time hose streams poured down on Banta and Soden, protecting them from the nearby flames.

It was about 3:45 a.m., an hour and a half since the collapse occurred, when Banta made the final cuts. Fireman David Soden was freed. Ropes were gently placed around the injured man, and he was carefully pulled up. Moments later, Sam Banta was helped up. Soaking wet, his eyes bloodshot and his voice rasping from the smoke, he took a sip of water. He was congratulated by the chiefs, officers and firemen alike.

The name Samuel Banta was placed on the Roll of Merit for his bravery. It would not be the last time.

On July 1, 1885, Samuel Banta was promoted to Assistant Foreman (lieutenant) and assigned to Hook & Ladder Company No. 10 at 191 Fulton Street in Manhattan. In 1887 Captain John Binns (now famous because of his daring scaling ladder rescue in 1884,) was given command of H&L 10 and Sam Banta was his lieutenant.

Sam Banta's next outstanding rescue effort was on January 22, 1887, when downtown companies were operating at a cellar fire at 84 Park Row. While directing his company's nozzle on the stairs leading to the basement, Fireman Francis Quinn of Engine 29 was overcome by the heat and smoke and fell headlong into the cellar. Sam Banta, now a lieutenant in Hook & Ladder 10, Fireman William Harrigan of Ladder 10 and Fireman James Rehill of Hook & Ladder 8 immediately attempted to descend into the cellar and bring up Quinn. Despite their valiant attempts they were driven back by the smoke and flames. Under the cover of two streams of water Banta again descended and saw Quinn floating face-down in the accumulating water in the cellar. Banta plunged into the water and grabbed the unconscious man. Holding his head above water Banta saw the preliminary signs of a backdraft bearing down on him. Banta dove underwater and pulled the limp fireman with him. He hoped they could remain underwater until the backdraft ended. Checking the air above, Banta held a hand up and was burned. Waiting a few more moments for the flames to pass he surfaced and towed Quinn back to the ladder.

There were no windows or openings in the rear wall for the escape of flames and smoke. This made exiting through the front extremely perilous. Despite the extreme conditions Lt. Banta carried his comrade to safety. But Fireman Quinn had suffered too much between the fire and the flooded cellar and could not be revived. The prompt and courageous actions of Lt. Banta and Firemen Rehill and Harrigan, allowed Fireman Quinn a chance at being rescued. All three members were placed on the Roll of Merit.

On May 26, 1889, the FDNY held a huge parade and exhibition in Union Square. Part of this festive event was the awarding of medals. Lt. Samuel Banta was awarded the Bennett Medal for his daring rescue of Fr. Quinn two years earlier.

It would be Lt. Banta leading the charge once again when FDNY units battled a cellar fire at 163 Chambers Street on May 6, 1897. The fire was in a five-story brick and stone building being used as a paper warehouse. Across the street from the fire building were the quarters of Engine 29, a double company. Many companies in this era were double companies, that is two completely outfitted units that shared the same firehouse and took turns responding to alarms.

The first section of Engine 29 responded to a report of a fire several blocks away. The second section moved up awaiting their turn to go to work. When a second alarm was transmitted for the first address, Lt. McGrath turned out the second section to respond to the nearby fire. Rolling out of the firehouse they were met with a blast of hot, choking smoke chugging from the basement of the building directly across the street. McGrath sent a man back to transmit this new alarm, which would send Engines 27, 7 and Hook & Ladder 7 to this new fire scene. These units arrived quickly and joined Engine 29 in the battle.

While 29 pushed the first hose line into the first floor, members of Hook & Ladder 7 broke into the sidewalk vaults and placed a ladder so Engine 7 could stretch into the basement. (Sidewalk vaults were building openings that extended past the property line and facilitated coal and other deliveries directly into the basement. These areas also afforded the firefighters an excellent point of ventilation during basement fires.) This second hose line could only move in 15 or 20 feet or so due to the noxious nature of the smoke. Nozzle teams inched forward and rotated their men on the hose as they advanced.

The ongoing battle was about an hour old when Capt. Kenny of Engine 7, and his men Firemen Reinhardt, Holahan, Keely, Horick and Lt. Cunningham, faced a blast of heat and smoke that pushed them back toward the ladder. It was clear to everyone in the basement it was time to leave and leave quickly. Grasping each other's arms or hands they moved toward the ladder, Lt. Cunningham and Fr. Horick each had a hand on Fr. Reinhardt, and both could feel his weight increasing as he slumped toward the floor unconscious. Both men tried to lift and carry Reinhardt, but conditions had become so severe they had to leave him to save their own lives.

Back on the street, the men who'd just escaped the basement lay gasping for air. They were suffering greatly from their ordeal and couldn't return to try and rescue the missing man. All those operating inside the building had been driven from the structure by the same expanding wall of heat and smoke. The sidewalks and street were filled with firefighters coughing spasmodically and gasping for breath or sprawled unconscious where they dropped. The unconscious firemen were carried across the street to the quarters of Engine 29 which quickly became a field hospital. With the numbers of unconscious men growing, calls were sent to nearby hospitals and the make-shift hospital was soon staffed by doctors.

The first man to try and rescue Reinhardt was Lt. Samuel Banta. He descended the ladder but was driven back twice. After his second attempt Banta dropped to the sidewalk, overcome by the smoke. Fireman King from Hook & Ladder 1 then attempted to reach the fallen man. King had been overcome earlier in the fire and was recovering on the floor of the firehouse across the street. When word of Reinhardt's predicament reached him, King leaped up from the floor and dashed across to the fire.

A rope was tied around his waist before he descended into the smoke-filled cauldron. After several punishing minutes he found the unconscious man and dragged him back to the ladder. Nearly overcome himself, King was unable to even climb the ladder and had to be hauled up by his comrades.

Fireman John Sheridan was the next to make a rescue attempt, but unlike the others he was equipped with a smoke helmet and a rope before he descended. Locating Reinhardt, he began to pull him by his legs, but the man's boot slipped off. Sheridan was driven from the basement before he could complete the mission.

Finally, Fireman John O'Connell of Hook & Ladder 1 made an attempt. He was wet down completely with a hose and taking the end of a rope climbed down into the basement. After Reinhardt's second boot slipped off, O'Connell was able to tie the rope around his legs and called for the rope to be hauled up.

Both men were pulled from the basement.

Reinhardt was placed in the middle of the street and was

quickly attended by doctors. He seemed to show signs of life and was removed to a hospital. Sadly, Fireman John Reinhardt could not be revived and died in the hospital. In all, dozens of men were overcome, with 23 firefighters taken to Hudson Street Hospital in serious condition including Lt. Banta. After a half hour in the hospital Lt. Banta demanded to return to the fire and continued working.

Lt. Samuel Banta, Capt. John J. Burns, Lt. William Cunningham, Firemen George K. Burns, Jacobs Eckes, John Higgins, Louis Horak, John T. Murphy, Joseph Mooney, Charles Sheridan, Robert Walker, and John O'Connell were all placed on the Roll of Merit for their courageous actions at this fire.

Banta would continue battling fires until his retirement on August 1, 1900. Banta, who was born in New Jersey, would again cross the river and live out his days in the Garden State. He passed away on May 18, 1916.

Andrew B. Sweet

In 1865, a two-year-old boy was brought to the United States by his Italian parents. Andrew B. Sweet became a butcher and lived at 38 Baxter Street in Manhattan until he was appointed to the New York City Fire Department on April 4, 1884, at the age of 21. He was assigned to Engine Company 31, before transferring first to Hook & Ladder 11, then to Hook & Ladder 15 and finally to Hook & Ladder 9. In 1888, Sweet married a young Irish girl named Margaret and they began to raise a family.

On March 13, 1898, an alarm was transmitted at 1:30 a.m. for a raging fire in the Bowery Mission and Young Man's House. Unlike other similar places in the neighborhood, this was a lodging house for young sober men with jobs. The five-story brick building was on the east side of the Bowery, a few doors north of Hester Street. The ground floor of the building was occupied by the Bowery Mission, where nightly prayer meetings were held. The four floors above were used as a lodging house, with rooms rented for 10, 15, and 25 cents a night.

On the receipt of the alarm, Engines 9, 55, and 17 and Hook & Ladders 6 and 9 responded. Flames were seen leaping above the fire building as the companies arrived. A second alarm was immediately transmitted followed quickly by a third alarm. Flames and thick smoke pumped from the windows at times obscuring the building. The front fire escapes were crowded with frightened men, many of whom were completely naked and had fled their beds in a panic.

Fireman Andrew Sweet pulled the ladder truck to a stop and raced inside the burning building. Seeing the main stairs cut off, he climbed the fire escape, broke a window and entered the thick smoke. He was able to rescue several men from inside and helped remove others clearing the fire escape.

Conducting another search Sweet found George Wilson, a 24-year-old-man, almost helpless with exhaustion and smoke inhalation. Sweet pulled him out onto a ladder just as the window exploded in flames. Sweet, despite being badly burned on the hands and face, held Wilson and was able to hand him down to another fireman below. After the rescue Sweet and other members of Hook & Ladder 9 were treated by a doctor who bandaged their badly burned hands. The injured firemen were relieved and sent home to recuperate.

On August 1, 1900, Sweet was promoted to lieutenant and sent to Hook & Ladder 6 on Canal Street. Two months later the department held their awards ceremony in the drill yard at Fire Headquarters. Lt. Andrew B. Sweet was presented the new Trevor-Warren Medal and Lt. Joseph Quinn received the James Gordon Bennett Medal for their heroic efforts at the Bowery Mission fire.

Following his transfer to Hook & Ladder 15, Lt. Sweet responded to a ship fire on October 8, 1901. Flames broke out in the hold of the bark *Criffel*, moored at Pier 12, East River. (A bark, or barque, is a sailing ship with three or more masts and rigged with square sails.) Arriving quickly the firemen, under the command of Chief Kruger of the First Battalion, learned the burning ship had explosives on board. The chief asked for volunteers and Lt. Sweet stepped forward along with seven other firemen.

After the hatches were removed and a ladder was placed into the hold, Lt. Sweet and the men descended into the smoky hold and set up a line from the stored explosives back to and up the ladder. One by one 250 cases of gunpowder-filled cartridges were removed by hand from the blazing ship. Most were stored safely on the pier, but several were dumped directly into the river.

In 1907 Andrew Sweet was promoted to captain and given command of Hook & Ladder 21 on West 36th Street before moving down to Hook & Ladder 10 on Fulton Street. While captain he also served as acting battalion chief in Manhattan's First Battalion. Eventually, Captain Sweet moved closer to his home and was given command of Engine Company 249 on Rogers Avenue in Brooklyn. He continued working there until he retired in September of 1921 with 37 years of service in the FDNY.

Thomas Lally

Born in Ireland on November 16, 1847, Thomas Lally's family emigrated to this country when he was very young and settled on the east side of Manhattan. He was appointed to the FDNY on August 10, 1870, and assigned to Engine 25. A month later he was transferred to Hook & Ladder 9. Lally was promoted to lieutenant on April 21, 1873, and assigned to Hook & Ladder 6 on Clinton Street on the lower east side of Manhattan.

On the evening of May 20, 1874, fire broke out at No. 18 Clinton Street. Lt. Lally saved the lives of two children who were on the fourth floor of the burning building. He carried them down a portable ladder placed against the building. This was the first time his name was placed on the Roll of Merit. On the night of March 13, 1877, Hook & Ladder 6 responded to a fire at 24 Ludlow Street after a kerosene lamp overturned in a second-floor front room of the five-story tenement. As the mother and child fled the burning apartment, the door was left open, and flames extended up the stairs blocking the exit of those above. On the top floor a husband and wife were able to grab three of their youngest children and dash down the burning stairs, escaping with painful burns to their hands and feet. Two other children, boys aged six and eight, ran toward the roof but found the door to the roof locked. They returned to their apartment and hid in a rear bedroom.

Lt. Thomas Lally led a two-pronged attack as part of his crew laddered the building while others dash into the adjoining building and crossed to the roof of the fire building. Lally dashed down the heat and smoke-filled roof stairs and plunged into the apartment. Crawling on his hands and knees he found both boys and carried them to the roof. Sadly, the eight-year-old was dead from the smoke. The unconscious six-year-old boy was hurried to the street and with medical attention, he survived. Lally's men continued the rescue work and were able to remove several families to safety. Lt. Lally, Firemen Dwyer, Grey and Foley were placed on the Roll of Merit for their rescue work.

Lieutenant Lally transferred to Hook & Ladder 10 at 193 Fulton Street in Manhattan. On November 1, 1881, Thomas Lally was promoted to captain and given command of Hook & Ladder 1 on Chambers Street. On July 21, 1882, Capt. Lally and his men rescued four women trapped at the third-floor window of 103 Washington Street. When the company arrived, the women were seen at the window screaming for help. With their exits inside cut-off by flames their only chance was to be removed by portable ladder. All four were safely taken to the street.

On May 1, 1884, Thomas Lally was promoted to battalion chief and placed in charge of the Fifth Battalion in Manhattan. This part of the city was known as the drygoods district which included an area of lower Manhattan that would become known within the department as "Hell's Hundred Acres." Here some of the most difficult and dangerous fires were faced, including cellar and sub-cellar fires. On August 30, 1884, Lally's headquarters was moved from the quarters of Engine 18 on West 10th Street to Engine 30 on Spring Street (the current home of the New York Fire Museum). Chief Lally would spend the next six years responding to fires from this firehouse.

One of the ongoing problems faced by the fire department was election night and the bonfires that followed. The men of the department did not look forward to a night of chaos as fires were set and streets filled with rowdy men and boys celebrating the election. On election night November 5, 1895, they would be tested with an extremely dangerous and difficult fire situation that had nothing to do with the elections or the bonfires.

A few minutes before nine o'clock a fire broke out inside a six-story building on the southeast corner of Broadway and Bleeker streets. The first floor of the building was occupied by the Empire State Bank, while the upper stories housed manufacturing firms, and were filled with flammable materials. The building extended through to Crosby Street, as did the adjoining building. Within minutes the six-story building was a mass of flames that extended to the adjoining structure.

Arriving first was Engine Company 33 who took the hydrant in front of the building. As the engineer of steamer made his connections, an explosion within the fire building caused conditions outside to became extreme. Driven back by the flames, firemen scrambled as waves of heat threatened to ignite the pumper. Seeing the horses were being burned they grabbed axes and chopped the feeder hose free so the rig and the horses could be moved to a safer place.

The conditions became so dangerous so quickly, that a third alarm was transmitted, followed quickly by a fourth and fifth alarms. Battalion Chief Lally was soon joined by Deputy Chief Francis Reilly; together they led members of Engines 14 and 21 inside the building and made their way to the upper floors to battle the extending flames. Reaching the fifth floor they opened their nozzles and directed water on the growing fire.

Suddenly, the staircase above them began to collapse, showering those below with flaming debris. Sensing further danger Chief Lally ordered the men to pull back. Realizing their exit was now cut off by flames Lally ordered them to move to the windows. With large sections of the burning building collapsing around them they reached the windows and called for help. As ladders were positioned, Chiefs Lally and Reilly and Fireman George Coleman of Engine 13 were injured as a large section of the floor above fell on them. All three were dazed but held their ground and helped with the on-going evacuation.

Reaching safety, Fireman Coleman was immediately sent to the hospital with a suspected skull fracture. Reilly and Lally refused to leave the scene. Both would later be relieved by Chief Bonner and sent home to recuperate. A tremendous backdraft in the original fire building caused the windows to fail and the huge building across the street was soon ablaze. The battle continued for hours with four large buildings being destroyed and 25 firemen injured.

On September 18, 1900, Thomas Lally was promoted to Deputy Chief by Commissioner Scannell and assigned to the Brooklyn Division. Then on January 19, 1904, while still holding the rank of deputy chief, he was given command of Brooklyn and Queens. Chief Lally was now in charge of 63 engines, 19 hook & ladders and two fireboats. This growing area of the city was filled with factories, commercial, educational, and ecclesiastical buildings. There was also a large waterfront, with the Brooklyn Navy Yard, the Erie Basin as well as numerous docks, wharfs, and warehouses. Plus, large ships from around the world moored there. The population of Brooklyn was 1.1 million people living in apartment houses, hotels, tenements and private homes.

Shortly after taking command Chief Lally and his men responded to a smoky fire that would have catastrophic consequences. It was just after 9:30 on the night of January 31, 1904, when Brooklyn fire companies responded to a reported fire in a two-story commercial building at the foot of Noble Street in the Greenpoint section. The American Manufacturing plant produced jute (rough fiber made from the stems of hemp plants and used for making twine and rope or woven into sacks or matting.)

Arriving first was Engine 138 (now Engine 238, see Glossary for Brooklyn company number explanation.) They were under the command of Captain Rickenberg. Conditions were so bad that a second alarm was immediately transmitted followed quickly by a third and fourth alarms. As members of Engine 138 pushed in they began feeling the debilitating effects of the noxious smoke. Without warning a backdraft rocked the building sending waves of heat and smoke through the structure with explosive force toppling the firefighters. A dozen men lay unconscious on the floor of the smoke-filled building with a dozen more staggering or crawling around trying to find breathable air.

Outside, Chief Lally had just arrived and quickly sized up the serious situation. Realizing that close to the entire first alarm assignment was in jeopardy; he ordered the firefighting to stop and directed all efforts to removing the overcome members still inside the smoke-filled building. Inside, Capt. Rickenberg tried his best to get his bearings and ensure his men were safe. He found two men, Dressel and Renk unconscious on the floor. Grabbing each by the collar he began dragging them back toward the front entrance. Lally watched the front entrance and saw twenty men stagger from the thick smoke and slump to the sidewalk. Rickenberg appeared dragging two men into the clear air where they collapsed in a tumble of unconsciousness. Battalion Chief McCarthy was shouting orders and directing the rescue efforts as he too dropped unconscious.

The smoke was having strange effects on many of the men. Carbon monoxide or some other chemical in the smoke was causing the men to act in unusual ways, some even staggered back into the smoke-filled building. Battalion Chief Rogers, the last man to leave the building after checking all firemen were safe, had to be restrained as he attempted to re-enter the thick smoke. As the sidewalk filled with firemen and officers stumbling and falling senseless to the pavement, men from the large crowd that gathered to watch the smoky fire, dashed to help the downed men as first aid efforts began.

Sadly, three members of Engine 138: Firemen Christopher Dressel, Peter Gaffney, and Arthur Renk died from the effects of the smoke. Eighteen other firefighters were also rendered unconscious by the smoke but revived and returned to duty.

Keeping up with the motorization of the FDNY, in 1904 Chief Lally was given a 1904 Locomobile touring car. This bright red, 24 horsepower automobile, could reach speeds of 45 miles-per-hour. At about the same time, Fireman Thomas D. Doran of Engine 218 became the chief's aide and chauffeur. They would spend the next 17 years together racing around Brooklyn and Queens battling fires.

Weather became a major issue for the fire department on January 21, 1904, when a snow and ice storm coated the streets with a glaze that proved extremely dangerous, especially for the horses. The headlines proclaimed that all vehicular traffic had come to a standstill, the street cleaning department was struggling to keep up, and the only apparent remedy was warmer weather. The Society for the Prevention of Cruelty to Animals had carted away more than fifty horses that had been killed on the streets of Brooklyn. One report stated that, "150 horses of the street cleaning department were injured by falling on the ice."

The fire department was experiencing delays between five and 20 minutes when responding to alarms. When questioned about the icy conditions Chief Lally said:

> It's only the principal streets that were cleaned after the heavy snowfall, and even some of those like Sixth, the Street Cleaning Department did not get around to. This

makes it necessary for us to make detours and of course delays our reaching a fire. The streets are so slippery that it is impossible to drive the horses at full speed. We were delayed in reaching a fire this morning in a flat at the corner of Lafayette and Classon avenues on that account.

The article went on to describe the special shoes worn by fire horses in such situations:

All of the Fire Department's horses are fitted with hollow rubber pads, and the suction of the air under these pads when the hoof touches the ground helps the animal to keep their feet. The shoes are resharpened every time the horse returns to the barn.

It was also mentioned that cobblestones were especially rough on the horseshoes.

One of the biggest challenges facing Deputy Chief Lally was keeping up with the growth of Brooklyn and Queens. His first annual report to the fire commissioner stated:

I again respectfully call your attention to the fact the Department in the boroughs of Brooklyn and Queens is not increasing proportionately with the growth of those boroughs. This vast increase in the number of buildings (6,000 in the borough of Brooklyn and 226 in Long Island City in the borough of Queens during 1904) demands additional protection. The number of fires has increased 10-1/2 per cent over the preceding year. Since 1898, up to the present time, a period of six years, only three engines and three hook & ladder companies have been organized, an average of one per year.

He also requested a new fireboat, stating the two boats in service needed complete overhauling. Lally also championed better water supplies and alarm box capabilities and oversaw the conversion of some of the volunteer fire companies still operating in Queens.

On the afternoon of April 21, 1905, Chief Lally responded to a working fire at the corner of Belmont and Thatford avenues in the Brownsville section of Brooklyn. Screeching to a stop in his red chief's car, Chief Lally took one look at the extending flames and immediately sent in third and fourth alarms. Strong winds were blowing smoke and embers across the neighborhood and threatening rows of wood-frame apartment buildings and tenements.

Flames spreading from the initial fire building soon had the entire street corner ablaze. Twenty minutes after the initial alarm the original fire building collapsed, minimizing the wall of flames that were threatening the neighborhood. Chief Lally's quick call for reinforcements paid off as companies were able to halt the spreading fire. A few minutes after the fire was brought under control a rainstorm rolled in and drenched the remaining embers. It also dispersed the huge crowd of spectators.

The new chief's car was moving Chief Lally around his command in record time. But with speed comes danger. A case in point was his June 5, 1905, response to a reported fire on Court Street. The chief's car was being driven by Fireman Edward Tarlton, with Fireman Thomas Doran along for the ride. Approaching the corner of State and Smith streets, Tarlton could see they were about to hit another vehicle and swung hard to avoid it. This caused their vehicle to strike a trolley car and throw the chief from his seat. Despite cuts and bruises, the chief jumped back in his car and zoomed off to the fire.

Four alarms were struck for a fire in a three-story-brick macaroni factory at 190 Seabring Street in Brooklyn on February 13, 1907. Flames quickly spread to the adjoining four-story building occupied by a cork company. The dense smoke from the greasy macaroni soon gave way to the blaze of a thousand feet of lumber used to construct the burning buildings. Hoses from various engines filled the surrounding streets stopping street cars from delivering passengers to a nearby ferry boat. Passengers had to walk the distance while negotiating snaking hose lines.

Members of Engine 126 (now Engine 226) were working on the third floor of the cork factory when the floors above them collapsed. Fortunately, a void was formed when the floors fell encasing the firemen. In the street Chief Lally heard their cries for help and called for volunteers as he dashed up the stairs trying to reach the trapped men.

They managed to climb the burning stairs but found their way blocked. While working with a pickaxe one of the firemen found a small opening in the debris. He was able to crawl through to the trapped men and lead them back to safety. Dazed but uninjured, the men were taken to a nearby engine house.

This was but one of the major fires battled by Chief Lally and his men that day. Two four-alarm, one three-alarm and one two-alarm fires tested the department. At one point 38 of the downtown fire companies were at work, nearly half of the entire force under Lally's command. Working at each fire, Chief Lally contracted a cold and could barely speak by the morning. Answering reporter's questions after the fires, the chief could barely whisper his reassertion of the fact that Brooklyn and Queens needed more fire protection.

> We need more companies, and we need a considerable number of them. What we have now is first class, but we haven't enough. We have every reason to expect that our requests will be granted at least in part. And as soon as they are... Brooklyn will be capable of handling most anything in the nature of a fire that could possibly come.

Fire Commissioner Wise agreed completely with Chief Lally and said he was doing everything in his power to accomplish the additions.

The newly installed high pressure hydrant system in downtown Brooklyn was given an operational test by Chief Lally and his companies on March 31, 1908. With a large crowd of curious people watching including officials from the water department, city government, the fire department, and members of the insurance companies, a simulated conflagration was staged.

Two minutes after the "alarm" was transmitted Chief Lally's red automobile dashed down the street heading toward the India Wharf. The chief was followed by a small army of fireman riding on hose trucks. Within minutes six lines had been attached to the hydrants and were operating. The streams at first were not very powerful, working with the normal hydrant pressure. But as soon as Chief Lally called the pumping station by telephone, 100 pounds of pressure were added, and the streams of water swelled with power.

Lally then directed the water tower be placed into operation as additional handlines were stretched from other nearby hydrants. The water pressure was increased several times and the streams grew in strength and reach. At the high point 18 lines were in play with 8,500 gallons of water a minute pouring through deck nozzles, the water tower and attack hoses. Chief Lally and his men were happy and confident with the new hydrant system.

Danger seems to be everywhere when you are a firefighter. This became very apparent on June 17, 1910, when Chief Lally smelled gas in his Brooklyn Fire Headquarters. He sent his trusted team of Firemen Joseph DeMoll and Thomas Doran, who teamed up with Captain Thomas Robb and Firemen

Southwick and Shaughnessy of Hook & Ladder 68 (now Ladder 168), to investigate the cause.

They knew a 100-gallon tank of gasoline was beneath the concrete floor of an airshaft, and to reach it required crawling through a cellar window. As they crawled through a darkened area to reach the tank, DeMoll apparently lit a match to help him see. This ignited an explosion that hurled the men across the space and into a wall. DeMoll landed in a foot and a half of water at the bottom of the tank area.

Even though they were all seriously burned, the other men searched in the blackness for DeMoll. They were able to remove him to safety and a doctor was called. DeMoll was a mass of burns, and it was feared he might lose his eyesight. Doctor White bathed his body in olive oil and ordered him to the hospital. Despite his burns he would later return to duty.

Chief Lally's health began to fail prompting his retirement from the FDNY on January 1, 1918. Special Oder No. 230 dated December 31, 1917 stated:

> Deputy Chief of Department Thomas Lally, in charge of Boroughs of Brooklyn and Queens... is retired at two-thirds pension because of his unequalled length of service in the Department and because of his distinguished record of usefulness. No man has ever served in the New York Fire Department as long as Deputy Chief Lally. He is now in his forty-eighth year-of-service. His entire service has been in the busiest fire districts of the entire city. For the last thirteen years he has been in charge of the fire fighting forces in the boroughs of Brooklyn and Queens, as Deputy Chief, and before that he was located in the downtown district of Manhattan in a territory which included the most active fire district in the city. He has distinguished himself as a commander and disciplinarian and as a practical fireman, and it is in recognition of his long faithful, and

useful service that he is retired at two-thirds pay. ($5,000 per year)

Also retiring on the same order was Lally's aide and driver for more than 17 years, Fireman Thomas D. Doran who was also in his 48th year of service. It was mentioned that he never had a charge against him in his long career. He too was granted two-thirds retirement pay and would receive an annual pension of $1000.

After a long illness Deputy Chief Thomas Lally died at home surrounded by his four daughters and three sons on October 14, 1920, at the age of 75. When Lally began his command of Brooklyn and Queens in 1904 there were 1,200 firemen. Upon his retirement the number had doubled.

Henry W. McAdam

The ship *City of Limerick*, arrived at Ellis Island on September 25, 1871. It had sailed from Europe with stops at Queenstown, Ireland, and Liverpool, England. Onboard was a 17-year-old young man named Henry McAdam and his brother William. Henry had been born in Ireland to a Scottish father and Irish mother. When they settled in, they both worked at a foundry where they made metal type for printing companies. Henry joined the New York City Fire Department on September 18, 1874, and assigned to Engine Company 5 at 340 E. 14th Street in Manhattan. This old firehouse was the former quarters of United States Engine 23 of the volunteer department. Hugh Bonner was the first captain of Engine 5 back when the company was organized in 1865.

On November 1, 1881, McAdam was promoted to assistant foreman (lieutenant) and assigned to Hook & Ladder 2.

Word went out within the department about the commissioner's plan to establish and train a Life Saving Corps. On January 24, 1882, Chris Hoell of the St. Louis Pompier Corps was engaged to instruct the members of the FDNY in the use of scaling and ordinary ladders and lifelines and other life-saving appliances. The training would be held at the Old Sugar House at the foot of West 158th Street. In late February the training began in earnest with six athletic young members of the department chosen from those who'd volunteered. They were Samuel Banta, John McLeod Murphy, John Needham,

William H. Jones, Edward J. Broderick, and Henry McAdam. After a week of concentrated training, they were ready for a public demonstration.

On the afternoon of February 27, 1883, the first exhibition of the Life Saving Corps was held at the quarters of Engine 47 on Tenth Avenue. This demonstration was for the benefit of the commissioners and chief officers. The members of the corps assembled on the third floor and warmed up their muscles with exercises, then began raising and lowering scaling ladders with precision. At the direction of Chris Hoell, teams scaled the ladders, showing great strength and dexterity. Assistant Chief Bonner (in charge of department training) reported his pleasure at the results.

Two months later a huge public exhibition was held downtown at Printing House Square across from City Hall Park. FDNY and city officials were joined by thousands of New Yorkers who filled the park as the demonstration began promptly at 2 p.m. The Life Saving Corps (LSC) consisted of 13 members under the direction of Assistant Chief Bonner and Chris Hoell. Each man wore a stout canvas belt with a spring hook. They also carried a hatchet and a steel spike that could be driven into the building and used as an anchor point.

Upon Hoell's signal six team members composing the first squad stepped forward. Each held a scaling ladder in hand and waited a moment while a portable ladder was placed against the building. They climbed to the top and placed their scaling ladder into the window above. The team utilized two rows of windows up the front of the seven-story building for their chain of scaling ladders. The squad quickly climbed up and disappeared into the top-floor window. They then reversed the operation and quickly climbed safely to the ground bringing the scaling ladder down with them.

A number of variations were displayed with teams of two

climbing up seven stories and back down, three minutes up and three minutes down. With the chain in place Chris Hoell climbed to the next to last ladder reached across and pulled the base of the last ladder across to him. He stepped onto the bottom steps and let go allowing the ladder and himself to pendulum across the face of the building. When it stopped moving, Hoell climbed to the top and into the window to the cheers of the crowd below.

Members then began sliding down ropes and lowering other firemen from the upper story windows. The display continued for an hour to the delight of the assembled crowd. At the conclusion Commissioner Van Cott said:

> These men have been under instruction but six weeks, and you see how they are perfect in every detail of the work. Within a year we will have 300 men equally competent, and a corps of them will be attached to every engine and truck in the city. When this is done the loss of life by fire will be reduced to a minimum.

The Life Saving Corps had a profound effect in the FDNY. With ropes and scaling ladders placed on ladder trucks and hose wagons the members of the department were ready to save those imperiled by flames regardless of the height. For their dedication to duty and for being the first members of the department to accept the challenge, the original members who volunteered for the extra duty were rewarded with promotions. Assistant foreman Henry W. McAdam was promoted to foreman (captain) and Firemen John McLeod Murphy, Samuel Banta, Edward Broderick, William H. Jones and John T. Needham were promoted to assistant foreman. (This was prior to civil service rules.) McAdam was given command of Engine Company 21, before transferring to Hook & Ladder 15 in August.

While working in Hook & Ladder 7 McAdam responded to a

fire at 63 East 12th Street. It was March 24, 1884, and inside the burning building Mrs. Maxwell attempted to exit her third-floor apartment and found her way blocked by flames. She returned to a front window and cried for help.

Arriving at the scene Captain McAdam yelled up to the woman who was clearly about to jump. He calmed her as a portable ladder was placed in position. McAdam quickly ascended the ladder to her window, as the flames closed in around them. In the words of Battalion Chief John Fisher:

> Taking into consideration the helplessness of the woman and the activity and good judgement displayed by Foreman Henry W. McAdam, and, in fact, the great personal risk he incurred by carrying this helpless woman down the ladder, I consider it not alone a perilous, but as brave an act as ever came under my observation... I would recommend that the name of Foreman Henry W. McAdam be enrolled upon the Roll of Honor.

Several months later, Captain McAdam was working in Hook & Ladder 2 when they responded to 931 Third Avenue. It was 1:30 in the morning when flames broke out in the four-story building. Numerous people were trapped at windows calling for help. McAdams and his men swarmed into the building rescuing people hanging from second, third, and fourth-floor windows. The also rescued people using the fire escape, stairs, and ladders. They rescued eight adults and five children from sure death. McAdam was again placed on the Roll of Merit.

In 1886, a fraternal group, the Order of American Firemen, was organized. The group was to serve two purposes: act as a fraternal organization bringing together volunteer and paid firemen from across the country and around the world, and to lobby with united action matters affecting the interests of firemen.

The local councils sent members to the national council to vote and represent their members. In the first year the association grew to 10,000 members. In the FDNY a local chapter called the Hugh Bonner Council was formed with 1,000 members. Henry McAdam was elected president. The Order continued for several years before it dissolved on a national level in 1889. Some local groups continued for years under the name, but the idea of a nation-wide organization never really took hold.

As Capt. McAdam continued working in the field, the training aspect of the FDNY was growing. The school of instruction was training not only new recruits but was also teaching current members of the department the proper use of scaling ladders and ropes. This training paid off when the first successful scaling ladder rescue was made by Fireman John Binns in 1884.

On June 1, 1897, Captain Henry W. McAdam was named chief Instructor. McAdam was now in charge of all departmental training. He held this position until his retirement in 1903. McAdam's became famous across the country as his training also included chiefs, assistant chiefs, and firemen from all parts of the United States who travelled to New York City to be trained at the FDNY school. Since the start of the LSC in 1883 until his retirement, it was said that McAdam had trained 25,000 men with only two accidents. Quite a safety record.

Following his retirement McAdam was hired by Luna Park, the famed amusement park on Coney Island. McAdam was placed in charge of the Luna Park Fire Department. This department was designed specifically as part of a huge attraction for the summer of 1904 called Fire and Flames. This attraction featured the burning of an entire city block daily.

The audience was seated in an outdoor auditorium across from a 520 X 250-foot stage that featured the façade of a four-story tenement building and a cast of 657 men, women and children. The "controlled fire" would be ignited, the actors would appear trapped and helpless at various windows as McAdam's four fire companies responded in and rescued those trapped and extinguished the fire.

Actors leapt from windows into nets, as others were rescued by ladders or were lowered with ropes. The action was reminiscent of the demonstrations of the Life Saving Corps that McAdam helped develop. Fire and Flames proved to be the most popular attraction at Luna Park.

Sadly, on the evening of March 29, 1905, Henry McAdam was standing on a street corner talking with a friend when he suffered a stroke. He was taken home to recover, but after three days was transported to Presbyterian Hospital. While unconscious in the hospital, his wife died due to complications during surgery, and his daughter also died from consumption. On April 27, 1905, Henry W. McAdam passed away at 51 years of age.

George L. Ross

In 1888, George Ross was running a cigar stand in Manhattan when his uncle persuaded him to join the New York City Fire Department. Born upstate in Tivoli, Dutchess County, his father John E. Ross was a postmaster in Albany. Following his uncle's advice, he became a member of the FDNY on December 23, 1888, and worked at Engine 18 and then Hook & Ladder 12. Ross was promoted to assistant foreman (lieutenant) on January 1, 1894, and was assigned to Engine Company 1. Ross was then promoted to captain on December 1, 1897, and was assigned to Engine 13, then Engine 19.

Shortly after his promotion to captain in 1897, Ross responded to a blazing loft building on Wooster Street. During the battle Ross fell 35 feet down an airshaft seriously injuring himself. He was rushed to the hospital where his injuries left his legs paralyzed for a time. His recuperation was long and painful but he made his way back to full duty.

He was promoted to battalion chief on July 15, 1900, and assigned to the Eighth Battalion.

On February 22, 1902, Manhattan fire companies faced one of the most difficult and dangerous nights of their careers. The city was in a week-long cycle of snow, rain, sleet and freezing rain. As soon as the roads were made somewhat passable, the weather moved back in and filled the streets and sidewalks with more snow and slush. So, it went as night fell on Manhattan.

Asleep in the Eighth Battalion night headquarters on 33rd Street, near Lexington Avenue, Chief Ross heard above the storm the sound of a woman's voice screaming. Looking out his window Ross saw hail being driven against the glass by a strong wind. The voice outside was getting louder and weak pounding started on the front door. Ross sent his driver John Gaw, to answer the door. With the racket continuing, Ross lifted the window and stuck his head outside into the raging storm.

"The armory's on fire!" shouted the exhausted voice below. Ross leaned out the window and looked up the street. One hundred yards away Ross could see a column of flames. Below he heard Gaw open the door. Ross yelled down for Gaw to send in the alarm as the chief quickly got into his fire gear. He hurried to his wagon and rolled out onto 33rd Street. As Gaw ran back through the deep snow and slush returning from the fire alarm box on the corner, he met the chief and his buggy. Ahead they could see flames bursting high into the air from every window on this side of the huge armory.

Ross and Gaw arrived alone, the nearby fire companies just starting out for the fire. It would take five long minutes for first of the horses and firemen to push, pull, and drag the heavy apparatus through the snow and slush-filled streets. Seeing the magnitude of the fire, Chief Ross transmitted a third alarm. The 71st Regiment Armory was a massive 200 X 250-foot, three-story brick and granite stone structure with imposing castle-like stone towers, turrets, and gables that sat at the very top of Murray Hill, a steep glacial hill on the east side of Manhattan. This last leg of the exhausting horse-drawn fire apparatus response was a painful reminder of the limitations of the poor animals.

As Engines 16 and 21 moved into position, Ross, realizing how advanced the fire conditions were shouted, "This is a terrible hole, boys. Get at it!"

Chief Ross led the way. The flying sleet stung the hands and faces of the firemen as they pulled their hoses toward the flames. Captain King of Hook & Ladder 1 pulled up, the exhausted horses chugging clouds of steam from their nostrils as firemen pried their frozen hands from the icy railings. Ladders were raised and hoses carried upwards their streams directed on the growing flames.

In addition to the mounds of snow and large puddles of slush, the streets were filled with piles of paving stones pulled up for the subway excavation work being done along the length of the street. This left only narrow paths for the placement of apparatus, hoses, and ladders.

When Chief Croker arrived, he took one look at the growing fire and sent in a fifth alarm. This would send 24 engines, 6 hook & ladders, 2 water towers, and the searchlight engine struggling through the snow-filled streets to join their frozen comrades already fighting a losing battle.

Fire companies battled the huge fire for an hour, the sleet, snow, and water hose spray slowing some of the fire's spread. Despite the horrible weather, large crowds gathered to watch the growing fire and ice spectacle. Sensing the building was becoming unstable, Chief Ross yelled to his men operating hose streams from ladders. He ordered them to drop their hoses and climb down. As this slow process was unfolding Ross saw pieces of the building topple to the frozen ground.

"Run for your lives!" Ross shouted. His men listened and did as they were ordered. So did Ross. Moments later the wall fell with a thunderous crash filling the very spot where they'd been working with a huge steaming pile of stones and bricks. On the other side of the fire, companies were moving in with hoses when a tremendous explosion rocked the building. Rumors spread through the crowd that the stored munitions inside the huge armory were about to detonate. Firemen believed the blast was caused by a backdraft but continued their attack carefully.

Under the direction of Chief Ross, firemen and subway construction workers moved 40 pounds of dynamite stored in an excavation work shanty only feet from the fire. As the last of the subway explosives were removed safely, the munitions inside the armory began to light off with the regularity of a Gatling gun.

It was decided at this point the residential hotel at 135 East 33rd Street, diagonally across from the armory, should be evacuated. Croker sent Captain Kenlon of Engine 72 to initiate the evacuation. As this was being accomplished, it became clear the collapse of the armory had forced clouds of embers across the large eight-story iron and brick, 200 X 225-foot building. The negative pressure of a moving elevator apparently drew the flaming embers through air vents igniting fires inside the elevator shaft. The flames were spreading quickly as firemen turned their attentions to this new problem.

Battalion Chief Ross was sent to help fight the growing fire in the hotel. Ross was more than familiar with the hotel with his family having an apartment on the fourth floor. Dashing inside he found the place almost deserted as all the staff were outside watching the armory fire. Seeing a light in the elevator shaft he went to investigate. He found the shaft on fire, with flames and sparks shooting up to the roof. Ross hurried outside and directed hoses to be stretched inside the hotel to the fourth floor.

As the lines were being dragged into position, Ross dashed up the stairs to the fifth floor, where he found a man and woman unconscious on the floor. Ross called downstairs to Acting Chief George Winter (captain of Hook & Ladder 12) who was directing the placement of the hoses on the floor below. He immediately joined Ross and they crawled on hands and knees to the unconscious couple. Despite the clouds of thick, noxious smoke, they dragged the victims back to the stairs and then carried them down until they were handed off to other firemen who took them to the street. They returned to continue searching the fifth floor but were driven back by the heat.

Unable to work on the fifth floor Ross decided to check his family's fourth-floor apartment. "Then I went to see about the safety of my wife, who was in a room on the fourth floor… I rushed to our rooms, but had not gone far when I fell, overcome by smoke. I recovered in a moment, as the air near the floor was not yet heavy with smoke. Then I crawled on my hands and knees toward the doors of our rooms. Again, I was overcome, and the next thing I knew somebody was carrying me down a back stairway."

Regaining his strength, he found out his family was safe and went back to the battle.

As the sun rose over the smoldering ruins of the armory and the hotel, exhausted firemen moved carefully, dousing hot spots and searching the rubble. Despite the heroic efforts of the firemen (numerous dramatic rescues had been performed) the death toll was staggering. Twenty-one guests in the hotel had been killed by the smoke and flames.

It was 8:02 p.m. when the FDNY received an alarm of fire for the Parker Building on the southeast corner of Fourth Avenue (now known as Park Avenue South) and 19th Street in Manhattan on January 10, 1908. The fire started on the fifth floor near the rear stairway of the twelve-story 125 X 150-foot building. The initial alarm from a special building alarm box located inside the building was followed immediately by several street alarm boxes.

Fire companies rolled out into the 28-degree temperature unaware that the fire had at least a 10-minute head start before the alarm was even transmitted. Inside flames were spreading rapidly via the rear stairs to the upper floors. On arrival Battalion Chief Shea took one look and transmitted two more alarms and special called two water towers.

In what would be a series of unfortunate events, the water towers got stuck halfway up and firemen had to climb up the masts like a jungle gym and then use a block and tackle to free them up. Despite their elevation the water tower streams could not reach above the sixth floor. Sadly, this was the lowest level of the expanding flames. Then the attack hoses began to burst.

As the men trapped on the roof were being rescued, (a rope was shot over their heads, made fast and then used to slide down to safety) about 50 firemen were making a push inside. It was now about 9:30 p.m. and under the direction of Deputy Chief Langford and Battalion Chief Ross, Captain Davin of Engine 72 and the men of several companies were attempting to advance against the growing flames in the rear of the fourth floor.

Ross and Langford were in the smoke-filled hallway when suddenly the building collapsed around them. In a matter of seconds both men were in pitch-darkness, half-buried in collapse debris. Ross slowly regained his senses and dug himself out. He then moved to help his buried comrade and realized that Langford was unconscious. After digging him clear, Ross, operating solely by feel while engulfed in extreme heat, smoke and darkness, dragged the unconscious chief officer toward the stairs. Just as Ross was about to step onto the stairs, they too collapsed beneath his feet.

Amazingly, Ross kept his footing and located another exit and was able to remove himself and Langford to the street safely.

Sadly, three men were killed in the collapse: Firemen Thomas Phillips and George O'Conner of Engine 72 and Fire Patrolman John Fallon. Later, Chief Ross, despite his own injuries, led a mission into the dangerously damaged building in search of the trapped men.

For his heroic rescue of Chief Langford, the following

year Battalion Chief George L. Ross was presented the James Gordon Bennett Medal, the FDNY's highest award for valor. The medal was presented at a ceremony held in the commissioner's office in FDNY Headquarters on East 67th Street. The room was filled with dignitaries, government, and fire department officials and the families of the members receiving the awards. As the report was read, the mayor pinned the medal on Ross' chest.

On December 14, 1918, George Ross was promoted to deputy chief and assigned to the Third Division. He was in charge of all the fire companies from 14th Street to 59th Street, river to river. He continued in that capacity until his retirement on July 1, 1939. Upon his retirement newspaper accounts of his career mentioned he "whipped out orders like a machine gun spewing bullets," recalled one lieutenant, "sometimes he'd just look at the men like a stern father and they'd know what to do."

He died two years later after a brief illness.

Every Picture Tells a Story, or Two – Thomas Kain

A newspaper photograph captioned, "Deputy Fire Chiefs John O'Hara (left) and Smoky Joe Martin (right) wish Lieutenant Thomas Kain a happy 44th birthday after fighting a blaze in Astoria." (See page 126.) The photo credits include January 10, 1900, as the date it was taken. In the photograph, the two chiefs stand on either side of a helmeted fire officer of medium height, a slight belly visible beneath his rubberized fire coat. His helmet frontpiece identified him as a lieutenant of Engine 212. The group wore similar attire, rubber coats and boots, and winter gloves. Their fire helmets differed slightly; O'Hara and Martin wore the white helmets of chief officers.

Despite the caption, if the date was correct, John O'Hara was not yet a deputy chief having been appointed as district engineer in the Brooklyn FD on December 6, 1897. (This was the equivalent rank of the FDNYs battalion chief. After the two departments consolidated O'Hara became an FDNY battalion chief on January 28, 1898.) He would become a deputy chief in 1907.

Despite the differences in rank, Thomas Kain was the senior man in the group. Kain joined the fire service on January 12, 1882, and was assigned to Engine Company 21 of the Brooklyn Fire Department.

Kain was promoted to driver in January of 1885. His job then included getting the horse-drawn steam pumper to the scene as quickly and safely as possible. Drivers and engineers were also responsible for the care of the horses and apparatus. Steam fire engines required near constant attention, maintaining water temperatures and steam pressures as close to operational as possible while the rig stood in the firehouse ready to respond.

On January 15, 1894, Kain was promoted to lieutenant (assistant foreman) and assigned to Brooklyn Engine 112, which became FDNY Engine 212 when the departments consolidated in 1898. He'd spend the remainder of his very long career working in the Wythe Avenue firehouse. Kain and his company routinely responded to fires and emergencies in their Williamsburg neighborhood and multiple alarms where assigned.

One of the most memorable fires Kain operated at was the Diamond Candy Factory fire. He was commended for his outstanding service at this difficult and dangerous fire. The November 12, 1915, blaze went to four alarms and took the lives of a dozen people.

On January 24, 1917 Kain celebrated his 30th year in the fire department. As was the custom, the members of his division presented him with a diamond-studded badge. It was noted he'd been in Engine 212 for 25 years already.

John Francis O'Hara

John O'Hara was born in Ireland in 1860. He came to the United States at the age of 14. After attending Saint Joseph's School on Pacific Street, young O'Hara got a job making deliveries for a feed and grain company. Several of the stops included local firehouses and he quickly became interested in the fire department. O'Hara joined the Brooklyn Fire Department on January 30, 1882, and was assigned to Engine Company 114 on Herkimer Street. Five years later he was appointed assistant foreman (lieutenant) and stayed in Engine 114 until he was transferred to Hook & Ladder 5. O'Hara was promoted to captain in 1889. He returned to command Engine 114.

O'Hara was promoted to the rank of district engineer (battalion chief) on December 6, 1897, and served in the 29th Battalion. In January of 1898, the Greater City of New York was formed. The municipal governments, including the fire departments, of Brooklyn, Queens, Richmond (Staten Island) and the Bronx merged with Manhattan. All the Brooklyn fire companies became part of the New York City Fire Department. John F. O'Hara was now a battalion chief in the FDNY.

On January 30, 1902, Chief O'Hara reached his 20th anniversary in the fire department. As was the custom, he was presented with a gold badge, studded with diamonds during a testimonial dinner given by the men of his battalion, at Briethopf's Hall on Jamaica Avenue and Bushwick Avenue.

In 1907 he was promoted again, this time to deputy chief of the 13th Division. In 1918, Deputy Chief Thomas Lally, retired as chief in charge of Brooklyn and Queens. John O'Hara was chosen as his replacement. Known to all as "Gentleman John" the chief had the uncanny ability of "maintaining unfailing courtesy on occasions of extreme excitement."

The chief's home life was pleasant and loving as he and his wife Catherine raised four sons and two daughters in their home on Hancock Street. But of course, the life of a deputy chief had odd and long hours. Days were spent at his headquarters on Jay Street. Nights were spent at home, until a multiple alarm came in.

It was 3:50 a.m. on December 22, 1922, when flames were discovered in a building at Bartlett Street and Harrison Avenue in the Williamsburg section of Brooklyn. Arriving fire companies were faced with heavy fire in the large building known locally as the Teutonia Hall. The former political meeting house had been subdivided into commercial spaces. Flames were raging from the windows of a baby carriage store and spreading in every direction. Deputy Chief Patrick Maher arrived and conferred briefly with Battalion Chief John Foley, before transmitting second and third alarms. Within minutes, 20 additional fire companies and Deputy Chief John O'Hara were responding to the growing fire.

On the fire ground flames were extending to nearby structures including several three-story-frame buildings housing six families each. In the rear, two other tenements were also igniting. Arriving with the third alarm companies, O'Hara directed firemen to clear all the nearby dwellings. Hoses were stretched to the rear of the carriage store in hopes of controlling the extending flames. O'Hara took personal command of this dangerous position. Operating were Captain John Westrich and members of Engine 211 along with Captain Henry Sullivan and members of Hook & Ladder 102.

Three top fire officials: Commissioner Thomas Drennan,

Deputy Commissioner William Thompson, and Chief Fire Marshal Thomas Brophy joined O'Hara for an update, before moving to a safer position.

By 4:30, the growing flames were taking their toll on the original fire building. Without warning the roof collapsed into the top floor, toppling a large section of the wall onto the 12 firemen operating below. The commissioners and every available fireman scrambled into the smoldering rubble and began to dig out the trapped men.

The first man uncovered was Chief O'Hara. His face was covered in blood, and his breathing was labored. They all feared the worst as the work continued. Brophy jumped into his car and raced to the Saint Louis Roman Catholic Church on Ellery Street. The marshal soon had Father Mellon out of bed and raced back to the scene. There he found Father Richard Hamilton, an FDNY chaplain, already giving the last rites to the injured men as they were uncovered. Fifty firemen worked frantically, by hand, clearing the tangled debris. One by one they were uncovered, all but two were unconscious. One man, Fireman Fitzsimmons of Engine 211, was in critical condition with a skull fracture.

O'Hara rested, still partially covered in bricks, as Father Hamilton moved in close and began his prayers. As he anointed the chief's forehead with oil, O'Hara's eyes slowly opened. He looked up at the priest and Tom Brophy standing above him. "Tom," he said weakly, "don't mind me. Look out for those other boys. They're still under the wall. I'm not as badly hurt as you think."

The chief was assured that all the trapped men had been removed before he lapsed again into unconsciousness. He was rushed by ambulance to St. Catherine's Hospital. The chief and his injured men would spend Christmas in the hospital. O'Hara would spend two weeks on medical leave. Several men were so badly injured they would not return to fire duty.

The chief resumed his job as the highest-ranking officer in Brooklyn and Queens.

Deputy Chief O'Hara would have another close call while his men battled a blaze in an old building known as New Plaza Hall, at the corner of Havermeyer and Grand Streets.

It was 11:50 p.m. on August 6, 1923, when Brooklyn Box 423 was transmitted for a cellar fire. The three-story fire building, now a hotel, was built in 1848 as a Masonic Temple, and was a landmark in the Eastern District of Brooklyn. The building occupied the entire block, with stores on the ground floor and the hotel and a dance hall above. The ground floor stores included a bedding supply dealer, a butcher shop, and a baby carriage company.

Upon his arrival, Deputy Chief Patrick Maher transmitted a second and third alarm as the flames spread from store to store. Arriving on the third alarm, Deputy Chief O'Hara conferred with his chiefs and transmitted a fourth alarm. This filled the streets with an imposing array of fire apparatus from across the borough.

Large crowds of curious onlookers formed, held in check by police reserves manning the fire lines. The dense smoke-filled streets allowed only brief glimpses of the firemen at work.

Several companies, under the direction of Battalion Chief Isaac Ludgate, were driving streams of water into the building, when suddenly, without warning, a huge section of the brick wall fell over. In a matter of seconds, a 50-foot high and 30-foot wide a wall of bricks, timbers and girders was hurtling toward the firemen-filled street and sidewalk below.

Chief O'Hara was seated in his car, directly in line with the Havermeyer Street wall when the collapse occurred. His driver, Fireman Walter Doolan, sensed the situation as it occurred. As the wall toppled, the fireman shoved the chief to one side, as he jumped from the automobile. Both narrowly missed serious injury. Others working nearby were not so lucky.

The rumbling of the collapse faded as the sky filled with a thick cloud of dust. Within seconds the muffled cries for help came from the pile of bricks and debris. The dust began to clear, and mangled, brick and beam-covered fire engines continued pumping. Firemen, police officers, and even civilians swarmed in, removing the bricks by hand searching for the 50 trapped firemen.

Sadly, two men were killed: Fireman Raymond Farrell and Fireman James Sullivan, both of Engine Company 230. Sixteen others, including Chief Ludgate, were seriously injured, and required hospitalization.

Deputy Chief O'Hara faced many difficult and dangerous fires in both Brooklyn and Queens including: a five-alarm wind-driven blaze in a six-story factory building at Sterling Place and East New York Avenue on St. Patty's Day 1924. At the height of the fire, a wall buckled, and a mass of brick and timber plunged into the street. All the working firefighters remained unscathed, a hose wagon however, was destroyed. When O'Hara arrived, he was faced with the collapse, live trolley wires falling into the street, and exploding stores of gasolines in an adjacent burning building. Chief O'Hara transmitted a borough-call, five-alarms bringing 18 engines, 10 truck companies, and 250 firemen to the scene.

Then O'Hara and his fire companies responded to a fire that affected fire history itself. It was just after 7 p.m. on January 15, 1924, when a fire was reported in the two-story building at 156 Grand Avenue in Astoria, Queens. The structure was home to the Veteran Firemen's Association, their clubhouse, and storage area.

Responding firemen, faced with a quick-moving basement

fire that was spreading upwards, pressed a frantic effort to salvage as many historic relics as they could. Among the historic items saved were: "Boss Tweed's Big Six," the hand-pumper used by Engine 6 of the New York Volunteer Fire Department (William M. Tweed, the notorious Boss of Tammany Hall was captain 1852 to 1854,) and the Rumsey & Company-built hose cart of Mohawk Hose Company.

Sadly, numerous pieces of equipment, and six valuable oil paintings of veteran Brooklyn and Manhattan fire companies were destroyed by the flames. The association's losses were estimated at $10,000 as the club's first floor was gutted.

Often the smoke was worse than the flames.

In the early morning hours of December 18, 1926, Brooklyn fire companies responded to a smoky fire at 225 Water Street. O'Hara arrived on scene at 6 a.m. with the first alarm units. Sizing up the difficult fire he transmitted second and third alarms, then went to work leading the battle against the flames.

As the fire was brought under control the chief laughed and joked with his men before leaving the scene and heading home at 8:30. After a brief stop at his headquarters, he arrived at his home on Hancock Street and advised his wife Catherine he had a heavy "dose of smoke" and felt ill. He told her he'd feel better after a nap. Knowing her husband she became anxious, but he assured her he'd be alright, he'd been through nothing worse than he'd endured dozens of times before.

The chief climbed into bed at around 10 a.m. Catherine went to wake him at 6:30 p.m. and found him dead. His was a major loss to his family, the fire department, and numerous groups he belonged to including the Knights of Columbus, the Brooklyn Elks, the Holy Name Society of the Fire Department, and his local church.

Fire Commissioner Dorman said:

I was very sorry to hear the sad news of the death of Deputy Chief John O'Hara. He was a great and a noble man, loved and respected by all the members of the department. I have known Chief O'Hara personally for more than a quarter of a century. He lived an exemplary life and was a credit to men of his type. May I say also that on behalf of the greatest firefighting force in the world we shall miss him. His death is a distinct loss to the great City of New York.

Thomas J. Ahearn

The respect of your peers is the greatest reward a firefighter can garner. Many firemen over the years have developed well-earned reputations. Few stand out as much as Thomas Ahearn. When his name was mentioned, it was almost always linked with the term "Bravest." Former Chief of Department Hugh Bonner said that Ahearn was one of the bravest men the fire force has ever known. Born in New York City on November 12, 1851, Thomas attended both public and parochial schools before joining the fire department on May 9, 1873. He was promoted to assistant foreman (lieutenant) on April 1, 1881, and was assigned to Hook & Ladder 11 on East 5th Street in Manhattan.

The night of June 7, 1885, Hook & Ladder 11 responded to a reported fire at 49 Pitt Street. The alarm was raised at 8:45 after a kerosene lamp exploded in a second-floor apartment. Within seconds the entire room was ablaze. Fleeing occupants left the door open in their panic and the fire began extending into the public hallway. The responding fire companies found flames leaping from the second floor of a four-story tenement building. Inside flames had extended from the second floor and up the narrow stairway leading to the upper floors, cutting off escape for those trapped above. With reports of children trapped on the fourth floor, Lt. Ahearn dashed inside and found the stairs blocked by flames.

Returning outside he climbed up the fire escape to the fourth floor. Finding the window Ahearn dove inside and began a difficult search. Faced with clouds of thick, hot smoke he crawled forward feeling his way. Despite the growing heat and flames, Ahearn found little Anna, five years old, and her two-year-old brother Joseph, both burned and unconscious. Picking them up in his arms Ahearn crawled to a window his men had just laddered.

With heavy fire pouring from nearby windows, Ahearn mounted the ladder, with a child in each arm as the crowd below cheered loudly. He somehow carried them both down to safety and turned them over for medical attention. Lt. Ahearn was also treated for painful burns to his hands.

On that very same day Ahearn had also responded to a fire at 312 East Houston Street where he'd rescued another five-year-old. Arriving at the front of the building Ahearn climbed up onto the stoop's railing and used it to grab the fire escape above. Muscling himself upwards he was able to reach the child who'd been cut off by the fire inside. Ahearn grabbed him and carried him to safety.

Thomas Ahearn was promoted to captain on February 25, 1886.

On July 23, 1890, fire companies responded to the Consolidated Gas Works on 21st Street between Avenue A and the East River where a tank of naphtha (a flammable liquid hydrocarbon mixture used in gasoline mixtures or as a solvent) had exploded. The blast set fire to the two-story pump-house that also housed two large wrought iron tanks, which were nearly full of naphtha. The capacity of each tank was 1,000 gallons. The initial explosion ruptured one tank and caused the second to explode moments later. The burning liquid was showered in all directions. The pump tender, a middle-aged man, was set ablaze. Covered in flames, he staggered forward and collapsed.

Captain Ahearn was in command of Engine 5 as they moved deep into the blazing building. One of the firemen spotted the prostrate man and called to Ahearn. Pressed to the ground by the scorching heat building around them they thought at first the man was dead. Ahearn's sharp eyes noticed his chest rise and fall. "He is not dead, I am going to get that man out!" Ahearn stated as he left his men and crawled ahead knowing that additional explosions could happen at any moment.

With flames raging around him and the constant threat of another explosion Ahearn inched forward flat on his stomach. He was able to grab the man and drag him back across the floor. Upon reaching safety the seriously burned man was rushed to the hospital where he later died. For his daring rescue Captain Thomas Ahearn was awarded the James Gordon Bennett Medal.

On January 2, 1893, Thomas J. Ahearn was promoted to battalion chief and assigned to the Fourth Battalion.

Fifteen months later Chief Ahearn would respond to a fire with life-changing consequences. It was a minute before midnight on April 3, 1894, when he responded to Box 227, a reported fire at 232 Rivington Street. Ahearn rolled from his quarters with Hook & Ladder 18 on Attorney Street. Fireman John Froboese, the chief's aide and driver, urged their horse to a gallop with the ladder truck following closely. Arriving at the blazing tenement the chief saw flames from a first-floor fire were threatening the entire building. Ahearn leapt from his buggy, as he learned a child was trapped in the fire apartment.

The chief paused long enough to gain information on the apartment layout before plunging into the burning flat. Under severe conditions he searched two rooms but was unable to find the child. He decided to search the blazing kitchen. He pulled his coat's collar up around his ears and dove into the room and made a desperate search. Still unable to find the child he returned to the exit only to find it had closed and locked blocking his way.

With flames swirling overhead and the entire room about to ignite he tried to kick his way through the door. His boot broke through the wooden door and became stuck throwing Ahearn onto his back. Ahearn struggled to breathe as the flames ignited his clothing. Worried firemen crawled in and found his leg protruding through the door. Captain Thomas O'Hearn and Lt. Beshinger of Hook & Ladder 18 broke away the damaged door, grabbed the chief and began to pull him clear. Ahearn was able to say, "Oh, Tom, save me!" Before he passed out.

As the injured chief was rushed from the building the missing child was found safe outside. It was decided to transport the chief to the hospital in his buggy rather than wait for an ambulance. He regained consciousness just as they raced toward the hospital. Captain O'Hearn was cradling Ahearn's burned head in his lap when Ahearn's eyes reopened. He looked up at his friend, "Don't frighten my wife, Tom…" he said then passed out again. O'Hearn was worried this was the last thing his brave comrade would ever say.

Ahearn was taken to Gouverneur Hospital suffering severe burns to the head, neck and hands. Every hair had been burned from his head. A fireman was kept by his side 24 hours a day to help him if needed and to advise the chief of department of any changes in his condition. It was weeks before he could even speak again. The staff was busy trying to save his eyesight by constantly changing gauze pads that were cooled first by a block of ice. His face, especially his mouth and ears were heavily bandaged. He finally moved a little in bed, so the doctor removed the bandages and leaned in close. "Can you speak chief?" and Ahearn answered, "I can see the pencil." The pencil was in the doctor's pocket. They were all relieved realizing he would probably not lose his sight.

The chief then went through another difficult period for several weeks. Finally, he awoke and tried to speak as his aide leaned in close. "Did they get the child?" The aide looked to Ahearn's brother John, a state senator who standing nearby. "Tell him yes," he said. The chief replied, "Thank God." He would remain in the hospital for months. But true to form, Thomas Ahearn, despite some hearing loss from his burns, returned to full duty.

Back at work Chief Ahearn, even with his lingering injuries, continued operating as he'd always done—leading from the front. On March 22, 1895, while battling a blaze at 164 East 3rd Street, members of Hook & Ladder 11 entered the cellar to battle the smoldering flames. After a few minutes Captain Thomas Sullivan fell unconscious from the smoke and accumulated pockets of sewer gas. As the captain was carried outside, Ahearn, Capt. Fisher, and members of Engine 25 entered the cellar to complete the extinguishment. Ahearn and Fisher both were knocked unconscious by the debilitating smoke and gas. Both were placed on the sidewalk outside the building and soon recovered and went back to work.

In November of 1899 Deputy Chief Benjamin Giquel of the First Division passed away. At the time there was civil service list for Chief Croker to use in replacing Giquel. So Chief Croker conferred with Commissioner Scannell and recommended Battalion Chief Ahearn for the position. Scannell made Ahearn acting deputy chief.

Ahearn was officially promoted to deputy chief on March 1, 1900, and assigned to the First Division in Manhattan. On January 30, 1901, D.C. Ahearn and his aide, Fireman William J. Martin of Hook & Ladder 4 responded to a fire in the Hotel Jefferson at 102 East 15th in Manhattan. Arriving quickly the chief and his aide saw several people on the sixth and seventh floors trapped by the flames and calling for help. The duo raced into the adjoining building, the Union Hotel, and took the stairs to the sixth floor accompanied by a policeman and a civilian.

Chief Ahearn found one of the hotel's lifesaving ropes (mandated by law after the Hotel Royal fire.) Ahearn went to a window and passed the rope across to a woman sitting on a windowsill of the blazing hotel and urged her to tie the rope around her waist. But as soon as she was handed the rope, she attempted to swing across. The rope broke and she fell to the sidewalk below and was killed instantly.

Ahearn and Martin left the cop and civilian on the sixth floor and dashed to the seventh floor, where two other ropes were procured. Ahearn doubled the ropes and passed them across to a husband who was waiting with his wife in a seventh-floor window. The husband secured his wife in the rope and helped her swing across to the waiting hands on the sixth floor. The ropes were returned to the husband, who tied the rope about himself and he, too, swung across the gap to safety.

To give Chief Ahearn some well-earned down time he was transferred to the relatively quiet 7th Division in the Bronx. Several times in 1910, Thomas Ahearn served as acting chief of department while Chief Croker was away.

Upon the retirement of Chief Edward Croker in 1911, all the deputy chiefs prepared for a new chief of department test. Part of this process was a medical exam. The Civil Service Commission ruled that due to the burn injuries Ahearn received in 1894, his hearing loss would disqualify him from taking the test. They also urged Mayor William Gaynor that the deputy chief should be retired at full pay (an unprecedented recommendation.) The mayor agreed.

After 38 years of service, on July 7, 1911, Deputy Chief Thomas J. Ahearn retired from the FDNY at full pay. But his time in public service would continue. In 1911 the State of New York established a new office of the State Fire Marshal. The governor asked Chief Ahearn to take the new position. He accepted.

The creation of this new office was a direct result of the Asch Building Fire (known to most as the Triangle Shirtwaist Fire that occurred on March 25, 1911, and claimed the lives of 146 people, mostly young women.) This new state official, the fire marshal, would supervise the administration of laws regarding the prevention of fires, the storage of combustibles, the installation of safety appliances, the inspection of boilers, and the construction and maintenance of fire escapes.

Ahearn had to build this new office from the ground up, starting with office space. He hired staff, gathered the pertinent laws and regulations to be enforced, and created the necessary forms and documents needed to record actions taken by the office and various applications to be completed by companies and persons in compliance with the laws.

One area of responsibility that became contentious was the storage and sale of combustible liquids in private and commercial garages. The automobile had become a big business in only ten years, and the people and companies in the field had become a strong political lobby.

The garagemen, as they were known, fought the existing rules and lobbied for less enforcement. Ahearn's office strongly disagreed. One group in particular, the Automobile Trade Association of New York State fought the fire marshal's efforts to regulate the storage of gasoline in private and commercial garages. A political alliance with state Republicans provided so much leverage that an act was passed that repealed the actions taken to create the fire marshal's office. In a closed session of the assembly, bills were passed that abolished the state fire marshal's office and the Department of Efficiency and Economy. (The Republican Party was able to "steamroller" right over Fire Marshal Ahearn and Commissioner Delaney, both Democrats.)

So, Thomas Ahearn finally retired. He left Albany and returned to his home in Flushing, Queens. He passed away at home on February 16, 1933, after suffering a stroke a few days earlier. Thomas J. Ahearn, "the bravest of the brave," was 80 years old.

George J. Fox

On March 11, 1888, George J. Fox joined the FDNY and was assigned to Engine Company 14. He later transferred to Engine 21. On February 7, 1892, he responded to a fire that would become infamous, the Hotel Royal Fire. The hotel stood on the southeast corner of 40th Street and Sixth Avenue in midtown Manhattan. When Engine 21 rolled to a stop, Fireman George Fox was informed that an elderly woman was trapped on the second floor on the 40th Street side of the building.

Finding his way inside blocked by fire he returned to the street and grabbed a scaling ladder from the hose wagon and climbed up to the second floor and entered the smoke-filled room. Thick, noxious smoke filled the room, and the roaring sound of the flames could be heard in the hallway just beyond the closed wooden door. Fox began his grueling search. Reaching the bed, he swept his arm across the top then dropped to the floor to check below. Underneath the bed he found the unconscious woman, apparently hiding from the flames. He pulled her from beneath the bed and carried her to the window.

Carefully climbing out onto the thin wobbly ladder, he climbed down with the woman and placed her in the hands of other firemen in the street. Taking a breath, he looked back toward the raging flames and saw another woman, trapped at a third-floor window. Grabbing another scaling ladder, he climbed to the top of a 20-foot portable ladder and raised the scaling ladder to the third-floor window. Reaching the top, he was able to pull the woman out onto the ladder and carry her to safety.

Despite the heroic actions of Fireman Fox and the numerous other brave firemen, 28 people lost their lives at this fire. A large loss of life. But considering more than 150 people were asleep at the time of the fire, the number rescued reflected the excellent work of the firemen.

On July 10, 1898, George Fox was promoted to lieutenant and assigned to Engine Company 14 on East 18th Street. On April 19, 1901, Engine 14 responded to a reported fire at 252 Sixth Avenue. At the scene a woman and her daughter were visible, trapped at a fourth-floor window calling for help. Lt. Fox and Fireman Eugene Rable dashed up the stairs to the fourth floor. They found heavy fire conditions on this floor and crawled down the hallway as the smoke and heat built up around them. Finding the apartment, the firemen entered and began their search.

They found both the mother and daughter unconscious on the floor of the front room. Each man grabbed a victim and began dragging them back to the public hallway. The hallway had become untenable as flames were bursting from a transom window above the door to the fire apartment. Keeping low they inched their way past the flames, which were rolling overhead and reached the stairs. They brought both the mother and daughter to safety.

On August 15, 1903, George Fox was promoted to captain and placed in command of Engine 33. He later transferred to Engine 21 on East 40th Street in Manhattan. In 1904 Captain Fox was placed on the Roll of Merit for a rescue while working in Engine 21. Then, in 1906 while working as an acting chief in the Eighth Battalion, Fox made another rescue that would earn him a medal of valor.

On the morning of March 19, 1906, FDNY units responded to a smoky fire in the Pennsylvania Tunnel at the foot of 32nd Street in Manhattan. George Fox responded as the acting chief of the Eighth Battalion. Arriving companies were faced with thick smoke that was so suffocating and noxious it was nearly impossible to enter and operate inside the pressurized tunnel.

Acting Chief Fox entered the tunnel alone and was able to extinguish the fire himself by cutting away burning flooring and beams. He was also able to locate and remove the body of a suffocated watchman. Captain Fox suffered bleeding from the nose, ears, and mouth upon his exit from the tunnel. For his valiant efforts he was awarded the first Wertheim Medal during a ceremony at Union Square Plaza attended by Mayor McClelland and thousands of New Yorkers.

Christmas Day 1910 saw Captain Fox transfer to Engine Company 90 at 1841 White Plains Road in the Bronx. The company had been organized in May of that year with a lieutenant in command. Fox also became acting chief of the 15th Battalion. He remained in the Bronx until he transferred back to Manhattan and took command of Engine 44 in 1911, then took command of Hook & Ladder 16 on October 25th of that year.

November 10, 1916, saw George Fox transferred to Engine 49 on Blackwell Island. This posting was usually reserved for officers that were recovering from injuries. He remained there until July 2, 1924, when he was given command of Engine Company 264 on Central Avenue in Queens, not far from his home. He continued there until his retirement on June 6, 1925, after 37 years of service. He passed away in 1936 at the age of 70.

Charles E. Field

Brooklyn fire alarm Box 614 was transmitted on August 30, 1895, sending Hook & Ladder 7 (later known as Ladder 107) racing from their quarters on New Jersey Avenue toward a fire in a tailor's shop on Osborne Street. The new hook & ladder truck rolled out with Lt. John Hogarth in command, Horace Peason was driving, and Charles Field was on the tiller. The three-horse team gathered speed as the members riding the side steps held tight. The company raced down New Jersey Avenue to Liberty Avenue, to Vesta Avenue toward the railroad crossing. As the ladder truck approached the crossing the firemen could see a train approaching rapidly from the east. Peason pulled his reins back slowing the horses.

The railroad gates were up, because the fire truck had the right of way. Gateman William Clark holding a red lantern shouted to the driver: "Come along; you're all right!" as he dashed down the track signaling the locomotive engineer to stop. Peason urged the horses on as the ladder truck rolled onto the tracks.

The train's engineer did not heed the signalman's warning and continued ahead. The locomotive struck the fire truck just in front of the rear wheels, inches away from Field, who gripped the tilled wheel tightly. The locomotive sliced right through the ladder truck leaving the rear wheels by the trackside as the firemen went flying into the air.

Tillerman Field fell forward, directly under the wheels of a train car, losing part of his left foot and left arm. One man flew from the rig and crashed into a nearby storefront, the officer flew over the horses into the middle of Liberty Avenue. The remaining men were badly banged up but escaped serious injury. The horses, freed from their damaged leads bolted in a panic.

Fireman Field was rushed to St. Mary's Hospital in critical condition. The gateman and the train engineer were both arrested by police.

Back in 1891, Charles Field had taken the civil service mental and physical exams for the position of fireman and was third on a list of 247 eligible candidates. On July 17th he was appointed a fireman. After recovering from his life altering injuries he was promoted to assistant foreman (lieutenant) and given a desk job at headquarters. In 1906 Field was second on the list to be promoted to captain, which caused some debate within the department. Many felt he should be retired with a disability pension, others thought he should be allowed to continue his career.

The president of the civil service commission was questioned about the case, and he replied:

> When the examination for promotion to captain came on, he (Field) applied for exemption from physical examination and explained how he had lost his arm in the service. The commission decided that just because a man has lost an arm in the service of his city is no reason why he should be barred from promotion provided he is otherwise all right. So, the commission provided that if he could pass the physical examination in every particular, with the single exception of the arms it would accept him.
>
> He was subjected to precisely the same examination as all the other candidates and was found to be in good condition. It would be a crime to bar a man from promotion because he lost an arm in the service of the city and I

am surprised to learn that there has been any comment on the case at all.

Charles Field was promoted to captain on March 18, 1906. He was assigned to Hook & Ladder 107 but was again detailed to headquarters.

In 1915 Fire Commissioner Adamson invited the 5,000 members of the uniformed force to assist in the operation of the department by offering a medal to the member who made the best suggestion for the improvement of the department. The commissioner was flooded with good ideas. Deputy Chief Patrick Maher was awarded the first Administration Medal with his idea to keep records of each member to distinguish between the energetic and efficient members and those that were not.

A close second was the idea submitted by Captain Charles Field who proposed that members should be drilled in various physical exercises in order to keep them constantly fit for the arduous fire duty they faced. His idea was accepted by the commissioner and put into effect in firehouses across the city. Field had been a life-long advocate of athletic training and calisthenics. This may have helped him overcome the devastating injuries he'd received in the train crash earlier in his career.

Chief officers across the city chose men from each company that were sent to a YMCA on the west side of Manhattan and trained by drill instructors in the various exercises. Commissioner Adamson remarked: "The object of these exercises is to keep the men in as good physical condition as when they came into the department." The commissioner's office also provided an illustrated drill book to be used in conjunction with the training.

On August 1, 1937, Captain Charles E. Field retired from the FDNY after 46 years of service.

Luke Flanagan

Luke Flanagan was born in Roscommon, Ireland, in 1873. He came to the New York with his parents and later joined the U.S. Navy. He served on the battleship USS *Massachusetts* and attained the rank of Chief Petty Officer. The battleship saw combat in the Spanish American War and was part of Commodore Schley's Flying Squadron, protecting east coast American ports from the Spanish Fleet. She also took part in an attack on the fort at the mouth of Santiago's harbor, and traded fire with several Spanish ships, helping to sink the cruiser, *Reina Mercedes*. When his enlistment was up Flanagan moved to the merchant marine and earned a marine engineer's license which qualified him for any tonnage in transatlantic service. He returned to New York City and was appointed to the FDNY on April 1, 1901, and assigned to Engine Company 34 in Manhattan.

During his training he caught the eye of Captain McAdam, the drill master and soon found himself part the department drill team. Flanagan was noted for his daredevil leaps into life nets. A newspaper reported that in 1904, Fireman Luke Flanagan leapt from a window 89 feet above the ground, landing uninjured in a new spring net that was held by 15 firemen. The article also stated that Fire Commissioner Sturgis, after finding out it was Flanagan's 100th leap, ordered him to stop jumping as it was an unnecessary danger. It was also mentioned his leap was a record that would never be broken.

Flanagan was promoted to engineer of steamer on July 1, 1905, and because of his training as a marine engineer, he was assigned to Engine 77, the fireboat *Abraham S. Hewitt* stationed at the foot of Gansevoort Street Hudson River. On March 1, 1908, Flanagan was promoted to lieutenant and assigned to Engine Company 7 stationed at 100-102 Duane Street.

On July 16, 1910, a crowd of more than 10,000 people, most on their way home from work stopped to watch a major waterfront blaze at Pier 14 North River. It was 12:40 p.m. when a fire was seen burning among some off-loaded cargo 40 feet from the end of the pier. Driven by strong winds the fire quickly spread and the cries of "FIRE!" echoed across the pier. On board the passenger steamer *Harvard*, the crew scrambled to stretch their own hoses and began battling the flames with eight streams of water. Unfortunately, no one notified the fire department, allowing the fire to expand despite the efforts of the crew.

Nearby on Pier 15, the freighter *Altamaha* was loading cargo when the fire broke out. The captain was able to shove off from the pier with a lighter (barge) still attached by mooring lines and move into the safety of the river. Still moored to Pier 14, a large steam ship, the *H.F. Dimock*, was soon ablaze along with the Bush Terminal lighter *Katie*. Crew members scrambled for safety and several were forced to jump overboard. The flames moved so quickly that a taxicab driver who'd dropped off passengers could not crank start his cab in time and had to run for his life as the automobile caught fire and exploded.

With flames threatening the ship and literally blistering the paint from the hull, the crew of the *Harvard* was able to chop through their mooring lines to free the ship. Despite not having a good head of steam, the crew was able to move the ship clear of the flames. The *H.F. Dimock*, with her decks ablaze was also swung into the river and was rescued by several tugboats.

Meanwhile, the FDNY arrived and despite the advanced fire situation, commenced their attack. Chief Binns directed the battle until Chief Croker arrived and assumed command.

Croker transmitted the fourth alarm as the fire jumped from Pier 14 to Pier 15. Flying brands sailed across West Street and set several sections of the old Washington Market on fire. Radiant heat was also igniting the corrugated roof of Pier 13. A fleet of fireboats and tugboats moved in to battle the flames from the water side as the land-based firemen continued their assault.

Conditions on West Street were becoming extreme, as smoke, heat and flaming embers blew across the street igniting storefronts along the street. The huge crowd of onlookers were forced to move to side streets, and the ferry boat operating from Pier 16 had to stop operations for two hours.

Eventually, the firemen began to gain the upper hand. During the battle Lt. Luke Flanagan began pulling some corrugated metal away to allow his nozzle team a better shot. A section of the red-hot metal tore through his hand causing a deep, painful gash. Flanagan was directed to the aid station where his hand was dressed on the spot. When informed by Doctor Archer that he was being sent to Hudson Street Hospital, Flanagan attempted to convince the doctor he could return to work. The doctor insisted, and Lt. Flanagan was taken off for further medical attention.

The following year, 1911, Luke Flanagan was promoted to captain and was given command of Engine Company 33 on Great Jones Street. This was a double company, two complete engine companies each with a steam engine and hose wagon all pulled by horses. The company's district was bounded by Houston and Thompson streets, Fifth Avenue, 8th Street, Fourth Avenue and the Bowery. Flanagan was now in command of four lieutenants, five engineers of steamers, and 24 firemen. In April of 1912 he attended the Fire College for six weeks.

Being the commander of a double engine company, it so happened that Captain Flanagan took possession of two Mack high pressure hose wagons in 1913. He also received a Christie tractor that was placed under the company's 1906 American *LaFrance* steamer. Looks like the horses are done and gone from Engine 33.

In 1915 Rescue 1 was organized in the Great Jones Street firehouse. Two of the eight firemen chosen for the new specialized company were Captain Flanagan's men: Firemen Walter A. O'Leary and John P. Ryan, both of Engine 33. This firehouse was also the night offices of the chief of department.

It was while Flanagan was captain of Engine 33, that he began studying law at New York University. In between fires he read law books and journals. His name was placed on the Roll of Merit in 1916 for heroic actions in the line of duty. In 1918 he was promoted to battalion chief and assigned to the Sixth Battalion. A year later Flanagan graduated New York University with a Bachelor of Laws, (this was the first professional law degree. *Juris Doctor* would become the standard in the 1960s,) but he continued with the FDNY. In 1920 Flanagan became an associate member of the International Association of Fire Engineers (now chiefs—the IAFC.)

True to his busy nature Flanagan was splitting his time between studying for the deputy chief's exam and writing a technical book about firefighting called *Science In Fire-Fighting*. The book, published by S.L. Parsons & Company in 1920, covered three main areas of study: mechanics, hydraulics, and heat and combustion. Mechanics covered the scientific principles involved in handling appliances, raising and extending ladders and water towers. With the forces required to execute the various operations shown mathematically. Hydraulics dealt mostly with the loss of power due to friction. The heat and combustion portion discussed the scientific knowledge gained from the study of combustion, radiation, and heat diffusion.

On September 7, 1922, Battalion Chief Flanagan, even

though he was on the eligible list for deputy chief, retired from the FDNY. He then became an associate of Robert A. Fosdick at 41 Park Row. When he was not legally engaged, he also lectured fire promotion classes at the Titus Civil Service School on East 13th Street. (It is interesting to note that the Titus School was the only civil service prep school in the city until Michael Delehanty opened his own school on East 11th Street. Eventually 80 to 90 percent of the city's cops and firemen were graduates of "Delehanty U.")

According to an April 1926 article in *Fire Protective Service Magazine*, among his other clients, Flanagan represented firemen in at least two separate cases. One involved a fireman unfairly fired, a second was seeking damages from a gas explosion. This case, injuries from a gas explosion, Flanagan took all the way to the New York Supreme Court. The case involved Fireman James J. Burke from an unnamed Manhattan fire company and the Uniformed Firemen's Association and argued that firemen should have the same rights for damages as private citizens.

Justice Churchill wrote the opinion in which his colleagues concurred. It held that the gas company's employee's negligence was clearly shown. It declared the standing of a fireman before the court in such cases was the same as the standing of civilians, that they lose no right of such action because of their membership in the fire department. They further found the claims of injury could not be shown to the courts satisfaction to be linked to the negligence of the gas company employees.

Therefore, while the verdict of the court ended up against the fireman, it did uphold the UFAs contention that firemen stand equal under the law.

Luke Flanagan also continued lecturing student firemen. He never agreed with the theory that firemen only required brawn and muscle. "I believe that fire control demands the

service of men educated for engineering and similar professions."
Chief Luke Flanagan passed away on May 29, 1950.

Lines & Lions

It was four o'clock Monday morning February 8, 1904, and the man on watch aboard the 260-foot long, Steamship *Tremont* was making his rounds on the main deck when he discovered smoke. Closer inspection found flames among the cargo stored in the port-side forward hold where 156 tons of freight were stored.

The ship, a side wheeler, traveled back and forth between Manhattan and Providence. She was moored in the East River at Catharine Slip, almost under the Brooklyn Bridge. The ship arrived late Sunday afternoon, and the cargo was not scheduled to be unloaded until later that morning. When the watchman saw the flames, he awoke another crew member, and together they alerted the 45 members of the crew asleep in their bunks.

As the crew escaped the smoke and flames, a call was made to the FDNY. The crew began fighting the fire and under the direction of the ship's captain George Oelweiler, five hose lines were stretched and operating as the fire department arrived. Faced with an advanced fire, a second and third alarms were transmitted and the fireboats *New Yorker* and *Strong* responded.

On the main deck, Lt. Andrews and his Engine 12 nozzle team, Firemen Matthews, Siemes and Grady were directing their hose stream into the blazing hold when loud animal noises were heard from below decks. Unseen by the firemen, were two wooden cages in amongst the burning cargo. Inside the cages were two lions and a Great Dane dog. As the flames ate away the enclosure the lions escaped. The frantic animals leaped up onto the main deck and roared their displeasure.

The fire officer and his men stepped back, their mouths hanging open in surprise. There before them backlit by flames, stood two lions now only 20 feet away from them. "Turn the water on them and back away!" Andrews ordered. His men acted quickly and directed the powerful water stream into the snarling faces of the deadly animals.

On the pier below, the heavy smoke obscured the vision of the chiefs and firefighters. They could however hear the frantic shouts of alarmed firemen and the roars of the wild animals. New York City firemen prided themselves on being ready for anything, except one would imagine, dealing with apex predators. As the lions were driven back by the stream, Andrews and his men inched over to the railing. One by one they lowered themselves from the deck using a davit. The lions continued roaring and dashing around the smoke-filled decks until the flames closed in and eventually claimed the beasts.

The escaped firemen, near exhaustion from their hard work and the debilitating smoke, were helped to safety. The charred bodies of the lions, who'd been taken to the city for an exhibition in a museum, were found hours later.

The ship eventually sank at the pier.

Part 2

Steamers & Engineers

In 1648 Peter Stuyvesant, the Governor of New Amsterdam, appointed four fire wardens, starting the fire service in America. The wardens patrolled the streets at night and inspected chimneys by day. Their numbers increased as the city grew. In 1731, the good ship *Beaver*, arrived from England carrying two Newsham hand fire engines. Jacobus Turk, a gunsmith, was appointed to take charge of the engines and keep them in good repair at his own cost, after a 10-pound advance was provided to him. These engines were relatively small, hand operated pumps that developed a stream of water that could be directed at a fire.

The General Assembly of the colony established the New York Volunteer Fire Department in 1737 and appointed 30 firemen. In 1761 Jacobus Stoutenburgh was made head of the department in 1861 and was paid 30-pounds a year. The next year his title was changed from "Overseer of Fire Engines" to "Engineer" (the spelling at that time was Engenier.) He is also credited as the creator of the leather stovepipe fire hat, that would later evolve into the American fire helmet.

In 1786 the Common Council reorganized firefighting efforts with the establishment of a new 300-man department. Five engineers were named to run the department. In 1791, one of those engineers, William J. Ellsworth was placed in overall charge with the title of chief engineer. He commanded 15 engines and two ladder companies.

These hand-operated hand engines became larger and more powerful as their design and construction improved.

Meanwhile, the Industrial Revolution (mid-1700s to 1800s) was slowly transforming the world with new technology. In England, Thomas Newcomen made the first commercially successful steam engine (not firefighting related) in 1712. This was greatly improved upon by James Watt in 1769. By 1812, steam was being used to power railway locomotives. These improvements were used to initiate the invention of steam fire engines. In 1841 Paul Hodge, an American civil-engineer, produced a steam-powered fire engine he called "The Exterminator." That same year Philadelphia's John Agnew began production of some of the most powerful and widely-used hand pumpers. These Philadelphia-style double decker had twin sets of pump handles that were operated by two rows of men on each side. One row held the brakes (handles used to pump) while standing on the ground. The second row stood on the deck of the pumper. Manned by 48 firemen it could deliver a stream of water 180 feet horizontally.

The best of the hand-powered pumpers was almost an even match for the newly perfected steam engines. The tipping point however became the continuing rowdy behavior of the large number of volunteer firemen needed to successfully operate the hand-pumpers. Several conflagrations in major American cities, and the pressure applied by insurance companies pushed the municipalities to abandon the volunteer system and embrace paid firemen using the constantly improving steam engines.

Despite the power of Tammany Hall, and the large numbers of politically active volunteer firemen, the state government decided enough was enough and took the power away from the city. On January 16, 1865, a bill was introduced in Albany, known as "The Act to create a Metropolitan Fire District and establish a Fire Department therein."

The battle between the city and state continued in the courts until the Court of Appeals ruled in favor of the new department on June 22, 1865.

The head of the new paid department was Elisha Kingsland with the rank of chief engineer. He took command on August 1, 1865, with a force that consisted of 15 assistant engineers, 52 volunteer engine companies, 54 volunteer hose companies and 17 volunteer hook & ladder companies. This force totaled 3,778 volunteer firemen and officers.

The actual physical start of the. Metropolitan Fire Department (later called the FDNY) began the day before on July 31, 1865, with the organization of Engine Company 1. They began service in a former volunteer firehouse at 4 Centre Street in Manhattan. They were assigned a new 1st Class Steam Engine built by the Amoskeag Manufacturing Company of Manchester, New Hampshire. This large steamer and a hose tender were both drawn by horses. The steamer by a team of two, and the hose tender by a single horse.

The first company commander was Foreman (captain) William Corgan, with his Assistant Foreman Walter T. Furlong. The steamer was to be pumped at fires and maintained in quarters by the Engineer of Steamer James Gilchrist. There was also a stoker, who fed coal into the fire box beneath the boiler, as the engineer operated the various valves that fed water into the boiler to produce the steam that drove the pistons to pump water into hoses under pressure.

There was also a driver and five firemen assigned to the company. This was the only paid fire company until September 1, 1865, when Engine 2 was organized at 304 West 47th Street, and Hook & Ladder 1 was organized on September 8, 1865, at 28 Chambers Street. The needed manpower was supplemented by volunteer fire companies that were slowly being disbanded as the new paid companies came in service.

In the earliest days only the drivers, foreman and engineer rode on the rigs. Everyone else ran to the fire. It makes sense that New York firemen referred to their response to alarms as "a run!"

When the department was created in 1865 the pay rates were: company foreman $800, assistant foreman $750, steamer engineer $900, drivers, stokers, tillermen, and firemen received $700. These rates were adjusted slightly by the state legislature the following year: a foreman was now paid $1,100 per year, the engineer of steamer was paid $1,080, the assistant foreman received $900, and a fireman $840. The rules and regulations of the new department stated in Section 10:

> The engineers of steamers shall, under the foreman, have the care and management of the steam-engines of their respective companies, and shall be held responsible that the same are in good working order and ready at all times for immediate use.

It was understandable the foreman should be paid more than the engineer of steamer, since the company commander was responsible for every action taken by the members of his company including the engineer. The reason engineers of steamer were paid almost as much as their captain, was they were considered "key personnel" because of the huge responsibility they held. Steam fire engines were complicated machines, that became even more so when they had to be raced through the streets to the scenes of fires and then operated quickly and efficiently.

The engineer of steamer was responsible for the care and condition of the apparatus—greasing the wheels, lubricating the chassis, and polishing the bright work. The engineer of steamer also maintained a constant steam pressure within the fire engine's boiler of 10 pounds while in quarters. (This increased to 20 pounds as the buildings grew taller and taller.) The pressure was officially checked every three hours (day and night) and the pressure reading was recorded in the company journal. The engineer was assisted in this work by the stoker. The engineer and company chauffeurs accompanied the officer on duty every morning after roll call, and inspected the apparatus and motors for proper lubrication and to check that they were in good working order.

Every firehouse that stationed a steamer had a small potbellied stove in the cellar that was used exclusively to provide steam pressure for the engine. Piping was extended from this stove, up through the apparatus floor to the pumper. A special slip-joint was used to insure a quick and easy disconnection when the apparatus responded to an alarm.

Excelsior (soft wood shavings) and wood kindling were used as the base of the fire to be ignited inside the steamer's fire box. Cannel coal, a fast-burning, gaseous bituminous coal, provided the fuel. Department rules and regulations required the engineer to have a 30-minute supply of cannel coal on hand, but they usually carried as much as they could pile on. (A fuel wagon was assigned on multiple alarms to augment the supply.) As he boarded the rear of the steamer when answering an alarm, the engineer ignited the excelsior and kindling in the fire box to begin rapidly developing enough heat to build steam in the boiler as they careened through the city's streets.

The engineer of steamer's most important responsibility of course was to supply a good and sufficient stream of water. The lives of the citizens and the firemen both were in the engineer's hands.

This became apparent on the evening of June 18, 1868, when companies responded to a reported fire at 53 Bowery. Engine Company 1's Amoskeag steam pumper, recently returned from the repair yards, had been operating for a short while. It pumped water through a hose line and the small fire was successfully extinguished. During the operation, Engineer of Steamer Patrick Hand noticed the safety valve was leaking. He took steps to stop the leak. With the assistance of a fireman, Hand placed a strap on the valve and tightened it to stop the leak. The company was in the process of "taking up" (the final part of firefighting when all the hose and tools used were gathered and placed back on the rigs.) As the hose was being drained and pulled back downstairs, the audience from the Old Bowery Theatre was letting out, across the street from the fire, and near where the steamer was hooked up to a hydrant. The crowd of mostly boys and men was exiting on to the sidewalk and quickly became engaged with the spectacle of the fire apparatus and firemen.

Suddenly, as the engineer was opening an intake water valve, the steamer exploded. The heavy steamer was lifted into the air by the blast as mangled parts and scalding water were hurled in all directions, including into the adjacent crowd. The blast also lifted a passing streetcar from its tracks and extinguished all the nearby gas streetlights plunging the area into darkness. When the dust and chaos settled it was seen that three men and a teenage boy had been killed instantaneously. Two more died in the hospital. The blast also left more than 30 persons injured. Engineer Hand was found under the steamer with one of the front wheels pinning him to the ground. He was extricated and taken to City Hospital in intense pain and suffering serious burns.

There were numerous serious injuries including burns, broken bones, and contusions. The injured included Foreman Roach who was reported as being scalded by the blast. The injured were rushed to hospitals as the dead were carried to a nearby police station. A coroner's inquest was called for and a jury impaneled. Their verdict was:

> We find that the deceased came to their deaths from

injuries by the explosion of the boiler of Engine No. 1, of the Metropolitan Fire Department, on the 18th inst., in the Bowery; we also find said explosion to have been caused by an overpressure of steam, the result of mismanagement of said boiler on the part of engineer, Patrick W. Hand.

As a result of these findings the fire commissioners dropped Patrick Hand from the department rolls. Engine Company 1 was disbanded the same day as the explosion. (The company would be reorganized in 1873.)

The power of steam was proving to be a dangerous force to be reckoned with, not just in New York, but around the world. According to a magazine called *Engineering*, during the year 1867 there were 70 steam boiler explosions in the United States, with 247 persons killed. In the first four months of 1868 there were 32 explosions that left 143 dead. Things were no better in Great Britain where 48 explosions in 1867 left 70 dead.

These explosions included stationary boilers (inside buildings, factories and mills,) as well as train locomotives, steamboats and tugs, and even a portable sawmill boiler. The Industrial Revolution, and the steam power that came with it, was a very dangerous undertaking. As if firefighting wasn't dangerous enough, firemen now had to consider their very means of water supply as a possible source of injury and even death.

Before the start of the Civil Service, promotions to the rank of engineer of steamer were initiated by the recommendations of battalion chiefs. The candidate's qualifications were then determined by a board appointed by the chief of department. Examinations both oral and written were then conducted by the board. In August of 1899, the Civil Service Commission took over these examinations.

The job of the engineer of steamer occasionally became more than pumping the steam engine at the scene of a fire. As a member of the uniformed force, they were at heart—firefighters. When duty called, they were ready to perform. Many performed acts of heroism, had their names added to the Roll of Merit, and even received medals for their valor.

The first to be recognized for his heroic conduct was Engineer of Steamer Seneca Larke, Jr. of Engine Company 20, who was detailed to drive and operate the searchlight unit (a steam engine equipped with large theatrical lights to provide fire ground illumination). At the height of the Equitable Building fire on January 9, 1912, the building collapsed, taking the life of a battalion chief and trapping several firemen. Also trapped were William Giblin, president of the Mercantile Savings Deposit Company, three of his clerks and a watchman. They were in a below grade vault that had barred windows at the sidewalk level. Their plight was noticed by firemen and a rescue effort was begun. Faced with a screen of bowed out steel bars, two inches in diameter, the ill-equipped firemen struggled to gain access with borrowed hacksaws.

With daylight breaking, Larke left his searchlight and volunteered his services to Chief Kenlon. He explained as a former ironworker, he knew the techniques that would enable him to do the job. Although reluctant to put the 37-year-old father of six into such a hazardous position, Chief Kenlon agreed.

With a new hacksaw frame and several fresh blades. Larke laid on his stomach by the barred window and began cutting. Water from outside streams, was pouring down the face of the building and splashing onto Larke by the barrelful, freezing as it fell. Broken stones, glass, flaming embers, and debris also fell on Larke and the chaplain who had taken a position next to Larke to give the Last Rights to the imprisoned if the rescue failed.

Firefighters directed hose streams into the cellar from time to time to control fire near the trapped men. Larke talked to Giblin, giving him encouragement as he worked to get through the bars. Giblin was a sickly shade of white and was clinging to the bars; next to him in even worse shape was the clerk named Campion.

After nearly an hour, one bar was cut free, but the opening wasn't large enough. Larke continued cutting, stopping only to change worn or broken saw blades, an interruption that was necessary 15 times.

A large stone fell on Larke's back and paralyzed him for a moment, but despite orders from both the chief and the commissioner to withdraw, Larke refused to stop cutting. A fireman had stayed nearby with a crowbar to help bend the bars back and to chip the ice off Larke so his arms could move freely.

The rescue operation was almost an hour and a half old when Campion's head slowly dropped down. Larke yelled to the man, Giblin moved in close to him to check him. Looking almost near collapse himself, Giblin told Larke that Campion was dead. The chaplain began his prayers and Larke sawed with renewed vigor.

After nearly an hour more, the second bar gave way and was pulled clear. Larke called for help. Giblin and the watchman were pulled to safety and then hurried to a nearby hospital. Larke was also hospitalized. For his heroic actions Engineer of Steamer Seneca Larke, Jr. was awarded the Bennett and Department medals.

Also recognized for bravery at this fire was Engineer of Steamer Charles W. Rankin, of Engine Co. 33 who responded as Chief Kenlon's aide. (See his section of this book for details.)

On June 14, 1913, while battling a difficult blaze on Water Street that involved a shed filled with barrels of gasoline and petroleum, Engineer of Steamer William McAllister of Engine 15, teamed up with his officer Captain Patrick Walsh in the rescue of Lt. Harry Schoener, who had fallen into a large puddle of burning fuel. The duo grabbed the burning officer, pulled him to safety and extinguished his burning clothing. Both were awarded medals with Engineer of Steamer William McAllister receiving the Mayor Strong and Department medals.

Engineer of Steamer William J. Fealy of Engine Co. 33 was detailed as chauffeur to the chief of department, when he responded to a fire on May 28, 1914. With a woman trapped on the fourth floor and no lines yet stretched, it took ingenuity to survive the building heat. Fealy wrapped his coat around his face before passing through the fire-swept fourth-floor hallway. Bursting through the door he located the trapped woman. Wrapping his coat around her, they proceeded back through the fiery hallway to the stairs and safety. Both the woman and Fealy were badly burned about the face and hands. For his heroic actions Engineer of Steamer William Fealy was awarded the Trevor-Warren and Department medals.

The Bonner and Department medals were awarded to Engineer of Steamer Timothy J. Fitzpatrick of Engine Co. 224 for his heroic actions on June 5, 1919, at the Hotel Bossert, at Montague and Hicks Streets. When a woman suffering mental problems learned she was to be committed to a sanitarium, she left her home and took a room in the Hotel Bossert. She promptly barricaded herself in her room and sat with her feet dangling out the window threatening to jump. The fire department was called, and Engineer of Steamer Timothy Fitzpatrick and a crew of men went to the rooms above where a rope was tied around Fitzpatrick. He jumped from the window directly above and swung down and caught her around the body and forced her back into the room.

On March 7, 1938, Engineer of Steamer Edward A. Rose of Engine Co. 78, saw a boy helpless and floundering in the East River off 90th Street in Manhattan. Engineer Rose, fully clothed, swam to his assistance and succeeded in bringing the boy back with him to the fireboat McClellan, where both the child and the engineer were taken onboard and treated for exposure before being taken to the hospital. It is interesting to note that at the time of the water rescue, Engineer Rose was over 55 years of age and had completed more than 30 years of service. The following year the Crimmins Medal was pinned on Engineer of Steamer Edward Rose by Mayor Fiorello LaGuardia during a departmental ceremony at the Court of Peace at the New York World's Fair in Queens.

The last to receive a medal for valor was Engineer of Steamer Otto R. Kutzke of Engine Co. 57, the fireboat *Firefighter*. At 5:30 p.m. on April 24, 1943, the Jersey City Fire Department was notified of a fire onboard the steamship *El Estero*, which was docked at Caven Point Terminal at the foot of Chappel Avenue in Jersey City, New Jersey. The ship was loaded with ammunition bound for the war. Twenty minutes after the initial alarm was received, Jersey City requested help from New York City's fireboats. Engine 57, the fireboat *Firefighter* (now known as *Marine 1*), and Engine 86, the fireboat *John J. Harvey* (now known as *Marine 2*), responded with Acting Deputy Chief John J. Hurton in command. Hurton and Battalion Chief John J. Lowery responded to the fire in the tender *Smoke*.

The burning ship was being moved away from the Jersey docks by two tugboats as the FDNY boats arrived. Chief Hurton checked the tides and decided to have the *El Estero* towed toward Robbins Reef Light in New York Bay. It was hoped that if the fire caused the detonation of the munitions, damage would be light to the surrounding waterfront. During the towing operation, the entire New York Harbor area was in peril. At any moment, the *El Estero* could detonate and ravage the building and ships along both sides of the river.

Using hawsers (very thick ropes), the tugboats pulled the ship toward the lower harbor, as flames roared below decks in the ammunition ship. The fire obviously was gaining in intensity and fireboat crews were aware of the blazing ship's cargo. One hold contained blockbuster bombs, each of which weighed 4,000 pounds. Nearby holds contained magnesium bombs and other explosives.

Chief Hurton had two choices: either the fire had to be extinguished or the burning ship sunk before flames reached the stored bombs. The two fireboats moved in, monitors flowing. Twenty-five streams were directed into *El Estero*. The ship finally surrendered to the attacking fireboats and submerged to its superstructure about a half mile northeast of the Robbins Reef Light.

At this medal ceremony Mayor Fiorello H. LaGuardia pinned 26 Department Medals on the chests of the crew members of the two fireboats. Eleven of these men also were presented citizen's medals for their valor. Engineer of Steamer Otto R. Kutzke of Engine 57 was awarded the Johnston and Department medals for his part in this dangerous operation.

Sadly, the job of engineer of steamer also proved to be an extremely dangerous one. Eleven FDNY Engineers of Steamer have died in-the-line-of-duty. Nine were killed during responses where they were either involved in a collision or were thrown or fell from the moving apparatus. They were:

1873 — George A. Erlaher, Battalion 2
1887 — William Wray, Engine 54
1890 — John Bulger, Engine 43
1895 — Peter McKeon, Engine 5
1906 — William H. Rush, Engine 49
1909 — Charles E. Meadows, Engine 162 (now 262)
1912 — William F. Stanton, Engine 103 (now 203)
1913 — John B. Barget, Engine 234

1914—John B. Doran, Engine 156.

In 1922 Patrick Doherty suffered a heart attack while working in Brooklyn Headquarters.

In 1904 Mark A. Kelly Engine 16, died from pneumonia complications, contracted on the FDNY mutual aid to the city of Baltimore. He died at his home in New York City.

With the advent of FDNY motorization, the last steamers were purchased in 1912 and arrived the following year. The 1898 steamer assigned to Engine Company 1 (reorganized in 1873 on West 33rd Street) was motorized in 1912. The team of horses was replaced by a gasoline powered Cross tractor. This proved to be a very effective method. The existing apparatus could continue in service while the horses were literally "put out to pasture." Several companies were contracted to supply these powerful hard rubber-wheeled tractors.

The last FDNY unit to have their horses replaced was Brooklyn's Engine Company 205. A ceremonial "Last Run," was staged and photographed on December 20, 1922, as Assistant Fire Chief Joseph B. Martin, in full uniform, tapped the following code: 5-93-205 into the fire alarm box at the corner of Joralemon and Court Street. This was a special call for Engine 205 to respond to the box location which happened to be in front of Borough Hall in Brooklyn. When the bells in the Pierrepont Street quarters rang out, the three-horse team was quickly harnessed. As Driver John Foster (literally the senior whip,) took his seat and the reins of the steamer, they started out for the box with the company's mascot "Jiggs" the Dalmatian—running ahead of the team to clear the way. Captain Leon Howard stood in his usual position on the ash pan (the step-like box in the rear of the steamer). As they gained speed the captain pulled the steam whistle rope, sounding a long clear blast, as Engineer of Steamer Tom McEwen pushed coal into the fire box. It's notable that even on the last, ceremonial run, they were ready for fire duty as they rolled.

Waiting in front of Borough Hall were Fire Commissioner Drennan, and other politicians, along with Smoky Joe, and other FDNY brass. Also waiting was Engine Company 205's gleaming new American LaFrance pumper. After some speeches, handshakes and photos, the two teams of horses returned to quarters. The Dalmatian Jiggs took it the hardest as his five equine friends left the firehouse and headed off to retirement.

In 1958 the last Engineer of Steamer Otto Kutzke of Engine Co. 57, put in his papers after 45 years on the job. The title of engineer of steamer retired when he did. It is interesting to note the overlapping of history as the issue of *WNYF* (the official magazine of the FDNY) that reported Kutzke's retirement, also featured an article by Ed Kehoe and Frank Brannigan about Atomic Bomb Effects. Yikes, from steam power to nukes!

Chiefs' Drivers & Aides

When the New York City Fire Department became a professional force in 1865, the fire service was amid a great change. Taller and larger buildings were making firefighting more difficult and dangerous. In the words of John Kenlon, chief of the FDNY from 1911 until 1930:

> At about the time of consolidation (when New York City, Brooklyn, Queens, the Bronx and Staten Island all became one city in 1898) a new era in building construction set in. From a five-story city in 1887, New York had begun to grow skyward to 20 and 30 story structures. Naturally the problem of fire protection in these high buildings became acute…

In the earliest days of the paid department the chief officers literally ran to the scene of fires and emergencies. Horse-drawn buggies were eventually provided and soon after drivers were chosen so the chief could focus on the fire and not be concerned with the horse and buggy. The higher the chief's rank, the larger geographical area he covered. Multiple alarms would require the chief of department to travel great distances. For example, the distance between Fire Headquarters at East 67th Street to the engine house in Far Rockaway is 28 miles; to the one in Riverdale (Bronx) is ten miles, to Tottenville in Staten Island is 26 miles (including a five-mile ferry ride.) When responding in a horse-drawn buggy, the chief would have to stop and change horses at intervals.

So, in those early days when Croker started off for a

multiple alarm in a distant part of the city, an alarm would be sent to the department's Hospital and Training Stables, four miles away to have a relay wagon waiting. The chief and his driver would jump from one buggy to another and dash off. This would be repeated at various places along the route.

Firefighting by its very nature is a dangerous endeavor. With large horses pulling very heavy steam engines, massive hook and ladder trucks and hose tenders carrying lengths of heavy hose, even responding to fires could prove deadly. As a matter of fact, the first member of the FDNY (then called the Metropolitan Fire Department) to die in the line of duty was a driver. On August 14, 1865, Engine Company 1 responded to a fire at 148 Water Street. While laying hose from the fire building back to the engine, Fireman Robert Wintringham, driver of the hose tender, was thrown from his seat as the horse became frightened and ran away. Winteringham's legs became entangled in the reins as he fell to the pavement. The tender passed over his legs, breaking them both. He was then dragged a distance before the horse could be stopped. He was taken to the hospital where his mangled right leg had to be amputated. Fireman Robert Winteringham died ten days later of his injuries.

Another major difficulty the officers in command faced was communications. Speaking trumpets and megaphones had their limits, and portable radios would not become a reality until after World War II. So chief officers began using trusted members of the department to relay their orders and to gather information from sectors of the fire the chief could not readily see from the front of the building.

Battalion chiefs and deputy chiefs were assigned aides to help them run operations on the fire ground. They would provide a reliable second set of eyes and ears for the chief. The aide would run to the nearest alarm box and transmit additional alarms and special calls at the direction of the chief. (Inside the alarm box, a Morse Code key allowed the members in the field direct communications to the dispatcher.)

The chief of department not only had a driver, but also had at least one aide. As the FDNY entered the motorized era, Chief of Department Edward Croker led the way with the purchase of a Locomobile he put into service in late 1899. This two-seated, steam powered motorcar was nicknamed "The Black Ghost" by the chief, who used the auto at nights when the streets were less congested. He also kept his horse and buggy on stand-by just in case. An article in the 1901 magazine *Automobile Topics*, quoted Chief Croker:

> The automobile is certainly of great value to me in responding to alarms. For example, I often have alarms of fire at night of twenty or thirty blocks distance to respond to; I cover the distance in one half the time with my Locomobile that it would take me with the horse I use day times... Sometimes I no more than leave one fire than I have another to attend, when I used a horse, it would be tired from the run to the first fire. As it is, I can keep going all night and at a clip of thirty to forty miles an hour when the streets are clear.

When asked if he felt the automobile was a practical machine for responding fire chiefs Croker answered: "I fully believe that all chiefs will use them in all large cities in the next few years."

Chief Edward Croker was so impressed with his Locomobile he ordered a second, customized and more heavy-duty version of the vehicle. In 1903 he received this special Locomobile of strong and heavy construction, with an extra-wide seat which could hold three persons. He road tested the vehicle at 30 mph. Croker requested a more durable machine to better negotiate the city's streets where surfaces varied from asphalt to Belgian blocks. There were numerous other obstacles to deal with including trolley car tracks, horse-drawn buggies, wagons and trucks of various shapes and sizes, and of course the numerous pedestrians.

The original Locomobile barely resembled motor vehicles of today, but they worked in their own fashion. It was basically a rectangular box on wheels powered by a steam engine. The boiler produced steam that drove two pistons (like a train locomotive, hence the name Locomobile.) Croker transferred the practice being used by FDNY steam engines that attached the rigs to stationary boilers in quarters that continually fed hot water into the system. As the steamer left quarters the attachment was disconnected automatically as the rig rolled out. Croker had a similar attachment placed on his Locomobile so he could get a head of steam up almost immediately. (Pretty inventive for 1900.)

In August of 1904 the city purchased a new 45 horse-power American Mercedes touring car for the chief and commissioner. (The two Locomobiles were Croker's personal property donated to the FDNY.) Painted bright red it featured FDNY identification plates and a large warning bell. The speedy convertible became quite the curiosity among the city's citizens. Newspapers quickly dubbed it the "Red Devil." According to *The Motor World* magazine this vehicle was a regular stock model, with the exception that, in place of the forward *tonneau* seats, there was a large box for stowing fire gear and other items. (A tonneau was originally an open rear passenger compartment, rounded like a barrel. It comes from the French word meaning cask or barrel.)

A few months later, another 1904 touring car, this one manufactured by Locomobile was purchased for Deputy Chief Lally, in command of Brooklyn and Queens. Unlike Croker's earlier steam powered machine, this auto had a four-cylinder 24-horse-power engine that was capable of a maximum speed of

45 mph. This vehicle also had a distinctly "fire department" look due to its brilliant shade of red with black striping. The vehicle also featured a large bell and a large FDNY plate on the rear.

Deputy Chief John Binns was responding to fires in a 1906 Electric Stanhope. The vehicle's cylindrical shaped motor was placed in front under the dashboard. The batteries were located under the passenger's seat. There was a rear storage area for fire gear etc. The 1,860-pound machine could travel between 10 and 20 mph. A rheostat (a variable resistor used to control current) was installed in the firehouse to keep the batteries charged. Binns' former horse driver, Fireman Frederick W. Deissroth was taught how to drive and maintain the vehicle.

One of the new problems faced by fire chiefs in the earliest days of motorized response was identification. Even though their cars were bright red, when most of the automobiles were black, police officers often chased the official cars as they sped by, not realizing the vehicles were fire department automobiles responding to fires.

Another problem was speed. The new autos were travelling at more than twice the speed of the horse and buggy they replaced. But the streets they were driving on were becoming more crowded every day. Daytime responses were made through congested streets, but late at night the streets were empty and the new FDNY automobiles took advantage of the open road. In 1899, an article in *Fire and Water* magazine stated:

> Chief Croker now drives to fires in a locomobile, whose motive power is steam generated by gasoline, which, it is said, can attain a speed of 25 miles an hour within 100 yards, and 60 miles an hour within a furlong (an eighth of a mile or 220 yards), and can be stopped in its own length… It will be possible to reach Harlem from the engine house on Great Jones Street in 15 minutes. The other night the Locomobile, which left the house after the engine company

had got 200 yards ahead, passed the horses like a flash in the Bowery, and was first at the fire.

The new motorized chiefs' cars and how they worked is very interesting. To me however, the real story is the guys who drove them to fires.

John Rush

One of Croker's first drivers and aides was John Rush, who'd made a name for himself while a member of the New York Fire Patrol. Rush, born in New York City on February 21, 1871, was the son of a FDNY fireman, and joined Fire Patrol 2 in 1893. A year later he married Helen Patterson and became a father when his daughter Sarah was born in 1895. It was a few minutes before 9 p.m. on November 5, 1895, when Rush responded to a fire at the Manhattan Savings Institute. The fire was reported inside the six-story building at the southeast corner of Broadway and Bleeker streets. The ground floor front of the fire building was occupied by the Empire State Bank; the ground floor rear section housed an express office and a shoemaker's shop.

Engine 33 arrived first and took the hydrant in front of the fire building. Shortly after the front door was forced open a tremendous backdraft explosion occurred. The explosion blew out the front windows and doors of 636 and 638 Broadway, sending bricks and flying glass across the street. The blast was followed by a sheet of flame that sent waves of heat across Engine 33. The team of horses, still attached to the rig, were being burned by flames shooting from the front of the building. Firemen scrambled to save the horses by chopping the hose in half, freeing the rig from the hydrant. With great difficulty the rig and the injured horses were moved away from the fire. Their actions were so dangerous several firemen's coats were burning as they rescued the horses.

Several other pieces of apparatus, including the hose wagons of Engine 55 and 30, were also damaged by the blast and fire. Both teams of horses were so frightened by the blast they ran off dragging their wagons behind them. The fire grew so intense the occupants were driven from the surrounding buildings. The flames also ignited the eight-story Manhattan Savings Institute across the street.

The department was now faced with fire raging in several buildings. Numerous firemen and horses were injured by the blast and would require medical attention. A third alarm was quickly transmitted (bypassing the second) followed moments later by a fourth, and fifth alarms (said at the time to be the fastest transmission of multiple alarms in the department's history).

Teams of firemen battled the flames in the original fire building, which collapsed an hour after their arrival. Various exposure buildings were also burning intensely. Assistant Chief Reilly and Battalion Chief Lally led nozzle teams into the blazing Manhattan Savings Institution on the other side of Broadway. They were all working on the fifth floor when the upper floors collapsed on them. Despite their injuries, they made their way to front windows and were rescued by extension ladders. Unfortunately, Lt. Fitzsimmons of Engine 3 became separated from the others during the collapse. He too made his way to a front window and called for help. Fire Patrolmen Rush and Burnett were inside the adjacent building when they heard his shouts. Moving to a front window they saw Lt. Fitzsimmons trapped at a window above them. Seeing that no ladders could reach the trapped man, Rush climbed out the window followed by Burnett. The duo inched across the narrow window ledge until they were below the cut-off officer. Still several feet beneath the man, Rush climbed onto Burnett's shoulders creating a human ladder. The officer carefully exited the window and climbed down Rush to the ledge. The trio delicately made their way back to safety. A reporter for the *New York Times* stated: "It was a perilous undertaking, and looked as though all would fall to the street."

Chief officers, firemen, and a large crowd of people watched this daring rescue play out 50 feet above the sidewalk. Rush's bravery would prompt an unusual action; a short time later the New York State Legislature passed an act appointing Rush to the FDNY on June 8, 1896. He quickly advanced to engineer of steamer on August 22, 1898, then to lieutenant August 1, 1900, captain on April 15, 1904, and battalion chief on July 1, 1911.

Shortly after Rush joined the FDNY he was detailed to drive Chief of Department Edward Croker, one of those who'd seen Rush's bravery firsthand at the bank fire. The chief had his night offices in the quarters of Engine Company 33 on Great Jones Street. Rush, considered a skillful driver, was soon seen urging Croker's famed horse "Bullet" as they responded across the city to major fires. When Croker introduced his new Locomobile in 1899, Rush soon proved his driving skills with the steam-driven machine the chief nicknamed Black Ghost. Newspapers loved to recount his daring high-speed handling of the chief's car.

One night in January 1907, Rush and Croker were responding to a large fire in the Bronx and were travelling at about 40 mph, when a policeman saw the car flash by. Not familiar with the car he gave chase on his motorcycle. As Rush slowed the rig to avoid hitting a trolley car, the trailing motorcycle cop was unable to slow himself in time and hit the left rear wheel of the chief's car toppling him from his machine. Officer Haggerty was thrown 20 feet and knocked unconscious.

Rush stopped and hurried to the downed officer. Croker ordered the policeman placed in his car and the officer was taken to Fordham Hospital where he recovered.

On September 18, 1908, the new high pressure hose wagons got their first test. The deep-seated fire was in a rag and paper warehouse on Elizabeth Street in Manhattan. The gleaming new rig stopped in front of the fire building and several lengths of hose were pulled off and attached to the high-pressure hydrant. The hoses were then run inside toward the fire. When Rush and Croker arrived, the chief saw the flames were gaining headway and turned to his trusted aide and told him to grab several lengths of hose from the wagon, and to attack the fire from the rear. Rush and a team hurried into position on the Bowery side of the building. Attached to another high-pressure hydrant they knocked down the flames and prevented a sure multiple alarm from developing. Chief Croker stated he was very pleased with the versatility of the new hose wagons and hydrant system.

Capt. Rush in command of High Pressure Engine Company 18, responded to a fire at 24 Cornelia Street, a six-story tenement on November 12, 1910. Engine 18 arrived first at what seemed like a small routine fire. Twelve members of 18 scattered and began working. As a team pried open the iron grating of the cellar, others stretched a line into the basement of the building. Before water had swelled the hose, the light smoke condition had changed. Heat built up rapidly in the basement melting the connections on a gas meter, adding illuminating gas to the now thick smoke.

Within a few moments men began to fall unconscious. Other members of the company crawled in to help only to be overcome themselves. Seeing the seriousness of the situation, Capt. Rush called for the smoke helmet Chief Croker had recently obtained. As the gear was being donned, Fireman Walter McBride of Engine 18, appeared at the cellar opening with an unconscious man in his arms. Handing off the man, McBride fell backwards into the cellar, he too overcome by the dangerous smoke. The captain fit the helmet to his head and quickly plunged into the toxic cloud of smoke, appearing moments later with McBride safely in his arms. Handing off the unconscious man he returned to the cellar. Searching deep into the cellar he found three of his men unconscious on the floor. One by one he carried them back to the cellar opening and handed them out. All three were removed to the hospital in serious condition.

Chief Croker announced his retirement effective May 1, 1911. Also, effective that day was the end of Captain Rush's detail to the chief, and his subsequent transfer from Engine 33 to Hook & Ladder 4.

Rush was in command of Engine Company 54 on June 17, 1911, and arrived first at a fire in a huge warehouse building on West 54th Street that ran through to 55th Street. The five-story building housed piano factories, cabinet shops, a brass polishing company, and other companies that stored and utilized large quantities of resin, alcohol, explosive acids, and other dangerous inflammable materials. To compound the dangers, the building to the east housed a lumber yard and the structure to the west was an asphalt company. A watchman inside the building smelled smoke and discovered the fire on the first floor in a laundry supply company. On the same floor was a stable with 11 horses.

Upon arrival Rush was faced with an advanced fire extending toward the stacks of lumber, and a stable with trapped horses. His attempts to reach the horses proved impossible due to the extreme heat. Rush redirected his efforts and ordered the initial attack to protect the lumber yard and prevent the flames from spreading in that direction. As multiple alarms were transmitted Rush, and his team battled the growing flames. Explosions began rocking the building as the stored flammables began detonating. Hearing a roar from deep within the fire, Rush saw the walls wavering and ordered an immediate evacuation of the building.

Just as the last man exited the building the flaming walls caved in showering the area with broken bricks and flaming debris. Captain Rush saved several companies from certain injury or death.

Unfortunately, Rush's luck on the fire ground didn't seem to follow into his personal life.

Sadly, his father, Engineer of Steamer William H. Rush of Engine 49 died in the line-of-duty when he fell from the apparatus and fractured his skull on November 14, 1906. A short time after, Rush's wife became bedridden and died three years later. His oldest daughter then became ill and passed away a week after her mother was buried. His brother, Fireman Charles E. Rush passed away on January 16, 1912, after becoming ill during the department's battle at the Equitable Building fire a week earlier.

On July 1, 1911, John Rush was promoted to battalion chief and given command of the Fifth Battalion in Manhattan. Rush got his first big job as a battalion chief on September 13, 1911, when he responded to a commercial building fire at 117 Mercer Street. The fast-burning fire went to three alarms.

The dangers faced every day by members of the FDNY run from the extreme to the mundane. Having gained notoriety for his driving skills with both horses and then with the new automobiles, it was ironic that the ultimate danger would be faced on a leisurely drive to dinner. It was April 25, 1912, and Battalion Chief John Rush set out from his quarters at Spring and Houston streets and headed toward his home on West 11th Street. Accompanying Rush was his driver Fireman John Harvey, but the buggy was being driven by Rush himself. While attempting to pass a truck, the rear wheel of the chief's wagon caught the side of the truck. The jolt frightened the horse and started it galloping northward on Hudson Street. Despite Rush's best efforts to control the panicked animal they continued north out-of-control.

Reaching Christopher Street, the chief saw a group of children about to cross the street ahead of him. Realizing the danger they would be in with the frantic horse bearing down on them, Rush leapt to his feet and pulled with all his weight trying to slow the animal. The right wheel of the wagon caught on the side of a trolley track tipping the wagon precariously. The horse fell over, and the wagon followed, with both men being thrown from the rig.

Amazingly the children were unharmed, and Fireman Harvey was uninjured, but Chief Rush was not as lucky, striking his head violently on the pavement. The chief was rushed to a nearby hospital but died two hours later.

When Chief Kenlon heard of Rush's death he said,

> I regard Rush as one of the ablest battalion commanders in the service. No braver man ever stood in two shoes. I first noticed Rush when a young man doing rescue work at the Bleeker Street bank building fire. I am depressed by his death and regard it as a great loss to the fire department and to the city and a great personal loss to me.

Retired Chief Croker said,

> John Rush was a model man. He was absolutely sober. He had no bad habits. He was industrious, economical and very thrifty. He was brave, too. I remember that fire at the Empire Bank Building on election night back in the nineties… Rush had the greatest trick of smelling danger that I ever saw in a man. He rushed me to fires for eight years and he was working all the time… He had great fire judgement and was always on the job.

It seems a strange irony of fate that a minor accident

should have killed Chief Rush. I had almost come to think he bore a charmed life. One gets such ideas of men who pass through seemingly impassable dangers unscathed.
   —Doctor Harry Archer,
      St. Vincent's Hospital April 26, 1912.

Charles W. Rankin

Starting in March of 1909, Engineer of Steamer Charles W. Rankin was detailed to the Chief of Department's office. Rankin joined Captain Rush as an aide and driver to Chief Croker. Rankin, born in Maryland in 1872, joined the department in 1901. He served as a fireman in Engine Co. 11 before being promoted to engineer of steamer (qualified and licensed to operate the department's steam pumpers). He worked at Engine 2 on West 43rd Street until 1909 when he was transferred to Engine Co. 33 on Great Jones Street and his detail to the chief began.

Rankin would respond with Chief Croker to large fires, city-wide until the chief retired on May 1, 1911. At that time Capt. Rush, who was expected to be promoted to battalion chief in several months, ended his detail as chief's aide. Another famous firefighter and renowned driver of this era, Fireman Francis Blessing joined Rankin when he was detailed to drive Acting Chief of Department John Kenlon starting July 20, 1911. Blessing, who was a machinist prior to joining the FDNY, took several details early in his career driving chief officers.

Also detailed to the chief was Fireman Luke Henry who shared the driving duties with Blessing. This team of Luke Henry driving with Rankin acting as the chief's primary aide, responded to a difficult and dangerous fire at 10 Jones Street in lower Manhattan. It was May 7, 1911, and the smoky fire was in a seven-story loft building. Charles Rankin, Luke Henry and members of Hook & Ladder 5 rescued the nozzle team of Engine 24 after they fell unconscious on the third floor.

Their determined teamwork saved the lives of five firemen. They were all placed on the Roll of Merit with Class II awards.

January 9, 1912, was a freezing cold morning. Manhattan fire companies responded to a blaze in the huge Equitable Building on Broadway. A quick second alarm had Chief Kenlon and his crew: Lt. Charles Rankin and Firemen Blessing and Henry speeding to the fire's downtown location. They raced about a mile and a half toward the southern end of Manhattan. All three would be instrumental in life saving efforts at this dangerous fire.

At the scene Kenlon and his aides gathered around Deputy Chief Binns who presented the chief a size up of the fire. Kenlon turned to Rankin, "Put in a third alarm." Two minutes later, after receiving another report from inside the building, Kenlon caught Rankin's attention and held up four fingers. Rankin nodded and transmitted a fourth alarm. Kenlon entered the building with Rankin, Blessing, and Henry to see conditions firsthand. On the fourth floor they met Chief Walsh who was confident he could drive the fire back and confine it to the Pine Street side. (It should be mentioned that conditions inside appeared to be better than they were, as the strong wind was pushing most of the smoke out of the building.)

The chief and his aides returned to the street, where Kenlon noticed granite trimmings on the dormer windows of the upper floors flying off. This signaled to the chief that intense heat was affecting the unprotected iron columns holding the structure up. He ordered all companies out of the building. Kenlon knew shutting down the inside streams would intensify the fire, but the chief wanted to be able to throw a water curtain completely around the huge building to protect the surrounding buildings.

At 6:28 a.m. Kenlon ordered a fifth alarm and requested an additional 25 pounds on the high-pressure hydrant system.

At this point there were 23 engines, 6 hook & ladders, 2 water towers and a force of 275 officers and firemen at work. Rankin was dispatched with a second order that the men inside the Equitable should back down and get out with all speed, bringing their lines to the Nassau and Cedar Street side, where the exposure risk was the greatest.

Rankin reported back that all companies had reached the main staircase, except Engine Company 4 and a few men from Hook & Ladder 1, who, under the direction of Battalion Chief Walsh, were fighting obstinately, only receding inch by inch. Rankin returned with the chief's orders to leave the line. Then a portion of the roof on the south side collapsed, forcing out part of the wall of the inner court and burying the steps down which the last men were hurrying.

Captain Farley of Hook and Ladder 8 reported that he and his men had removed Capt. Bass and some members of Engine 4 and H&L 1 from the collapsed part of the building. The chief ordered a roll call and discovered Battalion Chief Walsh was missing. To add insult to injury, the temperature was rapidly dropping, as 70 mph gusts of wind buffeted the fire scene. Exterior hose and water tower streams were directed at the flames. The dripping walls of the fire building turned to ice and the sidewalks and streets became frozen lakes.

The outside attack was in full swing. Kenlon closed Pine Street to protect the firefighting force from possible collapses in that side of the huge building. Then word came that three workers were visible, trapped on the roof. Hook & Ladder 1, whose horses had been led away earlier, was rolled into position by hand and the wooden aerial ladder was extended up toward the men. As this was being accomplished Lt. Rankin, and Firemen Blessing and James Molloy of Engine 32 grabbed scaling ladders and began climbing the aerial. Using scaling ladders was always a dangerous operation, but the projecting nature of the window designs and the strong winds made it even more difficult and dangerous.

Molloy and Rankin were moving from floor to floor as Blessing reached the top rung of the fully extended aerial. On the roof of the building across the street, members of Hook & Ladder 1, under the command of Acting Chief Kelly, shot a line from a rope rifle that draped perfectly over the roof. The trapped men began pulling the line upwards when suddenly, without warning a major collapse occurred.

Kenlon stood in the street, a cloud of dust and debris surrounded him briefly before it was blown away by the strong wind. The chief feared the worst as he heard bodies hitting the ground nearby. It soon became clear his men were still alive as he looked up and saw Blessing holding the top of the aerial, Rankin had one foot on a window ledge and Molloy was standing on the highest ledge of the broken and badly bulging wall. Their rescue was not accomplished, but their bravery could not be denied. Kenlon gave a huge sigh of relief as they carefully made their way to the ground.

Word came that men were calling for help from a barred window at the sidewalk level. They were trapped behind two-inch thick iron bars in a basement vault with fire raging behind them. Firemen quickly sprang to their aid including Lt. Rankin. As a hack saw began sawing the bars a hose line was directed into the basement window to hold back the flames.

Kenlon transmitted a borough call. This brought a third alarm assignment from a Brooklyn box to the lower Manhattan fire. A trio worked on the bars including Engineer of Steamer Seneca Larke, Lt. Rankin, and Fireman Luke Henry. Freezing water and chunks of debris cascaded down on the fireman, who worked for more than an hour cutting the bars away. Finally, the imprisoned men were freed.

The Equitable Building fire was an historic moment in the

FDNY. The department was faced with a major fire in a huge building housing millions of dollars of cash, bonds, and securities. The blaze was held to the original fire building, but it did cost the lives of six people, including Battalion Chief William Walsh. The difficulty in sawing the vault window bars would start Chief Kenlon on the way to forming a special company within the FDNY trained and equipped to handle such difficult rescue work. This plan would not become a reality until 1915, when Rescue Company 1 was organized.

Chief Kenlon's aides had proven their worth once again. Operating at a large fire with many complications, they covered the fire ground providing reconnaissance, delivering messages, and relaying orders. At the height of danger, they immediately took lifesaving actions, performing their duties in heroic fashion. For their work at this fire, Charles W. Rankin, an acting lieutenant at the time of the fire, was placed on the Roll of Merit with a Class I. Blessing and Henry were granted Class II awards. Rankin who was promoted to lieutenant in December of 1912, was also awarded a medal for his work at this fire as was Fireman Molloy.

On August 20, 1913, Lt. Rankin responded with Chief Kenlon to a three-alarm fire in the water tunnel construction site on a triangular plot at 149th Street and Nicholas Avenue in the Bronx. A flash fire that started in a ground floor blacksmith's shop soon enveloped the entire superstructure above the tunnel opening. As the first due company, Engine 38 rolled in, the updraft from the tunnel below was causing the mushrooming fire to spread to buildings on both sides of the avenue.

Chief Kenlon and his aides arrived shortly after the transmission of the third alarm and set about coordinating the battle against the expanding fire front. Then word came that 60 workers were trapped in the tunnel below the flames and their lives, and the lives of everyone in the area, were imperiled by the proximity of 900 pounds of dynamite stored in the tunnel below.

As the last of the super structure above the tunnel burned away and was doused by streams, Kenlon selected eight men, including Acting Capt. C.W. Rankin, and led them on an extremely hazardous descent into the smoke-filled tunnel in search of the trapped men. After avoiding a localized collapse Kenlon and Rankin delved deeper into the tunnel and located the 60 workers. They developed a plan that would safely remove all the men to the surface. Rankin's name was again placed on the Roll of Merit.

On November 27, 1913, Charles Rankin was promoted to captain and assigned to Engine 33, with his detail as chief's aide continuing. Then on March 7, 1914, he was made acting battalion chief while continuing his work with Chief Kenlon.

On January 6, 1915, Capt. Rankin accompanied Chief Kenlon to a serious fire in the subway at Broadway between 53rd and 54th streets. It was the morning rush hour when flames broke out among electrical cables and wires producing thick, noxious smoke. One person was killed and 200 were taken to hospitals with severe smoke inhalation. This fire prompted Chief Kenlon to finalize his plan to organize and specially equip a new unit called Rescue Company 1. Fireman Frank Blessing would be detailed to drive this new company.

This fire also began Capt. Rankin's in-depth research into the safeguarding of passengers in subway tunnels during fires and emergencies. This study was submitted to the fire commissioner who in turn submitted it to the Public Service Commission. The commission later adopted the majority of the suggested improvements including: the prompt location of a train in trouble, the speedy removal of passengers, and the centralization of electrical power control to one office. For his outstanding efforts Captain Charles W. Rankin was awarded the Administration Medal by Fire Commissioner Adamson. The award took place at the annual medal presentation ceremonies that in 1917 were held at the stadium of the College of New York.

While working a fire in a five-story tenement building at 102 Delancey Street, Capt. Rankin was searching the top floor when he was accidentally struck with a hose stream knocking him to the floor. While on the floor he heard moans and followed the sounds. His search led him to a locked door. After breaking down the door, he found two unconscious men inside the small windowless room. One by one he dragged them to the stairs and handed them off to other firemen. For his actions at this July 14, 1915 fire, Rankin was once again placed on the Roll of Merit. He was also placed on the roll for another rescue he made on December 2, 1918.

In August of 1921, Capt. Rankin, Doctor Archer and a large group of FDNY officials attended a baseball game between the FDNY and members of the Chicago Fire Department in Chicago at a benefit for Chicago's Firemen's Mutual Aid Fund. The FDNY team was victorious. The following year the CFD team visited New York and a series of games were played at Ebbets Field for the benefit of the Honor Emergency Fund of the FDNY. This time the Chicago team won two of the three games played and took home a beautiful trophy.

Rankin had a close call on November 16, 1921, while operating at a warehouse fire at 310 West 143rd Street, between Eighth and Bradhurst avenues. The blaze destroyed the warehouse and 25 automobiles, before leaping the street and igniting several tenements. At the height of the fire a 35-foot portable ladder fell, glancing off Rankin. His helmet was crushed but he was otherwise unharmed.

Early on the evening of April 21, 1922, Capt. Rankin was at the wheel of Chief Kenlon's auto when it was struck head-on by a civilian's auto on Central Park West. The chief and his aides were returning to Great Jones Street after Kenlon stopped home for dinner. Chief Kenlon, Lt. Luke Henry, and Fireman John Mayr received only minor injuries. Rankin however suffered a head laceration. Kenlon's car then returned to fire headquarters where Doctor Archer was summoned to stitch Rankin's gash.

In May of 1925 Charles W. Rankin was promoted to the permanent rank of battalion chief. He had been serving as an acting battalion chief since 1914. Rankin was assigned to the First Battalion but continued his duties as Chief Kenlon's aide.

Five alarms were transmitted on December 20, 1928, for a fire in a six-story commercial building at 139 Fifth Avenue near 21st Street. A natural draft caused by the surrounding taller buildings caused flames to leap up through the fire building and shoot 30 feet into the air. A dense smoke condition fell over the neighborhood as firemen battled the stubborn flames.

With numerous streams and a water tower attacking the fire, Chief Rankin and Capt. O'Toole entered the first floor to observe conditions. As they moved in, the ceiling collapsed, knocking them to the floor. A squad of firemen dashed inside and pulled the two men from the rubble. They were both treated and went back to working the fire.

FDNY Special Order No. 44 dated March 8, 1928, announced that effective the following day, Battalion Chief Charles W. Rankin was designated as an acting deputy chief.

Special Order No. 34 dated March 3, 1931, saw Chief John Kenlon retire after 44 years of service, with 19 of them as chief of department. The detail of Lt. Luke Henry as chief's aide ended as he was detailed to Brooklyn. Battalion Chief Rankin continued as the aide to the new acting chief. On March 1, 1932 John J. McElligott became chief of department. On March 15, 1932, Battalion Chief (Acting Deputy) Charles W. Rankin was transferred from the First Battalion to the Marine Division. Now in charge of the FDNY fire boat fleet, he took up offices in the fireboat *John J. Harvey* stationed at the Battery. In mid-November Rankin and most of the FDNY battalion chiefs assembled for the deputy chief civil service exam held in the municipal building in lower Manhattan.

In early 1936 Chief Rankin was placed on medical leave and began battling a long illness. While convalescing at his Brooklyn home and surrounded by his wife and ten children the chief passed away.

On February 6, 1936, FDNY Special Order No. 24 stated:

> With regret, the death of Acting Deputy Chief Charles W. Rankin, in command of the Marine Division, which occurred at 8:15 a.m., February 6, 1936, is hereby announced to the Department.
>
> Chief Rankin at all times devoted his best efforts to the interest of the Department for a period of more than thirty-five years. Almost twenty-seven years of his service in the Department were spent as Aide to former Chiefs of Department Edward F. Croker, and John Kenlon, who have often been heard to refer to him as a most efficient, sincere and painstaking officer and assistant. These facts are well known to those of us who labored with him. His estimate of conditions at fires was almost uncanny, and his advice and comments with reference thereto were accepted without question. By his passing, the Fire Department and the City of New York have suffered a distinct loss.

The bell system sounded the 5-5-5-5 signal, ordering all department flags to be lowered to half-mast.

Luke E. Henry

On June 8, 1901, Luke Henry joined the FDNY as a probationary fireman and was assigned to Hook & Ladder 10. Henry quickly caught the eye of Acting Battalion Chief (ABC) Daniel Conway who asked the young fireman to be his aide and chauffeur. Henry's value would soon become evident when they responded to a fire at 42 Vesey Street on November 2, 1903. The five-story building housed a dealer in electric batteries, electrical supplies, automobile fixtures, and apparatus. Large quantities of carbon, batteries, insulation, and pitch were stored in the cellar.

First arriving units were faced with a very smoky cellar fire. The first engine stretched a line into the cellar, but soon found the thick noxious smoke too difficult to breathe and limited the time each fireman could spend in the smoke. One by one each member of the nozzle team staggered back to the street and fell to the sidewalk exhausted and nearly suffocated.

ABC Conway ordered the cellar door opened and called for a ladder. Before the ladder was dropped into position, the chief lost his balance and plunged head-first into the cellar. Luke Henry quickly dove into the cellar after him. In the smoke and heat-filled cellar Fireman Henry located the injured officer and dragged him back toward the opening and shouted for a line.

Cradling the unconscious man in his arms, Fireman Henry held Conway and tried to protect him from the waves of heat until a ladder was dropped into the cellar and other firemen helped pull the duo from the scalding cellar. Both men were seriously burned and rushed to the hospital. Acting Battalion Chief Conway was admitted with burns of the face, head, neck, and hands. Fireman Luke Henry had serious burns to his hands and face but was released from the hospital. Immediately after this rescue Henry was detailed to Chief Hugh Bonner.

On May 14, 1904, members of the FDNY and a huge crowd of curious citizens gathered at Madison Square to watch the annual medal presentation. For his heroic actions in saving the life of Acting Chief Conway the previous year, Fireman Luke Henry was awarded the Hugh Bonner Medal.

Fireman Henry was transferred to Engine Co. 57 (Fireboat *New Yorker*) and detailed to drive the chief of department in November of 1903. His day-to-day job was maintenance of the chief's automobile and driving him on his daily inspections of firehouses and of course to respond to multiple alarms. When Chief Croker retired, John Kenlon became acting chief of department and Fireman Henry continued his detail as chauffeur.

Flames broke out in a seven-story loft building at 10 Jones Street at 8 p.m. on May 7, 1911. Fireman Henry quickly wheeled the acting chief to the scene. Members of Engine 24 under the command of Lt. Decker were operating a line on the third floor. The thick smoke was difficult to breathe, but Decker and his crew held their position. Suddenly, a backdraft sent a hot thick flame-laced cloud of smoke that bowled the men over. Lt. Decker and Fireman Irving dropped to the floor trying to return to the nozzle but were soon overcome by the smoke. Firemen Foster, Broderick, and Gorry had also been toppled and struggled to regain the nozzle. Feeling themselves being affected by the smoke, they dropped the line and groped their way to where Decker and Irving lay.

Broderick and Gorry dragged the lieutenant behind them

to the stairs and carried him to the street. Their arrival on the sidewalk prompted an immediate rescue effort for the remaining members inside. Fireman Luke Henry was the first man to dash back into the burning building followed by the members of Hook & Ladder 5—they headed for the third floor.

Conditions after the backdraft had become so severe that Henry and the other firemen were forced to lay flat on the floor and inch forward. They followed the hose line deep into the suffocating smoke. Near the thrashing nozzle, Henry found Irving and Foster. With the help of 5 Truck, they were dragged from the deadly smoke and carried outside to the fresh air. They were treated in a firehouse turned field hospital across the street. Both men were so severely affected by the smoke they were given 36 hours leave. Two of the would-be rescuers from Hook & Ladder 5 were also carried out unconscious.

Fireman Luke Henry and several members of Hook & Ladder 5 were placed on the Roll of Merit with Class II awards for their courageous rescues.

In the dark early morning hours of January 9, 1912, Firemen Luke Henry, Frank Blessing, and Lt. Rankin accompanied Chief Kenlon as they responded to a second alarm at Box 24, at the corner of Nassau and Pine streets. The fire proved to be in the Equitable Building and would turn into one of the most infamous and dangerous fires the department ever battled. All of Kenlon's aides performed heroically at this blaze. During the early stages of the fire Chief Kenlon and his team entered the building to see firsthand the conditions inside. They checked the fourth, fifth, and sixth floors. Conditions inside at this time were deceiving as the strong wind was venting much of the smoke allowing a relatively easy hose stream attack. Their return to the street brought the escalating fire into better perspective.

It was then that Chief Kenlon ordered everyone out of the fire building. A short while later when men were seen trapped on the roof, Blessing and Rankin made a dramatic scaling ladder rescue attempt. During this operation a major collapse occurred trapping many firemen. Among the first to enter the tangled mass of burning debris was Fireman Luke Henry. He joined in the search and rescue of the trapped members and helped saw the bars trapping men in the basement vault area. As the men were being pulled from the vault, one man cried out, "For God's sake don't leave me, my arm is fast!" Luke Henry moved into the dangerous spot and began a 15-minute rescue operation to free the pinned man. He was later awarded a Class II for his heroic actions at this fire.

The following year, he was awarded another Class II.

Luke Henry was promoted to lieutenant but continued his detail driving the chief.

In 1931 John Kenlon retired as chief and the details of his aides and chauffeurs were ended. Lt. Luke Henry transferred from Engine Co. 57 to Engine Co. 276 in Brooklyn near his home and was detailed to the Brooklyn Public Assembly unit. He worked there until he retired in 1933. Luke Henry passed away on March 19, 1939, after a thrilling career. He responded to an amazing number of major fires and emergencies, and often found himself in the thick of things.

Daniel Healy

Born in Kilgarvan, County Kerry in Ireland, Dan Healy came to America with his parents when he was a young child. He joined the FDNY on March 1, 1901, and was assigned to Engine Company 32 on John Street in Manhattan. On October 31, 1901, short circuiting electrical wiring caused a subcellar fire at 54 Worth Street. As first due Engine 33 began pushing in their attack line, flames melted connections on the gas meter and illuminating gas began to mix with the smoke. One by one the members of Engine 33 dropped to the floor unconscious. Members of Engine 32 moved in and began dragging their unconscious comrades back toward safety. Several members of 32 also were overcome and had to be rescued. For his part in the rescue and removal of the downed firemen, Dan Healy was placed on the Roll of Merit.

On March 10, 1904, Healy transferred to Hook & Ladder 7 on East 28th Street.

A fire that started on the ground floor of a big six-story factory building at 213 Grand Street was reported at 7:15 a.m. on December 16, 1908. The flames raced upwards trapping 150 men and women at work on the upper floors. Problems with the high-pressure hydrant system left firemen unprotected as they rescued those trapped inside the blazing structure. Flames ignited the tenement houses in the rear forcing the transmission of a second and third alarms.

Fireman Healy rescued a young woman from the flames and smoke and was placed on the Roll of Merit.

Healy started his detail as driver and aide to Deputy Chief Martin of the Second Division on January 21, 1906. This began 21 years of driving one of the most famous and colorful characters in the history of the FDNY, Chief Joseph B. Martin, known to all as "Smoky Joe." A few months later Healy was transferred on paper to Engine 55. Then, in 1910, he transferred to Hook & Ladder 24 on West 33rd Street. The department order dated March 8, 1910, mentioned his transfer and included a detail as driver for the chief of the Third Division, as Chief Martin changed commands.

At first Healy drove the chief's horse-drawn buggy, but this would change when the department began purchasing automobiles for the chief officers. In 1911 the Third Division was assigned a Cadillac touring car but kept the chief's buggy and horses as a spare.

Fireman Dan Healy once again would be placed on the Roll of Merit, for his efforts on December 16, 1908, when he responded to a fire at 213 Grand Street in Manhattan. The fire started on the fourth floor of the huge "L-shaped" six-story factory at 7:15 in the morning. As the first due units arrived the flames had 150 men and woman trapped above the fire with no way out.

To make matters worse, the fire involved celluloid that produced noxious fumes. In the street, engines were having difficulty getting adequate water from the new high-pressure hydrants, allowing the flames to extend to the floors above and even drop down to the third floor. Members of the hook and ladder companies were hard pressed, raising ladders and removing trapped workers. Three alarms were transmitted for Box-33-168.

Among those cited for life-saving heroism was Fireman Daniel Healy who was placed on the Roll of Merit along with eight other firefighters.

In a case of domestic terrorism, members of the infamous

Italian gang known as the Black Hand, set fire to a five-story tenement building at 37 Spring Street at 2:30 a.m. on April 30, 1909. Earlier the owner of the first-floor grocery store was threatened by the gang but paid no attention to their demands for money. Igniting two cans of flammable liquids was their method of communication. The store owner was at his home miles away when the arsonist touched off the fire.

Flames quickly raced upwards trapping 20 families, about 150 men, women and children in the blazing cauldron of smoke and flames. Those trapped inside had little chance of escape as the roof of the building stood three stories higher the adjoining structures. Arriving fire companies immediately attacked the flames and made valiant rescues using nets, ladders and their bare hands in the choking clouds of smoke. Fireman Dan Healy made a dramatic and difficult rescue that would place him on the Roll of Merit yet again, this time with a Class II award.

Sadly, nine people, including six children were killed and more than 20 were injured.

A major fire tore through the Eastern District of Brooklyn on the night of December 22, 1911. A nightwatchman saw flames within the first floor of a six-story building at 134 North Eleventh Street on the corner of Berry Street at about 8:30 p.m. He transmitted the fire alarm and within minutes Brooklyn fire companies were going to work. Arriving units found the fire had already communicated to the adjoining building and was threatening the entire neighborhood. With low water pressure and strong winds whipping the flames Chiefs Maher and Lally transmitted additional alarms that also brought Acting Chief of Department Martin to the scene.

Realizing the scope of the fire, and the various water and exposure problems Martin decided to do something that had never been done before. He sent his aide, Fireman Healy back to Manhattan in the chief's car with detailed instructions. Arriving at Ludlow and Delancey streets, Healy transmitted a third alarm from the fire alarm box. As soon as the last unit arrived, Healy led them across the Williamsburg Bridge to the fire.

With one action, 15 engines, 4 hook and ladders, and one water tower were brought to the fire. This was the first time companies were brought from one borough to another. This action would later be called a Borough Call. It was Chief Martin's idea, but Faithful Dan put this idea into action, carving another piece of FDNY history. After a three-and-a-half-hour battle, the fire was under control. Sadly, the flames left two brick factories, and two wood frame tenements in ruins. Hundreds of people were left homeless and without jobs. Several firemen were injured by falling walls.

The FDNY generally concentrated on fires, their prevention, and extinguishment. But they did whatever was necessary when public safety was an issue. An unusual incident occurred around 3 p.m. on the afternoon of May 27, 1916, when an elephant named "Lucy" was being transferred from a ship to a train car. The pachyderm arrived in New York after crossing the Atlantic from England. She was on her way to Michigan, her final destination. After leaving the ship her handler, Luke Connolly, began to lead her by rope toward the New York Central Railroad yards at 34th Street and Tenth Avenue. As the huge animal walked down the street, a sizeable crowd formed, watching her every step. Even in Manhattan an elephant was unique.

Perhaps because of the noisy crowd around her, Lucy stopped at 32nd Street and refused to continue. Connolly grabbed a boy from the crowd and entrusted him with holding the large animal as he dashed into a nearby bakery. Returning with 14 loaves of bread he coaxed the animal toward the train yard a half a loaf at a time. The animal took one look at the train car and the gangplank and stopped short, slowly shaking her head. NO train for her!

Making up her mind that a train ride was out, she started walking toward Pennsylvania Station instead. Asking for help, many men and boys stepped from the crowd and tried to carefully "pull" the animal in the right direction. Instead, the huge animal gently pulled them all down Tenth Avenue toward 29th Street. At that point the crowd dropped the rope as the animal became excited. At the corner of 30th Street and Tenth Avenue Lucy kicked over a high-pressure fire hydrant, before continuing on her merry way.

In his office, Chief Martin received a phone call from the high-pressure pumping station at Gansevoort Street stating the hydrant system was down from the Battery to 34th Street. Chief Martin and Fireman Healy sent squads of firemen to check the entire new subway system below 34th Street in hopes of locating the break. Unaware of the elephant's antics the search continued until the damaged hydrant was found and repaired.

Martin had Dan Healy notify the dispatchers that until the service was repaired and working properly, any alarms in the affected district would be answered with the addition of steam pumpers to the assignment. Luckily, no alarms were transmitted.

The elephant continued causing chaos as she tried to enter the grounds of a school at 34th Street and Seventh Avenue. She reached out and pulled the gate off and backed into the large grassy area outside the school and began to eat peacefully. She was later lassoed and then put in chains. Brought back to the train car, again she refused to enter. She spent the night sleeping outside next to the car. The trainer said he'd try again in the morning.

One of the things the speedy new automobiles changed was the time it took the chief to arrive at the scene. Responding in autos was proving to be much quicker than the horse-drawn buggy ride. Sometimes the chief would arrive first, and the instincts of a fireman kicked in. Case in point: November 16, 1916, Chief Martin and Dan Healy arrive at 356 Seventh Avenue, a five-story tenement. Visible upon arrival were two women trapped at a top floor window crying for help. As the first hook and ladder truck arrived Martin ordered a portable ladder placed to the window. Before the ladder was touching the sill Martin was nimbly climbing up with "Faithful Dan" on his heels.

Reaching the top, they were surprised when the 18-year-old woman became frantic and began battling them, almost knocking the ladder away from the building. Both men held her in the window as they entered the smoke-filled flat. After calming her, Martin left her with Healy as he dashed into the adjacent apartment and found an unconscious woman on the floor. Both men then carried the unconscious woman and the frightened young lady to safety.

Both Chief Martin and Fireman Healy were placed on the Roll of Merit.

On Christmas Eve, 1918 Joseph B. Martin was named assistant chief by Commissioner Drennan. Of course, continuing his detail as the chief's chauffeur and aide was Fireman Dan Healy. The area of response for Healy and Smoky Joe had now expanded to the entire city. The assistant chief was second in command of the entire department, which in 1918 was 304 companies staffed by 4971 firemen and officers protected a city that had grown to 5.4 million people.

To put things in perspective, in 1918 firemen in the FDNY were still working a continuous tour of duty, of 151 hours per week with three hours off each day. The annual salary for firemen was $1,500. A major raise followed in 1920 bringing the annual salary to $1,900. Then in 1922 the FDNY began the slow process of creating the two-platoon system with firemen working "only" 84 hours a week.

On the afternoon of September 13, 1919, flames broke out

in the Standard Oil Company yards, a sprawling area of tanks, pipes, and buildings that covered over 20 acres in the Greenpoint section of Brooklyn. The yard was packed with numerous tanks—some as large as 35,000 barrels, vast stores of naphtha, gasoline, oil, alcohol, and more than 1,000 barrels of other explosive and flammable liquids.

Chief Martin was acting chief of department when the alarm was received and with Healy at the wheel they raced off to Brooklyn. Multiple alarms had been transmitted bringing companies from across Brooklyn. Arriving with the third alarm, Martin sent Healy to do a size up while he conferred with Brooklyn chiefs. Upon Healy's return Martin ordered a fourth and fifth alarms.

With flames spreading from tank to tank and threatening to jump the Newtown Creek, Martin had Healy transmit the first of two Borough Calls at 3:23 p.m. (This brought all the apparatus normally responding to Manhattan Box 389, Avenue A and 23rd Street to the Brooklyn fire.) Martin continued in command until Chief Kenlon arrived.

The huge fire was spreading. Flaming oil covered the Newtown Creek as exhausted fire companies attempted to halt the extending fire. A second borough call sent additional Manhattan companies to the Long Island City side of the creek. The fire was fought for days and over 1,000 FDNY firemen and officers worked some or all of the fire. In the official report to the Board of Merit, Assistant Chief Martin stated:

> The duty performed at the fire in the Standard Oil Plant... is deserving of the highest commendation for energy, efficiency, courage and fidelity displayed and the effective service rendered under the most hazardous and trying conditions.

Fireman Dan Healy and Chief Martin were both named

among the 400+ officers and firemen who were placed on the Roll of Merit for the actions at this fire.

Faithful Dan continued driving Chief Martin to fire after fire until his retirement in 1925. Healy lived a quiet family life until he passed away in 1940 after a long illness. He was only 66 years old. When Martin learned of Faithful Dan's passing, he said:

> He was the sort of man you could always depend on to do what you wanted. If you wanted a report of how conditions were on the opposite side of a big fire you could be sure Dan could size it up and tell you the things needed to know. If you had orders to transmit you knew when you gave them to Dan that they would be carried out correctly.

Lt. Samuel Banta on rig and Captain John Binns in Hook & Ladder 10 circa 1885

Capt. Andrew B. Sweet Hook & Ladder 10

Deputy Chief Thomas Lally

Life Saving Corps demonstration at Printing House Square in 1883

Chief McAdam observing rope rifle training

Battalion Chief George Ross
Chief Ross was said to be a direct descendant of Betsy Ross, famed American flag maker.

Chief John O'Hara, Lt. Thomas Kain and Smoky Joe Martin
On January 10, 1900, Kain's 44th Birthday

Thomas Ahearn

Captain George J. Fox

Capt. Charles E. Field Hook & Ladder 107

Captain Luke Flanagan

Stylized Maltese Cross Badge of FDNY Engineer of Steamer & Assistant

Engine Company 205 responding to Special Call 5-63-205, on December 20, 1922. Fireman John Foster, senior whip at the reins, as they respond to Brooklyn Borough Hall.
In the rear looking forward is Engineer of Steamer Tom McEwen.

Engine Company 205 and the new American LaFrance 700-gallon per minute gasoline powered pumper. Capt. Leon Howard stands between horses and new rig. Note trolley car tracks, just one of many hazards the horses and responding firemen faced.

Chief Croker and Lt. John Rush
In the second Locomobile 1903

Rush and Croker in touring car

Chief John Binns and Fr. Diessroth in the 1906 Electric Stanhope

Deputy Chief Lally in his Locomobile touring car

Capt. Charles W. Rankin
Note the "Bugs" on his sleeve denoting rescues

A dashing photo of Chief Rankin

Deputy Commissioner George Olvany, Chief Kenlon, Lt. Rankin and Doctor Archer

A newspaper image of Fireman Luke Henry

Chief Smoky Joe Martin and Fireman Dan Healy

High-Pressure Hydrant System Pipes, Valves and Parts Stored on Waterfront

High-Pressure System test on West Street June 28, 1908

Fire Stories 145

Union Square High-Pressure System Test July 12, 1908

Union Square High-Pressure Water Test July 12, 1908

High-Pressure Hydrant & Tripods Being Used at Union Square High-Pressure Tests

High Pressure Engine 72 the first motorized rig in the FDNY 1909

Chief Croker at the trials of the new motorized rig
High Pressure Engine 72 January 1909

Fire Stories 149

Water Tower 1 after electric motorization in 1911

Members of Engine 20 testing Fireman Halloran's Hose Mask 1911

Honorary Chief Robert H. Mainzer the Millionaire Buff

Deputy Chief Edward J. Worth
Commander of the FDNY Marine Division

Chief David J. Oliver

Fire Stories 153

Louis Tischler.

Newspaper photo of Louis Tischler
(Below) Tischler in Rescue 1 circa 1920

Roggencamp Docrite Tierney Larkin Fullam Tischler Conners Capt Lamb

Fireman John Conners on December 17, 1921, wearing smoke helmet gear.

Fireman John Kistenberger at the wheel of Rescue's 1914 Cadillac, Lt. Thomas Kilbride seated next to him donning his helmet. Photo probably made in 1921 when the new a truck went in service.

Fireman William A. Dorritie Rescue Co. 1

Fireman Richard J. Donovan Rescue Co. 2

Fireman James Smith Rescue Co. 1
Despite his Medal of Honor there are no photos.
Perhaps this is him wearing a smoke helmet.

Members of Rescue 1 in 1915 with smoke helmets and pulmotor

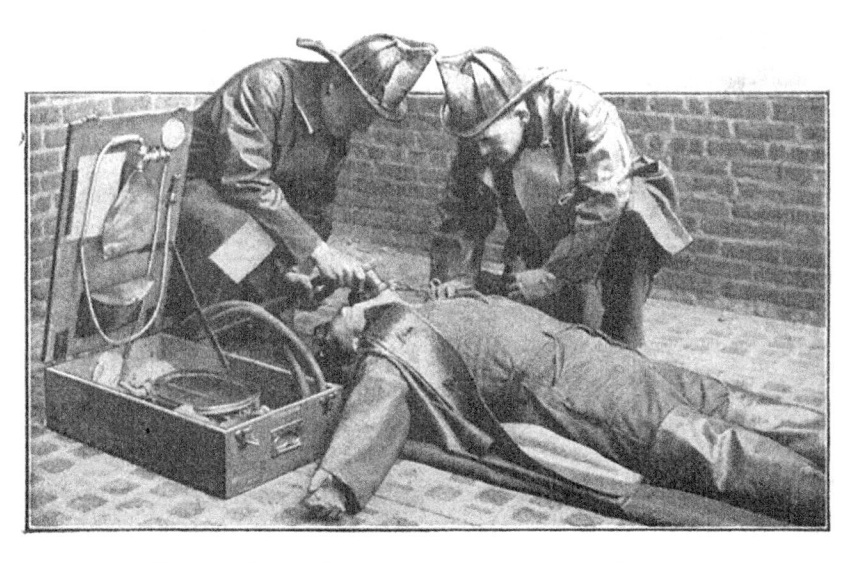

Rescue 1 members using pulmotor on fireman

Doctor Archer and his fully equipped medical car

Doctor Archer, unknown fireman, and Robert Mainzer in 1923

160 · *Fire Stories*

New ambulance delivery. On step is William Kenny, far right Edward Kenny, to his right Chief Kenlon with Doc Archer between them. January 29, 1923

New 1949 Ambulance, Doc Archer at door. In front of Engine 56

Part 3

The Parker Building Fire

The burning of the Parker Building on the night of January 10, 1908, caused the death of two firemen and a fire patrolman, the loss of millions of dollars of property, and the crippling of two great lines of transportation for two days. The worst loss however was the public's trust in the fire department due to political reasons. It all became clear as the fire and its aftermath unfolded.

The Parker Building on the southeast corner of 19th Street and Fourth Avenue (later called Park Avenue South) in Manhattan was completed in 1900. The 12-story high rise building had a cage frame with cast-iron columns and steel beams, brick exterior walls, and tile arch floors. The first two floors featured stone exterior walls, the third floor and above was brick. There was an interior 2-½-inch standpipe system, with hoses on each floor connected to a gravity water supply and fed by a small pump in the basement. There was also a perforated pipe system in the basement meant to act as a sprinkler.

The building was originally designed for office space. However, the building's occupants for years had been manufacturers, merchants, and printers. The first floor and basement held a stock of bar fixtures, billiard tables, furniture, refrigerators and upholsterers' goods and fabrics. The second floor held a large stock of hospital supplies, the third floor was filled with embroidery manufacturing and stocks of woolens. The fourth through seventh floors held large stocks of furniture, woolens, tailors' trimmings, books, and rugs. Manufacturing plaster art casts and gold pens filled part of the eighth story. Large stocks of books, editorial and business offices were on the ninth floor. The 10th floor was vacant. Printing and engraving companies filled the eleventh, twelfth, roof house and parts of the eighth floor.

The added weight of heavy printing presses, safes, and stores of paper were not anticipated in the original design. Each floor featured 17,000 square feet of undivided area. The building had many openings for elevators and other purposes that would provide a ready path for fire extension. There were also stores of varnishes, paints, furniture, rugs and other flammables that would only add to the fire load.

At 6 p.m., most of the tenants of the building had completed their day's work and departed the building. A half hour later the nightwatchman smelled smoke but was unable to locate the source. He made several trips through the building but was still unable to discover the fire. He had no keys to the fifth or sixth floors and had to bypass them as he searched the remaining floors. It was about ten minutes before 8 p.m., when workers on the sixth floor began noticing mice running frantically around the floor, and the distant sound of glass breaking. One employee Mr. C.J. Spaulding went to investigate. Spaulding observed a bright glow and as he grew nearer saw flames blazing among packing boxes and stored paper near the rear stairs on the fifth floor.

The night watchman by now had also seen the growing flames and pulled the special building alarm box inside, then dashed outside and pulled the street alarm box. Within seconds Manhattan units were responding to Box 361, it was 8:02 p.m.

The first arriving chief officer was Battalion Chief Joseph Shea who took one look at the fire and transmitted a second and third alarms, and then special-called two water towers. The first arriving companies stretched their hoses and soon found the rear portions of the sixth floor ablaze with flames extending toward the front of the building. For several minutes engine companies pressed their attack, but despite their aggressive efforts the fire pressed forward.

On the fifth floor fire patrolmen forced a door anticipating throwing covers over stock to prevent water damage from the hoses flowing above. They were met instead, by an advancing wall of flames. Attack lines were stretched on the fifth floor, but the nozzle teams were unable to push in due to the large and growing body of fire. They were quickly driven from the floor.

Outside, Chief Shea positioned Water Tower 3 on the Fourth Avenue side and Water Tower 2 on 19th Street. As the first water tower was being raised the top section of the mast jammed and would not extend. Firemen then climbed up and tried using a block and tackle to free the stuck section.

Deputy Chief John Binns arrived (Chief Croker was out of town in Pittsburgh on department business), Binns was acting chief of department. He conferred with Shea as he assumed command of the fire.

With reports of people trapped on the seventh floor, Captain Walter Gorgin of Hook & Ladder 7 and his men mounted the side of the building nearest the Hotel Florence and made a search. On the opposite side of the blazing structure a similar search was conducted by Captain William Keogh of Hook & Ladder 24 and his men. Both searches proved negative.

During the fire attack, several backdrafts rocked the building increasing the dangers firemen faced. One by one lengths of fire hose began to burst, a common occurrence of late. This caused delays and frustrated the hard-pressed firemen. Low water pressure and the constant failure of the new fire hose was hampering the attack on the fire and allowing the flames to grow.

Suddenly, far above the gathering crowd of spectators, four men became visible at the roof level. Their shouts alerted both the firemen and the huge crowd. Capt. Gorgin saw them and shouted to Fireman David Curley of Engine 14, Chief Croker's aide, for help. Together they hurried to the roof of the Hotel Florence with a mortar and lifeline. (A larger version of the rope rifle used to shoot a line with a rope attached, between buildings or ships as done by the navy.)

The trapped men yelled across that the roof was burning beneath their feet. "Don't jump! We'll get you. Keep up your courage!" Bellowed Captain Gorgin as the lifeline was shot across the roof. The men pulled it frantically and made it fast around a chimney, then prepared to slide down.

"Wait!" yelled Gorgin as he and Curley made a hitch around a chimney on the hotel roof making the rope taut. The men barehanded, inched hand over hand, from the fire building, across the 15-foot-wide alley, more than 120 feet above the ground and down two stories to the roof of the hotel. Their hands were burned by the friction against the rope, and their clothes were singed by the updrafts of heat from the flames below. But they all reached the roof safely.

Inside, more than 50 firemen were focused on the battle including Engine Companies 12, 16 and 18 who were back working on the fifth floor. Deputy Chief Thomas Langford, and Battalion Chief Ross were with Capt. Davin and the men of Engine 72 also on the fifth floor, but on the Florence Hotel (south) side. Capt. Shannon of Hook & Ladder 3 and two of his men were operating on the sixth floor. On the second floor the men of Fire Patrol 1 and 3, were throwing covers to protect stock from water damage while Fire Patrol 4 was doing the same in the basement. All hands were focused on their assignments and unaware of any added danger.

Unknown to the firemen the flames had weakened the structural steel to the point of failure. There were five heavy cylinder presses on the 11th floor, weighing some 15 tons, more than twice the load the floors were designed to hold. Suddenly, a heavy cylinder press came crashing down from the 11th floor. The cylinder press crashed through floor after floor on its way to the cellar, causing a major, localized collapse that pulled two firemen and a fire patrolman into the blazing abyss.

Capt. Gorgin, Fireman Curley and the men they'd rescued with the rope had just reached the street when the tremendous roar of the collapse was heard within the fire building. Firemen in the street ran to the 19th Street side of the building where several of the companies had made entrance. At these windows began to appear dust-covered firemen, some holding their unconscious comrades in their arms.

Extension ladders were rushed into position, and despite the flames raging from almost every window, the rescue work began. The ladders were becoming hot, and the rungs burned the firemen's hands as they ascended to reach the trapped and injured.

On the far side of the fifth floor, Deputy Chief Thomas Langford, Battalion Chief George Ross, Captain Davin and his men of Engine Company 72, and several other companies, battled their way to windows that overlooked the Florence Hotel. Firemen scrambled to place a ladder bridge between the two buildings and across the alleyway. Crawling across were Chief Langford, Capt. Davin and their men. One by one the firemen inched across the makeshift bridge, five-stories above the ground. It was then realized two men were missing, Firemen O'Connor and Phillips, both of Engine 72.

Davin had his hand on O'Connor and was dragging him toward the window when a second wave of the collapse drove them to the floor. Davin's right hand was crushed, and he was semi-conscious from the blow to his head. Unable to save himself the members of Engine 72 carried him across the ladder bridge.

Inside as the collapse occurred, Captain Vaughn of Fire

Patrol 3, (one of the heroes of the Hotel Royal fire) was working with his men on the second floor. They were covering goods with rubber tarps to prevent water damage, when suddenly the floors above came crashing down. After a moment of weightless dust and confusion, Vaughn found himself clinging to a girder. He moved toward the nearest window and bumped into one of his men, John Hutchinson. The dazed fire patrolman who'd been fully geared moments before now stood at the very edge of the chasm, helmetless, barefoot and in his shirtsleeves. He could only point to where his partner Fire Patrolman Tom Fallon had been seconds earlier. Vaughn grabbed him as he fell unconscious. He was able removed his injured man from the building.

The members of Hook & Ladder 3 had just reached the sixth floor when the collapse occurred. Captain John J. Shannon and two of his men Firemen Patrick Brady and Gustave Humbentel were toward the front of the building with the remaining men working their way toward them from the rear stairs.

Suddenly a large sheet of flames burst up into the faces of Shannon and his two men, as the floor collapsed. They realized immediately there was no way to reach the stairs, so the three of them moved to a window on the southerly corner of the building and climbed out onto the broad window ledge. The remaining section of the room behind them was quickly filling with flames and the smoke was pumping under pressure from the windows around them. Their shouts for help were lost in the noise of the fire trucks below, the heavy flames, and the thick clouds of smoke billowing around them.

Peering through the smoke, Shannon hoped to see help coming, but no one in the street below could see them. Shannon glimpsed a wire-framed sign projecting from the building ten feet below their position. It looked flimsy but was attached to the bricks by iron hooks. "Boys," he said to his men. "I'm going to take a chance. We can't stay here much longer. I'm going to jump for that wire sign. If it holds me, you fellows can follow. If it don't hold me—good bye."

With that he dropped down onto the sign. It twisted and strained but the hooks held fast. In a minute Brady and Humbentel dropped down to his side. They sat there, stuck on a sign, 60 feet above the ground obscured by thick clouds of billowing smoke. But it could have been worse, as they looked up at the ledge they'd just left, they saw flames now pouring from the window. The other members of Engine 3 had escaped to the street, and they began to search for their comrades until their captain's plight was noticed. An extension ladder was placed against the building but was too short so scaling ladders were used to complete the gap. Utilizing the six-foot hook Humbentel had refused to abandon, they were able to direct the ladder's hook in the window above their heads and climb onto the scaling ladder. The singed and exhausted trio descended the dangerous chain of ladders to safety. They had been trapped for nearly 20 minutes.

The dangerous work of fire extinguishment continued, but from a defensive position outside. Several attempts were made to approach the collapse area in hopes of rescuing the trapped men, but conditions became too severe. The flames were finally controlled, and the exhausted firemen could relax. The blaze had taken a severe toll: three men missing and presumed dead, nearly two dozen injured—some seriously, and the steaming shell of the burned-out building stood in mute testimony to the severe damage done inside.

Damages were estimated at $563,000.

The bodies of Fireman Thomas F. Phillips and Fireman George A. O'Connor, both of High-Pressure Engine 72, and Fire Patrolman John Fallon were later recovered.

The High Pressure Hydrant System

As stated by FDNY Assistant Chief Joseph B. Martin,

> The extensive fires and conflagrations up to and previous to the year 1904 in many large American cities caused officials, and among them New York, to view with alarm the possibility of a repetition of these fires and emphasized the necessity of installing ways and means of protection against such a calamity. The result was the preparation of plans for the introduction of the high-pressure service, which was inaugurated in 1904, and completely installed and ready for service in 1908.
>
> The first high-pressure system in Greater New York, installed at Coney Island, demonstrated its value in July 1908, when it was the dominant factor extinguishing a conflagration which would, no doubt, have reduced the almost complete frame building construction there to ashes.

The conflagrations Smoky Joe was referring to were: the Great Baltimore Fire ($150 million) on February 7 and 8, 1904, and the Great Toronto Fire ($10.5 million) on April 19, 1904. There were also major fires in Rochester, New York, and Shelbyville, Ohio, among other cities. The total cost of conflagrations in the United States and Canada for the year 1904 were estimated at $245.3 million.

On March 16, 1904, Water Commissioner John T. Oakley submitted to Mayor McClellan a plan for installing mains, pumping stations, and hydrants for a high-pressure water service for fighting fires. This plan included systems to be installed in lower

Manhattan, the Brooklyn waterfront and Coney Island. With pumping stations utilizing fresh water, but able to convert to salt water if needed. The idea was accepted, and the installation began with the Coney Island system which was completed in 1906.

The Coney Island high-pressure pumping station, unlike Manhattan and Brooklyn, was gas powered and had a limited capacity of 150 pounds per square inch. The high-pressure pumping station was located at 12th Street and Neptune Avenue. In Manhattan pumping stations were built at Oliver and South streets on the East River, and Gansevoort and West streets on the North (Hudson) River. In Brooklyn stations were built at Furman and Joralemon streets and at Willoughby and Saint Edwards streets. These were all electrically powered pumps and were each supplied by 48-inch and 36-inch water mains. These stations featured electrical pumps that together could supply 36,000 gallons per minute at 300 pounds. The water was distributed by 24-inch mains (two from each pumping station.) They fed 128 miles of high-pressure mains in Manhattan and 45 miles in Brooklyn. The Manhattan systems could also be divided instantaneously into independent systems if needed.

There were now about 49,200 hydrants in greater New York, 4,100 of these were high-pressure. It was stated the capacity of a single high-pressure hydrant could furnish as many hose streams as five fire engines, and that a 60-foot water tower stream could reach the 14th story of a building. When attached to a standpipe a good stream could be delivered from the top of a 40-story building. The continuing problem of defective and inadequate hose continued to plague the FDNY. As the high-pressure system was being completed the newspapers reminded the city of the rotten hose. On February 7, 1908 Fire Commissioner Hugh Bonner advertised for proposals to supply 100,000 feet of fire hose, with 40,000 feet strong enough to operate with the high-pressure hydrant system. Bids were to be opened on March 2.

The first test of the Manhattan high-pressure hydrant system was held on Sunday June 28, 1908 on West Street, near Gansevoort Street. Newspaper reports stated:

> Not only did West Street and several surrounding streets get a thorough and much needed bath as a result of the test, but Fire Chief Croker and his assistants were also thoroughly drenched. When the test was ended there was several inches of water in the streets. But Chief Croker was too enthusiastic to pay any attention to the drenching that he received. (NY *Tribune*.)

Twenty-four streams were operated for 20 minutes, and a thick mist reached the police lines at Jane and Bank streets. Several streams also reached the roof of the 12-story Western Electric Building. A second test utilized ten streams and a water tower. It was reported the flow of water was so great that it threatened to flood the surrounding steamer docks, especially that of the Wilson Line. (Subsequent news reports stated damage was done and the city was being sued for damages.)

The test, besides the water damage, proved so successful that officials from the FDNY and the water department decided to place the high-pressure system into permanent service on Monday July 6, 1908.

Chief Martin's earlier remarks also alluded to a fire in Coney Island that broke out on July 9, 1908. Flames, ignited by a careless smoker on the veranda on the east side of the Pabst's Hotel on Surf Avenue at 1 a.m., quickly jumped to the Vanderveer Hotel next door and soon both large wood frame buildings were ablaze. Luckily all those in the hotels escaped but were left standing in the street watching the fire in their bedclothes.

Arriving fire companies transmitted a second and third alarms but were able to stretch directly from the high-pressure hydrants to begin their attack. At around 2 a.m. the wind changed direction and spread the flames to the Brooklyn Rapid Transit station. The renewed fire was now threatening several nearby wood frame buildings. Deputy Chief Lally raced to the scene in his chief's car arriving in just 12 minutes. He transmitted a fourth alarm and took charge of the fire attack.

The wind died down and the fire was contained. The water pressure from the new high-pressure system proved sufficient and none of the responding steam pumpers were used.

Four days later, on Sunday July 12, 1908, Chief Croker and his men assembled in Union Square at 7 in the morning. About 100 firemen, small groups from each of the downtown companies were detailed to the demonstration. Hose wagons carrying 2,000 feet of hose were positioned. Water Tower No. 2 was set up and following Chief Croker's rapid-fire orders, members of the high-pressure companies began stretching lengths of the newly purchased high pressure hose. (The FDNY had bought 100,000 feet of specially designed hose able to sustain 400 pounds of pressure—each length having previously been tested to that pressure.) This test was designed to familiarize the firemen with the use of the new hydrants and apparatus, the hoses, pipes and pumps having all been tested to their capacity previously.

Forty-eight lines of hose were stretched 1,100 feet from nine hydrants. (Only 36 lines would be charged.) Each high-pressure hydrant fed four streams. Twenty-four streams were carried through 3-inch hose with 2-inch nozzles, 24 other streams were developed using 1-1/2 and 1-1/4-inch nozzles. The lines were positioned on three sides of Union Square, and the nozzles were directed east on 14th and 17th streets, and west on the other streets from Broadway. Double tripods were used with the 2-inch nozzles and the smaller nozzles were braced with prong-end holders.

On Croker's signal one after the other the lines were charged and the sound of the water rushing from the nozzles filled the square. Within seconds the black coats of the firemen shone with water spray. They shouted to each other as they struggled to control the heaving hoses.

In the first test the water pressure was raised to 250 pounds, then slowly increased to 290. At the nozzles, gauges read between 110 to 150 depending on the size of the hose and the number of lengths in the stretch. When the pressure reached the 290-pound mark, three hoses, one after the other burst from the pressure. The report of each bursting length echoed across the square like a rifle shot. The force was so great that each hose immediately was pulled from its brass coupling and swung in the air drenching everyone nearby. One line broke a window in a store injuring two men with the flying glass. The hoses were quickly controlled, and the broken lengths replaced. Two injured firemen were tended by Doctor Archer as the test continued.

The mist from the 36 streams rose like a cloud, and the morning rays of the sun created a beautiful rainbow over the square. Passing street cars were enveloped in the spray much like the little boats that approached Niagara Falls. Unlike those passengers, those on the street cars were not prepared to get wet. Most did however, with good humor.

The first test lasted for about a half hour. Then it was time for the ultimate test of the morning. Water Tower 2 was fed by four lines from one hydrant and the top nozzle drove a stream into Union Square Park soaking numerous spectators until it was redirected. While the lower nozzle directed its powerful stream, the top nozzle was pointed upwards and as the men stationed at the hydrant slowly increased the pressure, the powerful stream reached as high as the 30-foot flagpole atop the 17-story Metropolitan Building.

A cheer rose from the assembled crowd and the firemen standing near the water tower. The two men patted the hydrant as if in congratulations. The high-pressure hydrant test and demonstration had been a huge success. The firemen were happy and confident in the new equipment and the slightly damp spectators were impressed by the modern developments in firefighting.

On Thursday evening July 16th, just four days after the big water demonstration, Chief Croker strolled from the Broadway Central Hotel after enjoying his dinner. He stopped on the sidewalk and looked around the neighborhood. His eyes were drawn to the big six-story brick building at 1 Bond Street where he could see smoke coming from the building.

Croker ordered a citizen to pull the lever on a nearby fire alarm box as the chief hurried toward the burning building. In the nearby quarters of Engine 25 the bells directed them to respond to the pulled box and they arrived quickly with Engine 20 close at their heels. Above, fire had control of the two top floors. Chief Croker had found the place an inferno, with the growing flames held inside by the iron shutters. Croker sent teams to battle the fire from the front and from the alley in the rear, while he called for a second alarm and an increase in the water pressure.

Water Tower 2 rolled in and was positioned. Three 3-inch high-pressure lines were stretched to the tower. When all was ready those inside were warned and the tower was charged. A powerful stream of water drove into the flames and they quickly subsided. After only a few minutes the water was ordered shut off. Many looked at the chief in disbelief. So fast?

Moments later firemen appeared in the windows on the top floor and waved all was well. The flames were out. The high-pressure system had worked like a charm. Even the skeptics were becoming convinced—the system worked.

Then, on November 7, 1908, at 4:16 a.m., an alarm was received for a fire at 9 Walker Street in Manhattan. Fire companies responded to the location, including Chief Croker who rolled on the initial alarm. Accompanied by Deputy Chief Guerin and Captain Rush, Croker was on scene quickly. As firemen worked their way up the front fire escape, a call was made to increase the water pressure. Nothing happened. The water pressure being received was inadequate.

Captain Rush was sent by Croker to personally call the pumping station on Oliver Street and find out the problem. Rush was informed the pressure was on at the station, "Everything is working fine at this end." Meanwhile the flames were extending upward from the third floor. Conditions on the fire escapes was getting extremely hot and dangerous as the pressure below wouldn't allow streams to cover the firemen working above, and they were getting cut off by the extending flames.

Chief of Department Croker called the pumping station himself and was told the same thing Rush was earlier. The chief ordered the steam pumpers to take over. As quickly as possible, four steam engines augmented the pressure and hose streams were directed to protect the exposed firemen on the fire escapes as the water tower mast was raised and positioned. Its powerful stream tore into the fire and the fire was slowly defeated.

The aftermath dissolved into a finger pointing stand-off as fire chiefs blamed the pump house and water officials blamed the firemen. A physical examination of all the pipes and hydrants in use at the fire was completed and all worked fine. The logbook at the pumping station showed a call from the fire dispatchers at 4:37 ordering 125 pounds of pressure. (This was however 21 minutes after the arrival of the fire companies.) It also noted Captain Rush's call at 4:43 requesting an increase to 200. Both calls were apparently immediately complied with.

Obviously, something went wrong. It could never be proven if there was a communications failure, a mechanical error, or a human error on the fire ground. It was obvious the new system would take some getting used to. Despite the vast improvements, the high-pressure system was only a tool to be used by firefighters who still faced an extremely dangerous job.

The next big real-world test occurred on December 8, 1908, when flames broke out in the seven-story warehouse of the Western Union Company located at 152 Franklin Street in Manhattan. (Western Union was the main telegraph company in the United States from the 1860s to the 1980s. It pioneered such features as wire money transfers, and telex, a telecommunication service that provided text-based message exchange over the public telephone network. Their core business however was transmitting and delivering telegrams.)

When the first due units arrived, they found the flames were already well on their way from the basement to the roof, with the iron shutters on the ground floor glowing cherry red. To compound matters, the exposed buildings on either side were wholesale whiskey companies with barrels of spirits piled from floor to ceiling on all seven floors.

Deputy Chief Guerin transmitted a second alarm on his arrival and requested the Oliver Street pumphouse to increase pressure. As Chief Croker arrived lines were connected and being stretched into position. Even though the five lower floors of the building were in flames, and the window sashes of the exposed buildings were igniting Croker felt confident. Fifteen high-pressure attack lines were stretched, six along North

Moore Street leading to the rear of the warehouse. The rest were operating on Franklin Street.

With orders from the chief that no firemen were to enter the building, the exterior attack commenced. It was further augmented as the water tower was placed in front of the blazing warehouse. Three high pressure lines fed water into the tower and as the pumphouse pressure was again increased to 150, then 175 pounds, the towers stream easily drove into the flames showing at the fifth and sixth floors. This deluge then cascaded down from floor to floor further extinguishing the flames below.

Watching the battle with confidence, Chief Croker sent the steam engines assigned on the second alarm, back to their quarters. Two steamers remained and were used to pump water from the cellars of the exposed buildings. The chiefs and firemen were once again confident in the new system. An advanced fire that would have required a five-alarm response was held at two alarms. Deputy Chief William Guerin stated, "We are certain that we could handle six five alarm fires within the high-pressure zone at one time, whereas before we would have had a very hard time with two."

Prophetic words.

A worker on the fifth floor of the six-story commercial building filled with small factories, at 213 Grand Street, saw smoke and flames shooting from the transom above the door of the Kallenbock Comb Company, manufacturers of celluloid articles. He ran through the choking smoke to warn the 100 people working on the floor above. These workers, with their exit blocked by flames and the top floor quickly filling with thick smoke and heat, stumbled to the relative safety of the roof. Meanwhile, the flames were rapidly extending through pipe recesses, stairways, and burning through the floors.

On the street below fire companies rolled into position and

attached their hoses to the high-pressure hydrants, preparing to battle the flames. When the crews were in place, nozzlemen stood with limp hoses in their hands. Unknown to them a valve had blown off the deadhead of a main, suspended by chains in the subway excavation on Centre Street rendering the high-pressure system out of service. Thousands of gallons of water poured from the broken valve filling the excavation and reducing the pressure so dramatically it affected the entire system.

Engine men scrambled to get their steamers pumping and new attack lines were stretched and put into position as the flames above them grew. Members of the hook and ladders hurried with extension ladders hoping to reach those trapped above the growing flames.

On the roof, Sam Cohen decided to jump to the roof of the adjoining building. He found a 16-foot plank of wood and lifted it upwards to the roof. Men and women began to slide down through clouds of smoke and tumble to safety on the adjoining rooftop.

Members of Hook & Ladder 1 raised ladders from the roof of the other adjoining building and helped the near hysterical workers down. Several other ladders were also raised. One frantic man, who was pushing his way past women, attempted to climb onto a ladder and was calmed by the fist of a fireman. Rescue efforts continued with several unconscious workers carried down ladders to safety. Nine members of the department were placed on the Roll of Merit for their heroic efforts at this fire.

A sudden gust of wind whipped the flames that threatened to ignite the wooden fire ladders which were quickly removed as the last worker was brought to safety. The tenement house in the rear did catch fire and lines were repositioned to extinguish that blaze. It took three alarms to subdue the flames.

Chief Croker was livid with the failure of the high-pressure system. "I am heartily disgusted," he said. "If the high-pressure is to continue to be as unreliable as it has been in the past, we will have to go back to the old system or the whole city might burn up while we were waiting for pressure.

This was the second time the new high-pressure system had failed. But training and persistence prevailed, the system began performing as expected, and soon became a trusted part of the war on fire.

Three Corner Night

It was 7:22 p.m. on the evening of January 7, 1909, when the first alarm was received at the Manhattan FDNY fire communications office. The alarm was for a fire in a triangular six-story brick building at Franklin, Leonard, and Hudson streets, that was occupied by wholesale grocers. The fire started in the ground-floor offices of the Lipton Tea Company and spread quickly throughout the structure.

For the responding fire companies the winter weather would prove to be almost as difficult to deal with as the fires they'd face. Freezing temperatures and strong northerly winds would test the endurance of the firefighting forces. The daytime temperature reached 26-degrees but by night fall had dropped to 18-degrees.

The high-pressure hydrant system had been completed the previous year giving lower Manhattan excellent water pressure and the firemen an advantage they never had before. This water system and the importance of having double engine and ladder companies in this extremely high hazard section of the city would be reinforced before the night was over.

The sound of an explosion led Sergeant George Stevenson to look out the rear window of the Leonard Street police station. He was surprised to see a major fire blazing in the building to the rear of the stationhouse. He immediately hurried across the street and pulled the fire alarm box.

Just a few doors down on Franklin Street were the quarters of Engine Company 27, a double high-pressure engine company. Captain Jones and his men arrived quickly, and the officer immediately put in a second alarm. Battalion Chief Guerin arrived moments later and transmitted a third alarm. As Engine 27 began stretching a hose from a nearby hydrant, the building was rocked by a powerful explosion. The explosion coincided with the arrival of Water Tower 1, its team of horses near exhaustion after their response through the frigid streets. A sheet of flames shot across the sidewalk and into the street startling the horses so badly that two fell to the ground. Flailing and panicking on the ground they were unhitched by firemen and led away to safety.

Fire companies descended on the scene and immediately began stretching lines from the high-pressure hydrants. Flames were pouring from every window and a thick pall of black smoke hung over the neighborhood. Sparks and embers flew through the air as firemen struggled to battle the growing flames, and explosions continued inside the blazing building. Determined efforts helped protect the Borden Condensed Milk Company and other companies occupying the buildings on either side.

In the initial scramble to establish a fire attack the freezing weather only added to the danger. Fireman George Saich of Engine Company 20, slipped on the ice and a horse stepped on his hand, crushing his fingers. He was quickly tended by Doctor Archer. Fireman Robert Heirons of Engine 13 was run over by the hose tender crushing his legs, Doctor Archer had him removed to Hudson Street Hospital. Lt. George Copley, of Engine Company 6, was struck by a piece of falling coping and received a severe scalp wound. (Usually made of terra cotta, coping is the covering placed on the top of a brick wall to protect the bricks and mortar from the elements.) Fireman Victor Coakley was struck by a loose high-pressure hose, leaving him with a bad scalp wound and a concussion. Also added to the injury list was Police Officer William Cronideter of the

10th Precinct, who was run over by a fire truck. He too was taken to Hudson Street Hospital with a broken leg.

Three alarms brought 18 engines, five hook & ladders, two water towers and the searchlight engine to the scene. First the flames extended to the seven-story warehouse next door. Fifteen hose lines were stretched and were operating directly from the hydrants. Chief Croker arrived and had the pumping station at the foot of Gansevoort Street increase the hydrant pressure. He then transmitted a fourth alarm at 7:46 p.m. An hour later he would send in the fifth alarm.

Water Tower 1, being fed directly from a high-pressure hydrant, was doing good work on the upper floors when suddenly the nozzle at the top of the tower blew off. The force was so great that the heavy brass nozzle was blown over the building. Water Tower 2 was quickly moved into position and took over operations.

Firemen used specially designed tripods to place high-pressure hose streams in stationary positions. This allowed the stream to operate into the flames without needing men to hold the frigid hoses by hand. One tripod did fall over causing the six-man crew to wrestle the thrashing line until it could be controlled. The six soaked and freezing men staggered off to get warm and dry. Turret pipes on the hose wagons were also used to direct powerful streams into the fire building.

Late in the fire, Chief Croker noticed the cornice on the fire building about to fall and ordered all the firemen from the street. The last to leave their posts were the members of Engine 7 who were forced to drop their hose and run for their lives as the cornice fell and the roof collapsed into the building, toppling a sidewall into the street.

With the collapse of the fire building conditions improved quickly and Chief Croker was able to release companies to respond to the other fires nearby.

One remarkable sight was the line of steam engines parked and standing idle while hundreds of firemen battled the growing flames using only their high-pressure hydrant service as a water supply. Another was the firemen themselves, who within minutes of their attack, were covered in ice from the freezing water spray. The streets and sidewalks quickly became sheets of ice. (Two of these fires, because of the overwhelming volume of fire on arrival, were fought from the outside for hours.)

At 8:17 p.m., less than an hour after the Hudson Street fire started, an automatic alarm was received from 600 Broadway, a six-story commercial building. This was a loft building operated by a millinery and lace company. Engine 33, one of the few companies in the lower half of Manhattan still in service, responded from their quarters on Great Jones Street about a half mile to the Broadway address alone to check out the alarm. Nothing was visible upon arrival. The members forced the front door and began to search for fire.

Then two minutes after the automatic alarm for Broadway was received an alarm came in for a fire at 113 Bowery between Hester and Grand streets. This six-story commercial building was used as a clothing factory with coats being made on the top floor. Twenty tailors were busy working on the top floor when they noticed smoke coming up through the floor next to heating pipes. At the same time the building's night watchman noticed the glow of flames reflected in the windows on the second floor. He dashed to transmit the alarm.

The tailors working on the top floor found themselves cut off. Most went down the fire escape, while three were forced to the front windows and had to crawl out onto the window ledge. They crawled across the ledge toward the building next door and were rescued with ropes lowered from the roof of the adjoining hotel by police detectives from a nearby precinct.

A second alarm was placed upon the arrival of the first units. Deputy Chief Joseph "Smoky Joe" Martin arrived and transmitted a third alarm. With all the companies in the downtown section of Manhattan already heavily engaged at the first fire, companies from midtown had to respond to the scene. The tall, narrow building was becoming a chimney as heat and fire were pulled upwards. Conditions in the street were becoming so dangerous that Chief Martin had the elevated subway trains halted and the nearby station platform was used as a vantage point for fire hoses. Cops and firemen scrambled to evacuate the fire building and several nearby tenement buildings that were threatened by the wind-driven fire.

Back at 600 Broadway, members of Engine 33 located a fire on the fourth floor rear and a second alarm was transmitted at 8:29. A third alarm at 8:32, brought Chief Croker from the original fire on Hudson Street. He arrived quickly by automobile and took command of the Broadway fire. All the high-pressure companies in lower Manhattan were already at work and units from as far north as Harlem were dispatched to the scene. Croker transmitted a fourth alarm at 8:40 and a fifth alarm at 8:43. He also requested the high-pressure pumping station at the foot of Oliver Street and the East River to increase the pressure to 200 pounds. A half hour after the automatic alarm there were 20 high pressure hose streams being directed at the fire.

At 10:15, after nearly two hours of fire duty, a three-inch hose connected to a high-pressure hydrant at Broadway and Houston streets burst suddenly only a few inches from the hydrant. Two hundred pounds of pressure drove the water into a group of insurance adjusters who'd been allowed within the fire lines, pinning them to a wall. A young teen age boy was driven completely across the street by the water and was almost drowned by the cascading water until rescued by firemen. He was bruised, battered and soaked, but not too badly injured.

The total fire losses were costly. The Hudson Street fire was estimated at over a million dollars. The Broadway fire loss was placed at a quarter million dollars, and the Bowery fire at $75,000. Three major fires burning simultaneously, fanned by strong winds, with freezing temperatures sinking into the frozen gear of weary firemen, had presented the FDNY with quite a challenge. Amazingly, one they were able to win despite the odds against them.

After the fires were out, Chief Edward Croker explained to reporters:

> I told the mayor that never in my twenty-five years experience as a fireman have I ever known of such a severe test of the capacity of the fire department... Just think of it! Three corking big fires going at once! Why that Hudson Street fire under the old system would probably have been a two nine fire (a borough call within the same borough) and we might have lost the entire block. The fire at Hester Street (113 Bowery) was equal to a good three alarm, and the Broadway was surely a good five alarm.
>
> In all three big fires all going at once and not a single engine was used after the high pressure was turned on. That is the truth gentlemen, not an engine was used. Every drop of water came from the high-pressure service and there certainly could have been no better test of what the system could do, and no doubt should remain in any one's mind now of its absolute efficiency.

First Motorized FDNY Apparatus

In 1909 the FDNY was just beginning the motorization of their firefighting fleet. The first motorized rig to be received new was a Knox High Pressure Hose Wagon. This rig would be assigned to Engine 72 on East 12th Street in Manhattan. The high-pressure hydrant system was placed in service in 1908, with the idea being that specially designed hose wagons could respond to fires and work hose lines directly from special hydrants. This would allow the fire attack to proceed even before steam pumpers could reach the needed pressures. The pumps in the high-pressure system were started on the receipt of a box alarm in their areas. The pressure was raised to 125 psi until the order was given to increase, or to shut down. The initial areas were lower Manhattan and downtown Brooklyn. The system was later extended in 1911 and 1914.

At midnight on January 23, 1909, the rig was driven from Madison Square Garden (where it was on exhibition at an auto show) to the FDNY shops at 56th Street and Twelfth Avenue for its official inspection. From there it was driven, with all its equipment and 20 firemen on board, down Broadway and Fifth Avenue to 12th Street. The wagon was closely followed by the chief's 1906 American Mercedes touring car. Captain John Rush, the chief's trusted driver and aide was at the wheel. Also on board were Honorary Battalion Chief Harry Archer, and Fire Commissioner Whitney who'd accompanied Chief Croker during the test. The new five-ton hose wagon was watched carefully as it was maneuvered through the streets. Handling smoothly the new rig reached speeds of 30 mph travelling straight and maintained 12 to 15 mph on turns.

The next day the new rig was taken to the fireboat house at the foot of Gansevoort Street and was fed water at 300 psi by the fireboat *Thomas Willet*. The swivel nozzle, a fixed turret pipe like on a fireboat, was able to direct a stream 125 feet at all angles, from directly upright to straight down, and all around the compass. The test and the rig proved very successful.

Going Electric

Water Tower 1, stationed with Engine Company 31 at Lafayette Street and White streets, was motorized in 1911 using Webb-Couple Gear Tractor to pull the rig. The front wheels, poles, and other horse fittings were removed and the gas-electric semi-tractor with a ten-ton capacity was attached to the ladder truck. The fifth-wheel, or turntable was placed in the center of the tractor platform. The tractor itself was outfitted with a 50 horsepower, four-cylinder motor that generated electric current which supplied a storage battery placed under the chassis frame. This battery powered four motors attached to ends of the axles. The motor armatures revolved and the pinions at the ends of the armature shafts meshed with racks within the inner periphery of the heavy disc wheels. These gears then turned the wheels to any predetermined speed, according to the graduations of the controller. The battery was kept charged by power from the tractor.

The tractor was driven and steered by all four wheels, and since they were each independently driven there was always the same tractive effort by each wheel, no matter the arc of turning. Amazingly the tractor could turn in a very tight circle, the radius being the length of the water tower. The water towers being used by the FDNY at this time were about 45 feet in length, about the same length as a hook and ladder truck and weigh about 14,000 pounds. The tower was collapsible for easier maneuverability but could be elevated to a height of 65 feet.

The three-horse team the tractor replaced could only achieve about six-miles per hour. With the tractor geared to a higher speed (than other civilian) applications it could be driven at more than 15-miles-per-hour.

The following year, 1912, two new motorized 75-foot aerial ladders were delivered to the FDNY. The rigs were made with the combined work of Couple-Gear Freight Wheel Company of Grand Rapids, Michigan and the Webb Company of St. Louis, Missouri. The trucks were assigned to Hook & Ladder 2 at East 67th Street and Hook & Ladder 6 on Canal Street.

Both rigs were gas-electric four-wheel drive. The 50 horsepower Hershell-Spillman four-cylinder engine fed a directly connected dynamo that could be controlled from the front seat. Each of the disc wheels was powered by an individual motor. Like traditional ladder trucks the driver controlled the front wheels and a tillerman controlled the rear wheels while driving. Despite its 10-ton weight the truck could travel 25 mph on level ground.

It is interesting to note the two-sectioned wooden aerial ladder (40-foot bed ladder and a 35-foot-long fly ladder) was hoisted using an electric motor, along with a pair of heavy auxiliary springs to help take the weight off during raising and to protect the rig and ladder if lowered too fast. The bed ladder could be brought to a vertical position in four seconds. The whole ladder could be extended to its longest in just 15 seconds. There was a small separate rheostat (a variable resistor used to control current) for the hoisting motor and a separate throttle for controlling the engine that drives the generator, from the ladder platform.

This hook and ladder's wheelbase was 24 feet, and the overall length from front bumper to the projecting end of the aerial ladder was 46 feet. The rig also carried a complete compliment of firefighting equipment including: portable ladders, life net, axes and other tools.

1911

Some years seemed to become benchmarks in FDNY history, and 1911 was an important one. The New York City Fire Department had grown to 4,420 firefighters, officers and chiefs working in 258 fire companies. Along with the humans, 1,508 horses were helping to protect a population of 4.8 million people. During the year the FDNY would receive: seven high pressure hose wagons (a high-pressure hydrant system had been placed in service in 1908 allowing downtown engine companies to stretch lines directly from hydrants and begin their attack immediately, not needing to wait for the pumpers to gain enough steam pressure to charge their hoses.) Fourteen runabouts were placed in service for chief officers, a second sized gasoline powered steam engine, and one fire engine that was also propelled by a gasoline engine were placed into service on a trial basis. (Both rigs proved unsatisfactory and were later removed from service.) A gas-electric tractor was installed under Water Tower 1, stationed on Lafayette Street, replacing three horses. Ten horseshoeing wagons were also placed in service allowing horses to be shod right at their firehouse. But the department's change to motorization was well under way.

The FDNY also established the Fire College on January 1, 1911, to: "disseminate knowledge of firefighting and to establish and maintain the highest levels of professional standards. This was followed by the organization of a school in automobile instruction in September. Seventy firemen graduated and were considered to be expert operators. The fire boat fleet, now known as the Marine Division, had grown to ten fireboats.

The year started off with a difficult and extremely dangerous fire at 61-71 Greenwich Avenue, a five-story warehouse across from St. Vincent's Hospital on January 5, 1911. It was just before midnight when flames broke out in a fourth-floor wallpaper manufacturing company and quickly extended upwards toward the roof before dropping downwards to the floor below.

Upon arrival Battalion Chief Ross immediately transmitted a second alarm. Above the chief a dozen firemen were stretching lines up the fire escape to reach the flames. Crouching beneath pulsing clouds of thick smoke pumping from the third-floor window, they signaled for water and were able to push back some of the fire threatening their position. Suddenly, a backdraft drove a sheet of flames from the window enveloping the men. With the flames burning their eyebrows and hair, they dropped flat attempting to avoid further injuries. Despite their burns the nozzle teams held tightly and tried to direct water at the flames from their prone position. They were able to drive the flames back into the window as firemen below scrambled up ladders to assist them. The burned men were helped to the ground as fresh firemen continued the attack.

Fireman George Kitchen of Engine 72 was hurried across the street and admitted to the hospital with serious facial burns. Another man from 72, Fireman Thomas Ward was also treated for serious head and face burns but was sent home to recover. Three members of Engine 24 were also treated for burns and were sent back to quarters to recuperate.

The following morning, January 6, 1911, non-fire related emergencies also proved dangerous to the men of the FDNY. In the Williamsburg section of Brooklyn members of Engine Company 115 were asked by neighbors to help rescue a small black kitten that had spent the night stranded up a tree after being chased by a dog. Members carried a ladder to the tree in front of 103 Java Street and 25-year-old Fireman Anton Jiranek climbed up toward the cat.

The rescue attempt was drawing a crowd of onlookers from a nearby school. Around 200 children on their lunch breaks stopped to watch the action. They watched the fireman arrive at the cat's level and reach for the scared animal. The panicked kitten backed away as Jiranek stretched out further and further trying to grab it. Suddenly, the branch he was leaning on snapped and both the fireman and the cat dropped 30 feet to the ground below. The crowd of children screamed and scattered as the fireman plummeted to the ground just inches away. Jiranek struck his head and was immediately knocked unconscious. He was rushed to the hospital with a fractured skull. Sadly, he would pass away the following day, never regaining consciousness.

Later that evening in Manhattan, Officer Corcoran was walking his beat along Wooster Street when he noticed a red glare in a third-floor window of 69-71 Wooster Street, a new six-story "fire-proof" building that extended through to West Broadway. It was 7:30 p.m. He dashed to the nearest alarm box and pulled the lever. Three minutes later Engine 13 rolled in, followed by the chief's buggy being driven by Fireman John Stapleton with Battalion Chief Worth seated next to him.

As the horse settled down, Stapleton jumped out of the buggy and did a quick size up. He turned and yelled, "I don't like the smell here, Chief. You better look out for those men at the door while I get the horse out of the way!" As he galloped the horse to a place of safety near Spring Street, Chief Worth bellowed a warning at 15 firemen trying to enter the building, demanding they back away. A moment later an explosion rocked the building. The recently abandoned door was blown off its hinges. Nearby firemen were knocked to the ground and as they scrambled to their feet, a shower of broken glass, shattered window sashes and bricks rained down from above.

Flames were shooting out and threatening to ignite the nearby elevated subway structure on West Broadway just as Chief Croker arrived. (The elevated subway was commonly referred to by everyone in the city simply as the "L.") He ordered his aide, Captain Ross to: "Telephone the "L" people to shut off the power. We've got to get our lines up on the "L" or this fire will get away from us!" The power was cut a few minutes later.

After attacking the fire with numerous outside streams, Chief Croker sent a dozen men from Engine 13 to wet down the smoldering rubble. After operating only a few minutes inside the fire-damaged structure, the loud rumble and crash of a localized collapse was heard. Chief Croker and BC Worth darted inside and led the dazed men back through the mounds of smoking debris. Croker heard a voice cry out and shouted, "Who is it?"

"John Read of 13," came the muffled reply. The chief followed the voice to a tangle of beams, girders and rubble. With Worth's help the chief used hand tools to uncover the trapped fireman who was taken to a nearby hospital to be examined for internal injuries. Chief Croker remarked it was a miracle Read wasn't killed.

Later that day FDNY units responded to a reported fire at 12-14 Pell Street in the Chinatown section of lower Manhattan. The fire was in an old dingy five-story triple tenement known as "The House of Five Doors," a notorious address housing 200 occupants in single rooms. Besides the crowded housing arrangements, the building also included an opium den, and underground connecting tunnels that led to other nearby structures on Pell Street and the Bowery.

The fire started when the flame from a second-floor oil stove ignited a small Christmas tree sitting on a table. The fire quickly engulfed the room as the occupants fled with their caged canary. Flames then quickly spread throughout the 40-year-old wooden structure. Nearby gas company workers saw the fire, transmitted the alarm and evacuated numerous tenants.

The first arriving fire units found an advanced fire situation that had already communicated to the building next door. A second alarm was transmitted, bringing Chief Croker and Deputy Chief Binns, who were still working less than a mile away at the scene of the Broadway fire. Croker transmitted a third alarm as soon as he arrived. Despite the narrow street, advanced fire on arrival and the close proximity of the surrounding buildings, the fire was held to just two structures. The overhaul stage of the fire proved to be slow and dangerous. The smoldering ruins were wet down and a careful secondary search for missing occupants was begun. Later that night Chief Davin and a fireman found what they believed were human remains and requested assistance at first light. Sadly, the bodies of two people were found and removed from the rubble. It was feared more would be found.

It was 5:30 p.m., Thursday January 5th, closing time for most of the businesses in downtown Manhattan. As darkness was settling across the city, Police Officer Bennin of the Traffic Squad noticed unusually bright lights in the fifth and sixth floor windows of the Cook Building on Broadway across from City Hall Park. The officer dashed to the fire alarm box and transmitted the alarm. Arriving at the L-shaped building that ran through to Murray Street, fire companies saw flames leaping from the fifth and sixth floors.

Three woman and a man were noticed huddled on a

fourth-floor fire escape on the Murray Street side of the building. Fireman John Zeigler, driver of Hook & Ladder 10, heard of their plight and with the help of civilians hurried a 25-foot wooden portable ladder to their location. He raised it to the fourth floor and ascended to find one woman unconscious. He lifted her over his shoulder and ordered the others to follow him as he started down the ladder. Despite clouds of thick smoke swirling around them they followed the fireman down.

    The fire had apparently started in the basement and extended upwards inside an airshaft then mushroomed across the fifth and sixth floors. The leaping flames attracted a huge crowd of onlookers that filled City Hall Park. Police estimates placed the crowd size at near 100,000 people, most of whom had just emptied the numerous high-rise buildings in the neighborhood and had been on their way home.

    A half hour after the fire started, the roof collapsed sending a shower of embers and sparks from every window on the Broadway and Murray Street sides. The sound of the collapse and the blast of heat and sparks led the crowd to believe an explosion had occurred. Fearing for their lives, much of the throng hurried away from the scene. By 7 p.m., the fire was under control and the three top floors were in ruins.

Several days later, on January 11th, at 10:30 p.m. a truck driver was passing the five-story brick factory building at 108-110 Duane Street at the corner of Church Street. Looking up he saw flames and smoke bursting from a window. He jumped from his truck and began yelling as he dashed toward the alarm box at the corner. In his office, in the adjoining building, Deputy Chief John Binns heard the shouts and alerted the members of Engine 7. The chief and his men reached the street before the alarm was even transmitted. Binns led the men up to the third floor where they were stopped by heavy doors. Moments later

Ladder 1 under the command of Captain John Sullivan arrived and began forcing the doors with their axes and crowbars.

Waiting with a charged line, Engine 7 prepared to move in as the heavy doors were forced open. Binns, Sullivan and Battalion Chief Davin moved forward with the attack hose, when a backdraft sent a rush of flames at them. Driven to the floor, the men tumbled backwards in a confusion of flames and thick burning smoke. Firemen scrambled to remove their burned and injured brothers from the fire floor. In the street a quick assessment of injuries saw Chief Davin being carried into the quarters of Engine 7 with serious burns of the face and body. Capt. Sullivan suffered a sprained back in his fall, along with Fireman McCabe who'd received internal injuries. They were all taken into the adjoining firehouse and placed in the care of department doctors.

Deputy Chief John Binns, with singed eyebrows and burns to the face, transmitted a second alarm. Three alarms were required to slow the spreading flames.

On Saturday March 25, 1911, shortly before 4:50 in the afternoon, flames broke out in the ten-story Asch Building at the corner of Washington and Greene Streets. This infamous blaze would claim the lives of 146 persons, mostly young women, working in the Triangle Shirtwaist Company garment factory on the eighth, ninth, and tenth floors of the building. (The company made women's blouses known as shirtwaists.) The fire broke out under a cutting table on the Eighth floor and spread rapidly. Locked exits hampered evacuation and many young women were forced to jump from the upper floors. The FDNY was notified and responded quickly and found an advanced fire with numerous people trapped beyond the reach of their ladders.

As an aggressive fire attack was made inside, life nets were deployed in hopes of saving the jumpers. Jumpers were dropping in bunches overwhelming the net holders. "The little ones went through the life nets, pavement and all," Battalion Chief Edward Worth recalled. "The nets are good for low tenements, but nobody could hold life nets when those girls from the ninth floor came down." The chief ordered the nets abandoned, fearing his firemen would be killed by the falling bodies.

State and local laws followed, regulating labor rules and fire safety measures. In response to the deadly fire, the New York State legislature passed a carefully constructed act that provided fire prevention laws and gave the New York City Fire Commissioner the power to enforce these laws. The new fire prevention laws became effective October 19, 1911. Two days later the FDNY consolidated the bureaus of the fire marshal, violations and auxiliary appliances, and combustibles to form the Fire Prevention Bureau. In addition to those continuing in their previous roles, an additional 22 officers and firemen were detailed to the new bureau.

These efforts had immediate effect: in the first six months of 1912 the number of fires decreased by 1,850 compared to the previous year. In addition, the fire losses in 1912 were $3.5 million less than 1911.

On May 1, 1911, Chief Croker retired and on August 1st, John Kenlon became chief of department.

In September of 1911 the FDNY School of Automobile Instruction was established. By the end of the year 70 firemen had graduated and were considered to be expert operators of fire department motor apparatus.

In 1911 the FDNY received: 7 high pressure auto hose wagons, 1 second size steam engine—gasoline motorized, 14 auto runabouts for chief officers, 4 delivery trucks, 2 touring cars, 1 auto propelled gasoline pumping engine (on trial) and 1 tractor for water tower. The department also received

10 horseshoeing wagons. This solved a long-standing problem associated with the care of the fire horses: namely shoeing. Even though the department was fully committed to motorization of their apparatus, they still had 1,443 horses, and they'd all need shoes.

The solution was a squad of travelling blacksmith shops. Ten rigs were outfitted with complete horseshoeing gear including anvil, forge, and all the necessary equipment. They travelled from one firehouse to another and set up shop right in front of quarters. The horses were walked outside and shod right there. Previously, contractors were used, but the new method saved the department $40,000 a year. Money that could be better spent on purchasing motorized equipment.

The new Fire College began operations in 1911. Established the year before, to disseminated knowledge of firefighting, and to establish and maintain the highest professional standards, and to afford to men starting in the profession of firefighting the advantage of the experience of men who have devoted their lives to the profession. The Fire College consisted of: the officers' school, the engineers' school, probationary firemen's school, and the company school.

James D. Halloran

Firemen were known as "smoke eaters" or it was said they had "leather lungs." Neither statement was true of course. Smoke could be debilitating even to the most seasoned veteran. It just depended on what was burning. Some smoke was worse than others, but all smoke was bad. Various tools and methods were developed to overcome the need to breathe smoke. In 1911 (and for many years to come) firemen had no choice, they HAD to breathe smoke. There were several smoke masks or helmets, but each had its drawbacks. Imaginative firemen, however, would try to solve this problem. One intrepid man was Fireman James D. Halloran of Engine Company 23.

Before joining the fire department, Halloran worked with the Edison Company (later to be known as Con Edison) and with a gas company. While with the gas company he devised a method of preventing people from cheating the gas company's meters.

The other firemen in Engine Company 23 were not quite sure what their friend was doing when he disappeared after committee work. They'd find him in the locker room tinkering and drawing, surrounded by papers. Some thought he was studying for the lieutenant's test; others were not sure at all. While Halloran did not distrust his comrades, he did have good reason to be secretive about his invention. He'd tinkered with inventions before and twice had had ideas stolen from him. Before he'd even talk about his idea, he made sure he had the full protection of the United States Patent Office.

The other firemen were all pleasantly surprised to learn Halloran was inventing a new breathing device to make firefighting safer. His device featured an in-line attachment right behind the nozzle. It was a garden hose reinforced with spiral wire and stretched from the street into the fire building with the fire hose. The end of the garden hose (air hose) was attached to the in-line device, with smaller hoses branching off to nose cups that were fitted to the face of the nozzle team. As water passed through the attack line, the pressure caused a "Venturi effect," the water rushing from the nozzle end would cause a vacuum that pulled fresh air from outside through the small hose to the firemen inside. The initial tests were declared a success as the hose team was able to breathe the outside air.

What was needed was a real-life test.

Starting on September 1, 1911, Halloran was detailed to Engine Company 20 on Lafayette Street for 20 days to try his new idea. This busy downtown engine company responded to many cellar fires. These fires tended to be the most stubborn and smokiest types of fire operations. The company had also just been assigned a new rig, a Knox high pressure hose wagon.

Finally, the situation was right for a true field test when Engine 20 responded to a cellar fire at 62 West Houston Street on September 19, 1911. Under the watchful eye of Deputy Chief Martin and Battalion Chief Helm, Captain Biggers and Firemen Saunders and McGrath stretched the hose and the air hose into the smoke-filled cellar. The small fire was extinguished, but thick smoke banked down to the floor lingered. Using the new air hose, the men reported they could breathe easily and suffered no ill effects from the smoke. The crew had stayed in the thick smoke for 30 minutes.

The chiefs and officers on scene were also very happy with the new motorized hose wagon (its maiden voyage) and the new breathing device. It was planned to give the device further testing and his detail was continued for an additional 20 days. The story of the new device and its real-world test was reported in several of the city's newspapers and was picked up by other papers outside New York. It also was covered in *Scientific American*, *Fire Engineering* and other national magazines, complete with photographs.

After the testing period Halloran returned to Engine 23 until he transferred to Engine Company 289 on October 1, 1913. James D. Halloran was promoted to engineer of steamer December 16, 1918, and was assigned to Engine 53. In May of 1919 Halloran transferred to Engine 78, the fireboat *George B. McClellan*, stationed at the foot of East 99th Street and the East River.

Engineer of Steamer James D. Halloran's name was added to the Roll of Merit for his heroic actions at the Standard Oil Yards fire on September 19, 1919. He continued working on the fire boat until his retirement on August 16, 1927. While his patented idea was never adopted, it did prove the inventive nature of firefighters. Their imagination and their lungs would have to continue without benefit of breathing protection for many years.

The Millionaire Buff

Robert H. Mainzer was a successful New York City broker with the firm Hallgarten & Company, where his father Bernard had been a principal partner. Although he was successful in his own right, Mainzer inherited a fortune from his father, leaving him quite wealthy. He was also a classmate of Calvin Coolidge (30th President of the United States) at Amherst College in Massachusetts. Back in New York City Mainzer was a regular in the city's high society circles and enjoyed his subscription to the Metropolitan Opera. Robert was also a fire buff.

In 1902, Mainzer became a member of "The Ancient and Honorable Order of Buffs," a small group of wealthy men who responded to fires and supported the efforts of the department and the men who served in its ranks. Other notable members of this exclusive little band included: Dr. Harry Archer, Honorary Medical Officer FDNY, Col. N.B. Thurston, Chief Ordnance Officer of the National Guard, Howard Phelps (a steamship agent), James LeBaron Johnson (an insurance broker), and Simon Brentano (the famed bookseller).

These men routinely responded to second and greater alarms around the city. Several members had also been officially recognized for their efforts by the fire commissioner and chief of the department. Doctor Archer and Robert Mainzer were both made honorary battalion chiefs for their dedicated service to the department. These men could now enter the fire lines and observe the firefighting at close quarters. At times they actually became involved in the dangerous work of firefighting.

In 1903 he met Miss Iola Powell who'd travelled from her home in Peoria Illinois, to study music in New York. Mainzer heard her sing as a soloist in a church and became interested in the young woman. In 1905 their engagement was announced, with the wedding taking place in Paris, France. Returning home, they lived in the famed Ansonia Hotel on Broadway between 73rd and 74th streets. A number of famous people also lived in the building, including Babe Ruth of the New York Yankees.

After Battalion Chief Walsh was killed by the collapse at the Equitable fire in 1912, Mainzer spearheaded the fundraising to help supplement funds for Chief Walsh's widow and six children. They raised enough money to pay off the chief's mortgage—a cause he would spend numerous hours of devoted duty on. He raised money for dozens of firefighters' families after they were killed or seriously injured.

In June of 1912, Robert Mainzer's wife was the topic of a newspaper article describing her response to a four-alarm fire on Vanderwater Street. The article stated: Mrs. Mainzer was beautifully gowned and hurriedly pinned on a hat that was almost covered with plumes. The story explained that her husband had responded to a fire on Murray Street, and when she heard the fourth alarm come in on Vanderwater Street she just had to go. She was accompanied by "Tattie" her pet Pomeranian.

The Ansonia was the site of a lavish dinner party hosted by Mr. & Mrs. Mainzer on December 11, 1913. As the dinner began, a third alarm was transmitted for a fire in a four-story building on Broadway that ran through to Mercer Street. Faced with freezing temperatures and advancing flames Smoky Joe Martin transmitted the additional alarms. Mainzer and one of his guests, Chief John Kenlon, departed the dinner and raced to the scene. At Astor Place and Broadway, they stepped from their automobile. Kenlon glanced across the street at the blaze, then saw his aide holding his fire gear. Kenlon stepped from his evening shoes, tossed his hat to Rankin and took off his dinner jacket as he climbed into his rubber boots. Donning his rubber coat and fire helmet he took charge of the blaze.

In 1913 Mainzer donated a silver loving cup lined with gold to be presented to the winning baseball team in a series of games between the FDNY and the NYPD. Mainzer also was on the committee that would run the 1913 convention of the International Association of Fire Engineers (now Fire Chiefs.) This gathering would feature the chiefs of most of the major American cities. One of the most interesting features of the convention was the presentation and operational display of many new motorized fire apparatus.

One night, Mainzer was in his apartment when his private alarm system notified him of a serious fire downtown. (Several of the wealthy buffs had FDNY alarm bell systems wired into their homes with the permission of the fire commissioner.) He grabbed his boots, rubber coat and helmet and hurried outside. Reaching the sidewalk, he could see no cars in sight. He spoke briefly with a traffic policeman who told him the next trolley would be 17 minutes. Too slow for a fire response. As he pondered his next move Mainzer saw headlights approaching and flagged down the automobile.

The chauffeur stopped the vehicle and Mainzer jumped in. The owner of the car looked at Mainzer in amazement. Boots, fire coat and helmet at 3 in the morning! Mainzer advised him of his need to respond to the fire downtown and the owner invited him along as the driver headed south.

"Just think of it," Mainzer later told an audience of fire engineers, "In all New York, with its 5 million inhabitants, I managed to stop the one man who was going downtown to the same fire. He told me he was the owner of a factory next to the burning building and that his caretaker had just advised him of the danger."

This was not Mainzer's usual response to a downtown fire. He usually would respond in Doctor Archer's automobile. This bright red auto featured an FDNY placard and came complete with a fire bell. Mainzer would also equip himself of a similar vehicle. Later, the first department ambulance was purchased, and was quartered on West 83rd Street in Engine 56's firehouse only a few blocks from Archer's home. The ambulance's primary driver, Fireman John J. Deleney of Engine 56 would pick up Archer and Mainzer then respond to fires city wide. The trio tended to hundreds of injured firemen, and civilians alike.

On December 2, 1911, Mrs. Mainzer was summoned to fire headquarters without being informed of the reason. When Iona and Robert arrived Fire Commissioner Johnson called in Deputy Chief Guerin, Battalion Chief Howe and a number of other fire officers. Mrs. Mainzer was asked to take a seat. The fire commissioner then presented her with a gold badge making her an honorary member of the department. The badge would admit her within the police lines at any fire. She was only the second woman in the city to receive such an honor. (The first was Miss Helen Gould, who received her badge after the help she provided firemen during the Windsor Hotel fire.) Iona Mainzer had been very active helping with the FDNY exhibit at a recent budget show.

Special Order No. 196 dated October 9, 1913 announced the following:

> I. Mr. Robert H. Mainzer is hereby appointed an Honorary Officer of the Fire Department, City of New York, to serve without compensation—this in recognition of his services to the Department, first as a Special Investigator of Insurance Conditions in Europe, second as Chairman of the Financial Committee of Citizens which

gathered funds for the Forty-first annual convention of the International Association of Fire Engineers in this city during the week of September 1st to 6th, 1913.

Mr. Mainzer for several years has responded to second and greater alarms, and at fires of importance has rendered valuable assistance to the men on duty there.

Honorary Officer Mainzer will report to the Chief of Department, at Fire Headquarters, at 1 p.m., October 9, 1913, for assignment of duty.

By Order of John Kenlon, Chief of Department.

At that time Kenlon named him his personal aide.

For several years Mainzer had been on a special mission at the direction of Chief John Kenlon. After the Equitable Building fire proved the FDNY lacking in special tools and equipment, Mainzer began a study of the specialized firefighting gear being used by European fire departments. He travelled across the Atlantic and saw first-hand what was available and being used by our European brothers. He came home with notes, ideas and equipment.

After a serious subway fire on January 8, 1915, sent several hundred people to the hospital, it was time for the department brass to act. So, on January 18th a special company was formed called Rescue 1. The hand-picked crew began a month and a half of special training on the tools and equipment brought back by Mainzer. The new unit went into service on March 8, 1915, changing the fire service forever. It is believed that the special tools such as the smoke helmets, inhalators and a blau-gas torch were purchased by Mainzer and donated to the department. These tools and the techniques developed by the new company would set the stage for modern rescue work.

It was two o'clock in the morning on December 23, 1915, when Robert Mainzer responded to a blaze at 225 West 17th Street. Mainzer was at the chief's side watching the firefighting when the chief ordered the nearby buildings to be evacuated. Mainzer went to help. Entering the small house next door to the fire, Mainzer made his way to the top floor. He knocked on a door and attempted to help a 60-year-old widow to safety. She refused to leave without Little Eva, Crank and Baby.

Mainzer swept the darkness with his eyes but saw no crib or sleeping babies. The woman's frantic motions drew him to a small water-filled globe. He laughed and tucked the globe under his arm and led the woman and her three goldfish to safety.

A testimonial dinner was held to honor of Mainzer's efforts on behalf of the FDNY, especially his work in outfitting Rescue 1. The new company was just completing their first year of service and had already proved themselves extremely successful. The party was held on January 16, 1916, at the Hotel Knickerbocker. This hotel, built in 1906, by John Jacob Astor IV, played host to the world's biggest names in entertainment, politics, culture and high society. The hotel only lasted for 15 years but helped establish Times Square as a tourist destination.

One of the speakers at the 500-guest testimonial was Al Smith. At the time of the dinner Smith was Sheriff of New York County, having been a member of the NY State legislature for 11 years. He would go on to be President of the NY City Board of Aldermen (now known as the City Council), and the 42nd Governor of the State of New York. Smith ran for President of the United States in 1928 and lost to Herbert Hoover.

His speech at the testimonial dinner was a bit like a roast: "Times have changed. Here we are at a boiled shirt, claw hammered coat, plug hat banquet to a civilian fireman. When I was a citizen fireman the only banquet I ever got was the heel of a cheese sandwich from some uniformed fireman who dropped it to man a hose."

On the morning of February 17, 1919, employees arrived at

their four-story brick warehouse at the foot of East 48th Street and were confronted with a fire blazing inside. On the first floor, bales of jute (rough fiber made from the stems of tropical plants used for making twine, rope or woven into matting) were piled nearly to the ceiling. Bags of sulphur were stored on the second floor, and other chemicals were stored on the floors above.

The alarm was transmitted and the FDNY responded to the scene. Companies descended on the fire building and began laddering, venting and stretching lines into position. When the flames from the burning jute reached the sulphur, it too began to burn. Dense clouds of smoke laced with fumes and gases began to accumulate within the warehouse. Suddenly, an explosion tore through the second floor blowing the metal shutters right off the windows. Firemen on ladders either jumped or were thrown from the ladders. Two firemen on the ground floor were overcome and had to be dragged out by their comrades.

The flames were battled for hours with the debilitating smoke limiting the time anyone could spend inside the smoke-filled building. Conditions had become so dangerous, the only members to reach the second floor were members of Rescue 1 while wearing their smoke helmets.

Archer and Mainzer subjected themselves to "severe hazards in resuscitating 30 firemen who had been rendered dangerously sick and unconscious by reason of the deadly combination of poisonous and deadly gases generated by burning jute and sulphur." Mainzer and his good friend Doctor Archer were recognized by the FDNY for this work when they were "promoted" to Honorary Deputy Chiefs by Commissioner Frank Lantry and Chief Kenlon.

Huge crowds lined the East River bridges on March 28, 1920, to watch a spectacular warehouse fire on South Street. Three alarms were transmitted for the blazing six-story building filled with thousands of bags of pepper and fireworks. The debilitating smoke reddened the faces of firemen as they staggered from the clouds of noxious smoke. Inside the smoke-choked building Smoky Joe Martin led the men of Rescue 1 as they donned their smoke helmets, plunged into smoke and began lugging out bags of spices.

Firemen not able to utilize smoke helmets resorted to wetting handkerchiefs and wearing them across their nose and mouths as filters.

Mainzer arrived at the scene and saw the effects of the smoke firsthand. Knowing milk was a good antidote for such irritants he cruised the neighborhood, gathering every can and bottle available. He returned to the scene and helped at the first aid station.

The crowds at first seemed to enjoy the smell drifting across the city. Coffee and other pleasant spices laced the smoke at first, but when the flames reached the pepper the mood of the fire and its audience changed rapidly. Things grew dangerous very quickly. The crowds began to disperse of their own accord, but the firemen were not as lucky as they had to continue operating. At one point while passing a bottle of milk to Doc Archer, Mainzer took one breath too may and keeled over.

Mrs. Mainzer made the newspapers once again in 1922 when she took decisive actions to save the life of a young woman. Late on the afternoon of December 27, 1922, Mrs. Mainzer entered a Fifth Avenue beauty shop to get her hair done. She donned a robe over her dress (as was the practice) and took a seat awaiting her turn.

She was seated for about ten minutes when she heard a scream from the main room. She jumped up and hurried toward the growing chorus of screaming. In the main room she found a young woman standing in the middle of the floor her robe aflame from head to toe. Without hesitation, she grabbed towels and began beating out the flames. Her efforts were working when the woman fainted and fell against Mrs. Mainzer setting her robe on fire. Faced with her own emergency, she flung off her robe, and with her bare hands beat out the flames on her own dress then returned to the girl.

Mrs. Mainzer had the girl resting comfortably when a doctor arrived. He treated her burns and sent her home in a taxi. When later asked about the incident she laughingly refused to answer.

In 1923, the City of New York was planning a silver jubilee to celebrate the 25th anniversary of the formation of the Greater City. This month-long celebration would highlight the city's accomplishments and its plans for the future. Mayor Hyland appointed Mainzer, among others, as members of the Finance and Advisory Committee to help organize and raise the funds necessary for the celebration. The idea was to have the city workers do their regular jobs and let the volunteer committee members do the bulk of the work.

The Silver Jubilee was held between May 28 to June 23 and included daily broadcasts from the new radio broadcasting exhibit set up on the second floor of the exhibition hall. (Radio was gaining in popularity at the time.) The huge celebration culminated with a gigantic Fifth Avenue parade on May 26, 1923. The line of march took 40,000 city employees down the avenue to Madison Square. When the FDNY reached the reviewing stand at 59th Street the parade stopped, and members of the fire department turned to view the presentation of medals of valor to both the FDNY and the NYPD.

In 1925, Robert Mainzer celebrated his 50th birthday. He had made a point of recording every fire he attended, noting important facts of each job. He told newspaper reporters that at this point he'd responded to 5,000 fires in the city.

The chief of the Berlin Germany Fire Department arrived in New York City on the steamship *Columbus* on May 9, 1925. Chief Kenlon assigned Mainzer to meet the German fire officer at the pier. For many years Mainzer had been the liaison officer between Kenlon and visiting chiefs from foreign countries. Mainzer spoke most of the languages of continental Europe, was skilled in European diplomacy and knew the atmosphere which best suited the dignity of those who came to our shores.

Chief Gempp had written a series of articles about his department that Mainzer helped translate prior to publication in *Fire Engineering* magazine. In the article the chief stated that it had been 20 years since any German fire officer was sent abroad to study firefighting. The welcome he received in New York far surpassed his expectations. Gempp recalled that five years earlier when John Kenlon visited Berlin, the chief at the time sent an orderly to tell Kenlon he was too busy to see him. The Bürgermeister of Berlin (the mayor) later ordered the chief to apologize to the visiting chief. At the time Gempp was the first assistant chief and had some misgivings as to the reception he'd receive.

Chief Gempp was happily surprised at his reception. Not only was Honorary Deputy Chief Mainzer there to meet him, but Kenlon had also sent Lt. John Meyer of Hook & Ladder 20, and Fireman John Myer of Rescue Company 1 (both German speakers) and a department car for Gempp's transportation. Gempp would spend a month in the United States visiting Detroit, Chicago and Milwaukee. He spent most of his time with Mainzer in New York.

While he was noted for his generosity Mr. Mainzer did not like to be taken advantage of. He once objected to the price of a ham he purchased. Instead of paying the $25 bill, he sent the vendor only $14. The vendor sued, but in a highly publicized case Mainzer won the verdict. The vendor was Arnold Reuben, whose specially seasoned meat became the basis for his famous "Reuben Sandwich."

On the evening of November 14, 1926, flames broke out in the basement of a building on the northwest corner of 79th Street and Columbus Avenue several blocks from Mainzer's home. The building housed stores on the ground floor and the Emerson Drug Company on the upper floors. When the first due units arrived the smoke and flames were already spreading. As the firemen commenced their attack, about 300 men and women were happily dancing in the adjoining building the Academy Dance Hall.

As the fire progressed the smoke began to infiltrate the dance hall causing a panic. Firemen laddered the hall and began helping people escape through the windows. Others evacuated using the stairs. The fire had reached three alarms and conditions were deteriorating in the fire building and the exposures.

Ten minutes after the last of the people had been taken down the ladders word reached Mainzer that 25 dancers were still inside. Mainzer and Lt. Al Kinsella of Engine 74 (an original member of Rescue 1 who'd been promoted) climbed the ladder and entered the smoke-filled dance hall. Mainzer was familiar with the dance hall's layout and together they searched for the dancers. They found the group and Mainzer led them to a rear exit that led to an alley. And safety.

A gala dinner at the Biltmore Hotel was held on March 3, 1927, to celebrate Chief Kenlon's 40th anniversary in the department. He was presented a gold and diamond-studded badge by Deputy Chief McKenna, then Honorary Deputy Chief Mainzer presented Mrs. Kenlon a diamond bracelet. Letters of congratulations from Governor Smith, Cardinal Hayes, Mayor Walker, and the heads of the fire departments of Paris, London, San

Francisco and Berlin were read.

Fire Commissioner Dorman, Chief Kenlon and other fire officials were on hand along with the Fire Department Band, Bugle and Drum Corps, at the Central Park Mall on September 1, 1927, when renowned composer and conductor Edwin Franko Goldman was set to perform his new composition, "The Third Alarm." The march, complete with sirens, bells and whistles was dedicated to Honorary D.C. Robert Mainzer, who was also a musician. The piece recognized Mainzer's many efforts on behalf of firefighters and their families. The march was recorded and published in 1929 and Goldman went on to earn a star on Hollywood's Walk of Fame.

In September of 1927 Mainzer travelled to Germany and visited Chief Gempp at Berlin Fire Headquarters. To continue his 27 years of attending fires he was given a room at headquarters and responded with the Berlin firemen.

April 22, 1931, was a pleasant afternoon for a drive, and Robert Mainzer was rolling along on 57th Street when he noticed smoke ahead at the corner of Seventh Avenue. He pulled over and dashed toward Carnegie Hall where he could now see flames licking above the famous venue. He called to a traffic cop who ran to the alarm box. A minute later Engine 23 pulled in and were led to the roof by Mainzer. The fire appeared dramatic from the street but luckily was limited to roofing materials. The blaze was quickly subdued by Deputy Chief Ross and his men.

One of Mainzer's most prized possessions was a photograph of Chief Kenlon inscribed: "To my aide Robert H. Mainzer, who never failed me in the hour of stress or danger."

Robert Mainzer continued his fine work until his death in 1936. One newspaper article three years earlier stated he had donated over $100,000 to the department. He received a department funeral including an honor guard of eight fire companies and a pumper as a caisson. Commissioner McElligott stated:

During his thirty years of service he gave unstintingly of his time and of his wealth to the welfare of the department and its members. He was in every sense a fireman at heart.

Edward J. Worth

Born in New York City in 1862, Edward Worth was the son of an Irish mother and a Scottish father. As a young man Edward went to sea and became an able-bodied seaman prior to joining the FDNY. He was appointed on December 30, 1888. Worth was promoted to lieutenant on December 31, 1897, and assigned to Engine Company 17 on Ludlow Street in Manhattan. He also served in Engine Company 27 on Franklin Street. Then on January 1, 1901, Worth was promoted to captain and placed in command of Engine 18 on West 10th Street. He was later transferred to Engine Company 30 on Spring Street.

Nine months after his promotion to captain, Worth was made acting battalion chief. This was a common practice in this era, (and is still done to this day). When a chief went on vacation an acting chief was named by the deputy chief from among the senior captains. So, nine months after being promoted to captain Edward Worth found himself responding to a major fire at 142-150 Worth Street (of all places) as a battalion chief. The alarm was transmitted at 3:38 a.m. on the morning of September 22, 1901. The fire originated on the second floor and extended to the third, fourth, fifth floors and roof, and adjoining building, through open stairs, belt holes, pipe recesses and wooden chutes within the printing company. Three alarms brought 14 engines, 4 hook and ladders, 1 water tower and the searchlight engine to extinguish the hour-long fire.

The fire department held its annual parade and medal ceremony on May 14, 1904, they marched up Broadway from the

Battery all the way to the 23rd Street reviewing stand. After the medals of valor were presented, the mayor called the name: Captain Edward J. Worth of Engine Co. 30. With Chief Croker and Fire Commissioner Hayes at his side, Mayor McClellan pinned the Stephenson Medal on Worth's uniform. This signified having attained the highest standard of efficiency and discipline in his company for the year.

The evening before he was to be promoted, Edward Worth was working as acting battalion chief and responded to a four-alarm fire in a five-story brick building occupied by a paper box manufacturing company on Greenwich Street. The blaze started just after closing and spread throughout the building. The following morning, November 4, 1905, Edward Worth was officially promoted to the rank of battalion chief and was placed in command of the Third Battalion in Manhattan.

On July 16, 1910, Battalion Chief Edward Worth responded to a fire on Pier 14 North River that began around 1 p.m. Strong winds were spreading the flames to several lighters moored alongside the pier adding to the extension problems. While directing the attack on a blazing lighter, Worth heard cries for help. Unable to locate the victim Worth shouted to the fireboat James Duane about 300 feet away. Conditions around the pier were becoming extreme as the fireboat moved in near Chief Worth. The radiant heat was so intense that buildings 250 feet away were igniting.

The fireboat pilot Lawrence Healy nosed in close to the pier and Worth jumped aboard joining Deputy Chief Kenlon (in command of the Marine Division) and Captain John H. Kelly and his crew. Pointing back toward the blazing pier Worth explained he'd heard cries for help. Looking back at the mass of fire they realized any cries had to be coming from the water beneath the pier.

The two chiefs, captain and two firemen took crouched

positions in the bow as Pilot Healy edged the fireboat in close to the raging pier. The rope bumpers attached to the bow of the fireboat burst into flames prompting Kenlon to have two of the rear monitors (large fireboat nozzles) direct their streams onto them as the fireboat moved in.

Suddenly, two men became visible clinging to a piece of burned wood beneath the pier. As the captain turned to ask for volunteers, both firemen, John Walsh and William Mareck leapt over the side, boots, clothes and all and swam toward the trapped men. Walsh swam ahead with Mareck close on his heels. Despite blistering heat, low visibility, and adjusting for the back pressure from the many steams the fireboat was throwing Pilot Healy held this dangerous position.

The firemen swam beneath swirling smoke and flames. With fire raging overhead, and the smoke-filled air burning with each breath, each fireman grabbed a man and held him afloat. Ropes were thrown from the fireboat to Marek and Walsh, who were each supporting an unconscious man. They both grabbed ropes and held tightly as they were pulled from beneath the pier toward the fireboat. With great difficulty they swam the men to the side of the fireboat where they were wrestled onboard.

This combined rescue effort, under extreme conditions, surely saved the lives of the two men. The superb seamanship of the pilot, the strong leadership of the officers and the unflinching bravery of the two firemen, placed them all on the Roll of Merit. They were each recognized for their valor at a ceremony at Fire Headquarters on April 11, 1911. Battalion Chief Edward Worth, Deputy Chief Kenlon, Capt. Kelly and Pilot Healy were each awarded the Department Medal, with Fireman Walsh also receiving the Trevor-Warren Medal and Fireman Mareck the Hurley Medal.

In 1911 Worth was made acting deputy chief and placed in charge of the Marine Division. In 1915 Worth was promoted to deputy chief and remained in command of the Marine Division.

At 2:08 a.m. on Sunday July 31, 1916, a sudden violent explosion rocked New York City shattering glass windows that showered the streets and sidewalks from midtown to the Battery. Trolley cars were rocked from their tracks. Thousands of frightened people leapt from their beds and swarmed from tenements and hotels, shocked by the force of the blast.

The explosion wasn't even in the city proper, but rather occurred across the river and about a half-mile east of the Statue of Liberty on a mile-long peninsula known as Black Tom. The former island had been filled in served as shipping terminal and warehouses of the Lehigh Valley Railroad. Besides normal merchandise, the freight cars, barges and lighters were filled with explosives and ammunition on its way to the war in Europe. An estimated 1,000 tons of explosives were stored on 32 freight cars and 10 barges. A burning freight car exploded sending flaming debris across the terminal area setting numerous freight cars and barges on fire.

As the Jersey City Fire Department responded to the scene, tugboats attempted to fight the fires but exploding shells held them back. Yard workers scrambled to move explosive-laden train cars as fiery barges drifted into the open river. At 2:30 Joseph B. Martin, acting chief of department received a telephone call stating several blazing lighters were drifting in a strong current that was taking them toward Ellis Island. Martin called Deputy Chief Worth who immediately jumped on the fireboat *New Yorker* and headed from their berth at the battery toward the huge fire.

The *New Yorker* had just reached the scene when one of the drifting barges slid up against the Ellis Island Hospital pier. Chief Worth and a fireman got off the fireboat and helped the island fire brigade extinguish the blaze. At times the shrapnel (fragments of a bomb or shell) became so bad they had to lie flat to avoid being hit. At 2:40 a second more powerful explosion rocked the fire area. Worth and company briefly took refuge in a warehouse that was already riddled with bullet holes.

Chief Worth climbed back on board the fireboat and joined the other FDNY fireboats and pressed the attack as shells and bullets whistled around them. They moved in on the burning barges and towed them away, often needing to dive for cover on the steel decks of the fireboats. They poured water on the blazing barges until they sank near Ellis Island. They were marked with light buoys to show their locations. With the loose barges extinguished the FDNY fireboats moved in as close as they could to the blazing fires on land and directed their powerful streams at the growing flames.

In all, six persons were killed and explosions and fire left more than $20 million in damages.

With the war in Europe filling the docks and piers along New York harbor with munitions and supplies heading abroad, the waterfront hazard was recognized to be so serious that the FDNY organized an auxiliary fleet of fireboats, 143 in number, composed of powerful tugboats operated by the railroads that operated terminals along the waterfront. All these boats were equipped for firefighting, and the crews trained in fire extinguishment. It was estimated that during World War I years, Worth led the battle against 300 waterfront fires. As "admiral of the city's firefighting navy," he worked in cooperation with the Coast Guard and the US Navy.

Firefighting has always been a dangerous occupation, even when you attain the rank of deputy chief. On March 15, 1918, Chief Worth responded to a fire on the barge *Templar*, moored at Pier 37 Manhattan. The barge, loaded with 2,900 bales of cotton was towed across the river to the Brooklyn side and held at the foot of 37th Street as the fireboat the *New Yorker*, moved in to battle the stubborn, deep-seated fire. With three other fireboats working alongside, the operation commenced.

While standing near the stern of the *New Yorker*, a bale of cotton from the burning barge fell on Worth, knocking him to the deck. Firemen rushed to his side and helped the dazed officer to shore where he was examined by an ambulance surgeon who advised the chief to stop work and go home. The chief smiled, donned his helmet and returned to the fire.

In early 1920 Chief Worth was forced into sick leave when he battled a serious case of influenza. (The 1918-20 influenza pandemic took the lives of 25-50 million people world-wide.) After several weeks of recuperation he was able to return to his post, covering fires from the Harlem River to easternmost parts of Queens.

At the direction of Fire Commissioner Drennan, Worth prepared plans for a new fireboat and the refurbishment of the existing fleet. Work on the boats had been held up during the war years, but the commissioner gave Worth the order "full speed ahead" on this new project. Among the work to be performed would be the thorough overhaul on the fireboat *Zophar Mills*, which would almost be completely rebuilt at the estimated cost of $65,000.

The *New Yorker*, *George B. McClellan*, *Thomas Willett*, *Cornelius W. Lawrence* and *Abraham Hewitt* would all be repaired and repainted after their difficult battle at the Standard Oil Yard fire. The rest of the fleet of ten would also be refurbished as needed. The *Velox*, Worth's command launch, escaped damage at the fire.

On March 31st, the keel of the new fireboat the *John Purroy Mitchel* was laid. In attendance were Commissioner Drennan, Deputy Commissioner Thompson, Chief Treacy of the Bureau of Repairs and Supplies, and of course Chief Worth.

The completed ship was formally turned over to the city December 27, 1921, at a ceremony held at Battery Park. (The fireboat *John Purroy Mitchel* was named for the 95th mayor of New York City who served from 1914 until 1917. Mitchel joined the US Army Air Service as a flying cadet, completed his training in San Diego and obtained the rank of major. He was killed in a training flight over Louisiana on July 6, 1918.)

This was now the 10th fireboat under the command of Deputy Chief Edward Worth, "admiral" of the fireboat fleet. The new 132-foot boat cost $250,000 and was the first fireboat that was run on fuel oil. It also featured a 27-foot-high water tower, and four other water turrets, one atop the wheelhouse, another on the foredeck and two on the main deck aft. When operating at full capacity the fireboat will deliver the same amount of water as 12 land-based engines.

The new fireboat was officially designated as Engine Company 57 and located at Battery Park in Manhattan.

On the night of November 10, 1924, Deputy Chief Worth and his men were in their firehouse when a civilian ran to quarters shouting that a woman holding a child had jumped in the river a short distance away at Pier 1. Worth directed Lt. Owen Ryan and two firemen Thomas Whitman and Samuel Steinmetz, who dashed to the site and plunged into the black waters of the North River. The child was floating downstream as Fireman Whitman swam to her rescue. The mother was closer to the sea wall where Ryan and Steinmetz caught hold of her. Both were removed from the water but only the mother survived.

Four days later, on November 14, 1924, shortly after eight o'clock in the morning, an explosion in the subcellar of a chemical plant at Morris and Warren streets near the waterfront in Jersey City, New Jersey, quickly spread flames to the adjoining warehouses before igniting a dozen tenements. Explosions of saltpeter shattered windows and strong winds helped spread the flames. Three alarms were sent in rapid succession bringing the city's entire firefighting force to the scene. For an hour the flames were battled as explosions shook the neighborhood. The toxic smoke and explosions took their toll on the firefighters as dozens were injured or overcome.

At 11 p.m., fireboats from New York City under the command of Chief Worth arrived and help prevent the flames from reaching the waterfront. Worth's Marine Division stretched lines 1,200 feet to position their attack. In all, four city blocks were left destroyed. The fire reached 25 tenements, a sugar refinery, a box factory and a chemical works. The toxic smoke hung over an area of more than 30 blocks and forced everyone to seek fresh air.

A most unusual fire faced Chief Worth and his men on February 9, 1927, at four in the morning when flames broke out inside the aquarium at Battery Park. The priceless collection of sea creatures, animals and waterfowl were in danger of being killed, until the firemen from the Marine Division under Worth's command were able to control the fire and hold the flames back in the blazing carpentry shop adjoining the executive offices of the aquarium. Despite the extreme heat generated by the blazing lumber none of the animals were injured.

In 1928 Chief Worth again battled failing health and was placed on medical leave. During his absence, his understudy, Battalion Chief William Purdy was designated acting deputy chief in charge of the Marine Division. Worth fought his way back to full duty, but it was apparent the years of fire duty were taking their toll. On October 2, 1929, Deputy Chief Edward Worth retired from the FDNY. He was given a proper farewell at his headquarters at the Battery. Worth had spent more than 40 years on the job, spending all that time in the busiest area of the city, lower Manhattan. His name appeared on the Roll of Merit six times for personal bravery.

Chief Worth died from pneumonia, on July 13, 1936.

David J. Oliver

There are several different metrics to judge the success of a career in firefighting. One was, especially in the horse-drawn era, to make it to retirement in one piece. Another was to work in busy places, or to advance in rank by promotions, or to save lives at fires. One member of the department who excelled in all of these was David J. Oliver. Born in New York City on February 6, 1885, to Irish immigrant parents, he grew up on Washington Street in lower Manhattan. As a young man Oliver worked as an iron worker and rigger.

Then on February 1, 1906, David J. Oliver became a probationary fireman and was assigned to Hook & Ladder 10. He would also work in Hook & Ladder 15. Oliver's outside skills began to pay off as the department began motorization. While a member of Hook & Ladder 20, he was detailed along with Fireman Henry Fischer of Hook & Ladder 23 to travel to the Nott Fire Engine Company in Minneapolis, Minnesota, to be specially trained in the care and operation of the new motorized pumping engine being specially built for the FDNY.

Oliver remained in Hook & Ladder 20 upon his return from Minneapolis and received additional training at the department repair shops on March 15 and 16. On the 16th, a large contingent of FDNY brass arrived at the repair shops at 56th Street and Twelfth Avenue to witness the initial testing of the new fire engine. The huge red machine was 20-feet-long, with two seats in the front. A 110-horse-power gasoline engine was beneath the large front hood, with the rear half of the rig a regular steam engine guaranteed to pump 700 gallons of water a minute at 125 pounds pressure. The entire massive rig stood on four huge red wheels with solid rubber tires and chains to prevent skidding at high speeds.

In attendance for the test were fire chiefs from Baltimore, Washington, Roanoke and Norfolk Virginia, Pittsburg, and Patterson, New Jersey. Also present were the FDNY brass: Fire Commissioner Waldo, his deputies, Chief Croker, and Deputy Chiefs Howe, Lally and Guerin. Commissioner Waldo, who already had extensive automobile driving experience, invited former Chief of Department Charles O. Shay to join him on the first trial run. Shay had been a member of the volunteer department back in the days of hand pumpers before he began his 24-year tenure in the FDNY. Waldo took the rig out for a spin. They returned to the shops amid the throbbing and roaring of the engine, their frozen tears streaked across smiling faces.

The rig was then driven to the river for an hour-long pump test. Afterwards the new engine was put through a more serious road test when the Nott Company's master mechanic Herbert Penny rode alongside Fireman David Oliver who took the rig up Broadway to 110th Street, east to Lexington Avenue, up the steep Duffy's Hill at 105th Street, across the Queensboro Bridge, and out on Thompson Avenue. The rig maintained a speed of about 30 mph.

The following day, Oliver's transfer to Engine 58 went into effect, and on March 20th he began driving the new apparatus to alarms from the 115th Street and Madison Avenue firehouse. By the end of the year the Nott fire engine and a Waterous engine assigned to Engine Company 39 both proved unsatisfactory and were placed out of service. But David Oliver's time on 115th Street didn't slow his knack for being in the right place when he received a Class III award in 1913 for a rescue he made while working in Engine 58. This was his second time on the Roll of Merit having been awarded a Class II in 1911 while working in Hook & Ladder 20.

With the new apparatus trial completed, Oliver transferred to Hook & Ladder 15 where he went back to firefighting in lower Manhattan. On October 7, 1915, a ship was being fumigated while moored at Pier 13, East River at the foot of Wall Street. A still alarm brought Hook & Ladder 15 to the scene. The responding members were faced with a stevedore who'd fallen into the hold.

Despite heavy sulphur fumes and unfamiliar darkened surroundings two members immediately descended a 35-foot ladder into the ship's hold in search of the missing man. Firemen Frank G. Rowe and David J. Oliver began a difficult and dangerous search for the missing man. Without benefit of smoke helmets or help from the new Rescue Squad the men pressed into the noxious blackened atmosphere.

Under extreme conditions the team located and removed the lifeless man. Members on the dock immediately began artificial respiration and were able to revive the unconscious worker. Both Frank Rowe and David Oliver suffered from their daring rescue but were soon back to duty.

For their heroic exploits both men were placed on the Roll of Merit with Class I awards. Later, Fireman Frank G. Rowe was decorated with the Bonner and Department medals and Fireman David J. Oliver was presented the Trevor-Warren and Department medals at the annual medal ceremony held on May 3, 1916, at City Hall.

Eight months later, on December 24, 1916, David J. Oliver was promoted to lieutenant and assigned to Hook & Ladder 10. The following September he attended the FDNY Fire College for six weeks. Two years later, on June 19, 1919, he was promoted to the rank of captain and given command of Hook & Ladder 9 on Elizabeth Street in lower Manhattan. Then on May 1, 1920, Oliver transfered to Hook & Ladder 1. During this time Oliver was also serving as an acting battalion chief in the Second Battalion.

Capt. Oliver would be placed on the Roll of Merit twice for heroic actions on the same day. He was awarded a Class II and a Class B for rescues on August 24, 1920. The alarm for a fire at 47 Essex Street came in at 2:30 in the morning. Acting Battalion Chief Oliver with his chauffeur Fireman Ed Hegewald arrived first on the scene of the blazing six-story tenement. Oliver dashed inside shouting a warning to the families sleeping in their apartments. On the top floor he knocked at one apartment and receiving no answer, he kicked in the door. Inside, driven to the floor by the thick, hot smoke he found a family of four unconscious.

Opening the window Oliver called down to arriving firemen directing ladders be placed to his window. One by one he dragged the unconscious people toward the window. He was joined by his driver and Lt. Poggi of Engine 17. Carefully they lifted each person up and out the window into the waiting arms of firemen. The parents and their two daughters were treated by Doctor Archer prior to their removal to a nearby hospital. They all recovered.

For their heroic actions Acting Chief David Oliver was placed on the Roll of Merit with Lt. Poggi and Fireman Hegewald.

A very difficult and challenging fire was battled on July 17, 1921, when Manhattan fire companies responded to 345-347 Greenwich Street. The blaze broke out late Sunday night and raged all through the morning hours sending thick clouds of smoke pumping from the Phoenix Cheese Company factory building. Arriving units determined the fire was in a large refrigerator and Engine Company 27 stretched a line to the doorway. When the thick door to the refrigerator was forced open, dense clouds of smoke and fumes billowed from within.

Conditions deteriorated so quickly that Lt. Stapleton, choking and gasping for breath, ordered his men to withdraw to the street. In the swirling clouds of smoke some of the men who'd heard the order backed out, as others unaware of the decision moved in with the hose. Retreating to the street the men began dropping onto the sidewalk dizzy and overcome by the effects of the noxious smoke. Inside the refrigerator, the nozzle team was quickly overcome and dropped unconscious onto the floor. Outside, counting his crew Stapleton realized three men were still inside.

Members including Captain David Oliver and Fireman James Mulvaney of Hook & Ladder 1, and Fireman James Simonetti of Engine 27 pressed into the toxic atmosphere. Two members of Rescue 1 donned gas masks and plunged into the thick smoke in search of the missing men. One of the Rescue 1 firemen located the downed trio and shouted for help. Oliver, Mulvaney and Simonette joined the masked men and dragged the unconscious men from the refrigerator and carried them outside.

For their extraordinary rescue efforts three members of Rescue 1 were placed on the Roll of Merit with Class II awards. Class II awards and medals of valor were given to Captain David J. Oliver of Hook & Ladder 1 who received the Scott Medal. Fireman Mulvaney was presented the Brookman Medal, Fireman Simonetti was awarded the Crimmins Medal and Fireman Roggencamp from Rescue 1 received the Prentice Medal.

A few weeks before the annual FDNY medal presentation ceremony was to be held at City Hall, Acting Chief Oliver responded to another life-threatening situation. Oliver and his chauffeur Fireman William Fraser responded to a reported fire at 160 Greenwich Street a five-story tenement. As the fire companies responded to the scene, the tenants of the building were attempting to escape the smoke and flames. Mike Kramer, the father of three children took his family to the roof and used pieces of lumber to erect a bridge to the roof of the next building. The mother crossed with her small daughter, the father came next with another daughter and a neighbor came last carrying five-year-old Mike Kramer.

Approaching the other roof, young Mike slipped from the man's arms and fell into the smoky darkness below. The frantic cries of the adults drew in Acting Battalion Chief Oliver. He found a rickety wooden ladder that was lowered from the roof and held fast by Fireman Fraser, while Oliver climbed down into the swirling darkness. In total darkness Oliver locked his knees around the bottom rung and hung upside down to extend his reach. Dangling in this fashion he was able to reach down and grasp the boy who'd ended up in a deep puddle on a roof extension. With one hand he was able to lift the boy and gather him into his arms while above his aide struggled to hold the ladder steady. Back upright Oliver paused to catch his breath and allow the dizziness from his inverted rescue to pass. Acting Chief Oliver climbed up and hoisted the youngster safely onto the roof.

Manhattan fire companies responded to a reported fire at 814-816 East 5th Street on June 12, 1924. A fire that started in the basement of a wood turning factory spread quickly to the two adjoining buildings. Battalion Chief Donaghey took one look at the spreading flames and put in a second alarm. A third, fourth and fifth alarms soon followed. At the height of the blaze 17 firemen became trapped on the roof, cut off by the extending flames. Realizing their plight Acting Battalion Chief Oliver and Firemen O'Brien and Schneider raised a 40-foot portable ladder to the fourth floor. Oliver dashed up the ladder with a scaling ladder and placed it to the roof. With flames extending below them and threatening the rescue attempt streams were directed to protect Oliver and the men on the ladders.

One by one the men climbed down from the roof with Oliver remaining in position to help guide them across the gap between the ladders some 50 feet above the ground. Within a few harrowing minutes 16 of the 17 trapped men were safely on the ground. The last man was cut off by flames on the roof and was rescued by two firemen from an adjoining roof.

Oliver's next promotion came on May 16, 1925, when he was made a battalion chief and assigned to the Second Battalion. Later that year Chief Oliver was transferred to the 42nd Battalion in Brooklyn. Daring rescues followed him to that borough as well.

The dangers faced by firemen across the country have always been varied and grew more complex with each passing day. So, it was on the evening of November 12, 1925, when Brooklyn Box 2796 sent companies to 1416 66th Street where an illegal alcohol still had exploded in the basement. (With the adoption of the 18th Amendment to the Constitution it was illegal to produce, import, transport or sell alcoholic beverages from 1920 until 1933. This led to the use of illegal and often dangerous improvised alcohol distillation apparatus.)

Arriving at the scene companies were faced with alcohol burning across the floor and live steam escaping from an overheated furnace. Under the protection of a hose stream Chief Oliver crawled into the burning room and dragged Sal Nuccio to safety. The Board of Merit rated this daring rescue as a Class I. This was the eighth time the name David J. Oliver had been inscribed on the Roll of Merit. He now wore on his uniform: the Trevor-Warren, Scott, Kenny and two Department medals.

On January 10, 1930, Chief Oliver and Chief John P. Hederman swapped places with Oliver going to the 33rd Battalion and Hederman taking his place in the 42nd.

Even on his day off, David J. Oliver had a nose for smoke. On May 6, 1932, at around 7 a.m., thick clouds of smoke began filling the skies over lower Manhattan as one of the largest pier fires in the city's history developed. The huge Cunard Docks complex at Pier 54 in the North River at 14th Street was the site of the difficult fire. The creosoted pilings gave off acrid smoke overcoming almost 300 firemen. Oliver, off-duty, went to the scene and volunteered his services.

This fire raged out of control until 2 a.m. the following morning. Five-alarms were transmitted as well as calls for manpower only as the dense smoke took its toll on the firefighters. Flames burning in the spaces between the underside of the concrete floor and the wood deck planking eventually ignited the multi-story pier superstructure above, driving the firefighting force back toward the roadway. The fire continued until the once large bustling pier complex was left a smoldering ruin.

Chief McElligott then asked David Oliver to take over command of the department's training. On November 8, 1933, Chief David J. Oliver was named chief instructor of the FDNY School of Instruction. Another unusual job came with this assignment when in September planning and training commenced on a project to be known as The Midnight Alarm. This fire safety presentation was held in Madison Square Garden on November 23 and December 21, 1937.

Chief Oliver oversaw the various portions of the presentation including calisthenics done by probationary firemen, firefighting demonstrations, ladders, rescue tools and various specialized equipment. The proceeds of the show were used to purchase an additional department ambulance: a 1938 Cadillac used to organize Ambulance 2.

Chief Oliver had the unique experience in the fire department when on September 1, 1937, his son Richard, was appointed to the FDNY and assigned to Hook & Ladder 4. This appointment also required training and now standing before Chief Oliver was recruit number 88. "This fellow is No. 88, and is going to tow the mark, the same as everybody else." Oliver said he would treat all the new men the same. "I tell them they are all members of the New York Fire Department now. Their duty is to protect the life and property, no matter what the cost is. If it comes to giving their lives, that's their duty too. That's what I'll tell my son, that's what I tell them all."

Young Richard was following in the family tradition of service. He was named for his uncle, Deputy Inspector Richard Oliver, who has a distinguished record as detective chief. He also had two uncles on the job, Fire Lieutenant Matthew and Fireman Joseph Oliver.

Battalion Chief David J. Oliver continued in his role as chief instructor until his retirement on June 2, 1939. After a thrilling career where his valor was recognized 11 times, Oliver was asked if a fireman needed brains over brawn? His reply was simple: "It's not the muscles. It's the heart. That's what makes a fireman."

Frank C. Clark

Born December 2, 1881, in Newburgh, New York, Frank Clark was a motorman before joining the FDNY on July 11, 1906. He was assigned to Hook & Ladder 24 on West 33rd Street in Manhattan. This area of the city, known as the garment district, had many high-rise buildings and fire-resistive buildings and lofts. Just to the north was Times Square, the theatrical district, and the fashionable Fifth Avenue shopping district. At the time Hook & Ladder 24 was assigned a Dederick 85-foot wooden aerial ladder built in 1901.

It was 3:30 in the morning on March 3, 1909, when a fire was reported at 374 Seventh Avenue, a double tenement. The structure stood in the middle of a row of five tenements and was filled with mostly Italian families. The fire was discovered by a neighbor who saw flames pouring from the first-floor barber shop at number 374. He gave the alarm and soon the fire escapes were filled with panicked men, women and children clad only in their night clothes.

Flames had complete control of the center of the building when Fireman Frank C. Clark of Hook & Ladder 24 and Fireman John McCarthy of Engine 1 ascended 35-foot ladders to the fourth floor. Nasty, super-heated smoke was pumping from the windows.

Clark jumped, grasping a window shutter momentarily before diving into a window. In the street below, Deputy Chief Langford judged the extreme conditions Clark faced and said, "There goes a man to his death." Driven to his hands and knees

Clark began searching in dense smoke and heat as three other firemen raced up the ladder outside. Somehow Clark was able to find an unconscious woman and bring her back to the ladder. As he handed her off to other firemen he fell unconscious across the windowsill. The battered fireman was lifted off the windowsill, carried down the ladder and taken to a first aid station in the street by his comrades.

Fireman McCarthy of Engine 1 stood on the very top rung of the ladder, bracing himself against the building, the hot noxious smoke swirling around him. Despite the heat and smoke, he held that dangerous position as the children of two families were handed down to him. Balancing the small lives in his hands, he was able to hand them down to safety.

Fireman Robert Nelson of Hook & Ladder 24 remained at the very top of his ladder and was handed two babies found by firemen searching inside. Just then an excited occupant above dropped her baby toward the fireman below. Wrapping his legs around the top rung, Nelson held two babies in his left arm as the third child dropped from above. Leaning dangerously, Nelson caught the third baby. With the help of other firemen steadying him, he brought all three safely to the street.

After reviving in the street, Fireman Clark again returned to the top of the ladder. There he received two children from Fireman John J. Quinn, and quickly took them to the street.

On Friday April 7, 1911, the recipients of medals for valor for the years 1909 and 1910 were announced by Fire Commissioner Waldo. The men receiving the awards were chosen by a board composed of Deputy Fire Commissioners Johnson and O'Keefe, Chief Croker and Deputy Chiefs Lally, Kenlon, Ahearn and Maher. This committee informed the commissioner that they confined their consideration to acts performed in the line of duty.

The task of declaring one heroic act to be more credible than another is a delicate and difficult one and it is quite certain firemen have performed in 1909 and 1910 acts as fine as those of the medal winners, but the board has acted according to the official evidence submitted to it. The medal winners by no means include all those who deserve high praise for risking their lives in their efforts to save others.

Two hundred guests filled the third-floor assembly room ceremony in Fire Headquarters. The large gathering included relatives and friends of the firemen, and politicians and city officials. A unique group included civilians and fire officers whose lives had been saved by the honorees.

Deputy Fire Commissioner O'Keefe stepped forward and announced: Fireman Frank C. Clark, Hook & Ladder Company 24, For heroic conduct… The Hugh Bonner Medal. (This medal endowed in 1897 was considered the second highest award after the James Gordon Bennett Medal.)

On Wednesday, January 8, 1915, there was a serious fire in the subway below Broadway between 50th and 59th streets. Rescue work by the fire department was severely delayed due to the inability of firefighters to operate for any length of time in the heavy smoke. More than two hundred persons were hospitalized with smoke inhalation. It was becoming clear that special equipment and specially trained men were needed. The call went out within the FDNY, and hundreds of firefighters volunteered. All the applicants were checked out and members with experience as mechanics, engineers, electricians, iron workers, riggers and other trades were given preference, provided they were otherwise fit for the severe work they were expected to encounter. Of this number a captain, lieutenant, and eight firemen were chosen. Among the eight fireman was Frank C. Clark of Hook & Ladder 24.

Starting Tuesday January 19, 1915, at 10 a.m., the newly chosen members of Rescue 1 reported daily to the old headquarters building at 157 East 67th Street in Manhattan. There they were given extensive training in specialized tools, first aid and use of the new smoke helmets.

Their cache of tools included: Draeger smoke helmets, Lyle gun (rope rifle), rigging equipment, ropes, life belts, cutting torches, jacks, pulmotor, and an extensive first aid kit. The equipment was considered "state-of-the-art" at the time. The company was to be located centrally in lower Manhattan in a dense commercial district that was also a heavy fire activity area.

First and foremost in their training were the Draeger smoke helmets. These helmets would allow the wearer to venture into smoke and gases while breathing clean air. Two of the helmets were equipped with a hard-wire telephone system that allowed continuous communication to the outside. The company was issued eight smoke helmets, two of which had telephone comms. Four helmets were on the rig ready for immediate use. The others were overhauled and tested. The helmets were rotated weekly to ensure even wear.

In this era, probationary firemen received about four weeks of training. The members of Rescue 1 received 36 days of specialized training before being placed in service on Monday March 8, 1915, at 8 a.m.

During his first year in Rescue 1 Frank Clark worked four jobs that were mentioned on the Roll of Merit. The first was a fire on Delancey Street on July 14, 1915. Then he responded to an accident in a chlorine vault at the United States Rubber Company at 561 West 58th Street on September 7, 1915. A leaking tank of sulphur chloride drove back the first arriving units. Members of Rescue 1 donned their smoke helmets, and despite the dire warnings from the on-site chemist, they entered the cellar, located the leaking container, and raised it to the street where it was placed inside a new container and sealed tight.

On September 11, 1915, Clark responded with his company to a difficult blaze fed by stored film at the studio and offices of Famous Players Film Company, in the old Ninth Regiment Armory Building at 213 West 26th Street. Flames were leaping 200 feet into the air and were visible for miles around the city as the battle commenced. The toxic smoke from the burning celluloid severely affected both firemen and civilians. Five alarms were transmitted bringing 25 engines, five ladder companies and two water towers. Members of Rescue 1 donned smoke helmets and made their way to the adjoining roof, then climbed ladders to the roof of the blazing building attempting to complete roof ventilation. (This was most likely the first time in the history of the fire service that roof ventilation was accomplished by firefighters wearing breathing apparatus.) Moments after they opened the skylights and scuttles, an explosion occurred beneath them causing the roof to begin sagging. They hurried back to the ladders just as the roof collapsed into the flames below.

The department orders also mention a fire at 67 West 23rd Street on December 27, 1915.

On January 16, 1918, Clark responded with Rescue 1 to a fire at 345 West 36th Street. The delayed alarm allowed the fire to eat through the floor supports so that when the fire attack began, the floor began to collapse into the raging fire below. As the members of Rescue 1 crawled onto the sloped floor, Frank Clark was able to reach Lt. John Donaghey who was clinging onto the sagging floorboards, desperately trying to keep from sliding into the raging flames below. As Clark pulled him upwards then dragged him to safety, the other members of Rescue 1 rescued the remaining firemen trapped at the edge of the blazing floor.

 Rescue 1 was special-called to the foot of Barclay Street in Brooklyn on July 30, 1918, where fumes were coming from the lighter *Kingston*. The barge was filled with 25 tons of chloride of lime in large cans. With some of the cans leaking and the captain missing, Rescue 1 was called. Fireman Frank Clark and John Dorritie donned smoke helmets and explored the cabin searching for the captain. They found the captain's clothes but no other sign of him. The chloride of lime was to have been shipped to Europe but was rejected by the government. It was dumped into the ocean later that day.

Frank Clark was on duty Saturday October 5, 1918, when Rescue 1 was special-called to the Brooklyn Navy Yard for an explosion and fire onboard the submarine *O-5* moored at Pier 12. Sailors and first due fire companies had limited success in attempting to enter and battle the fire caused by the buildup of hydrogen gas after a valve snapped closed. A series of explosions continued as Rescue 1 arrived at the scene. Lt. Blessing split his men into teams. Blessing, Kilbride and Donohue donned masks and entered the rear hatch as Frank Clark, James Smith, John Mayr, and John Ryan attempted to enter through the conning tower and then helped off-load ammunition and fed a constant stream of hand extinguishers to fight the fire inside. All the men of Rescue 1 risked their lives as they extinguished the fire and rescued the remaining sailors. Class I awards were given to Blessing, Kilbride and Donohue (they later also received medals) Class II awards were given to Frank Clark, James Smith, John Mayr and John Ryan.

 A sharp-eyed police sergeant noted people coughing and having difficulty breathing on Broome Street. He went to investigate and found a cloud of greenish-yellow gas escaping from the J.M. Thompson & Company Warehouse at 521

Broome Street. It was 11 p.m. June 23, 1920. Almost overcome, Sergeant McKay found a telephone and called his Beach Street stationhouse. Arriving first was Deputy Chief Henry Helm who immediately special called Rescue Co. 1.

Arriving in minutes, Rescue 1, under the command of Lt. Thomas Kilbride, conferred with the chief as the gas cloud began affecting the entire neighborhood. As the members of Hook & Ladder Companies 5 and 20 and the police reserves began evacuating the surrounding apartment houses and tenements, Rescue 1 prepared to enter the building.

Helm led them to the front door, which was forced open. Helm entered the building and was driven to his knees by the gas. Staggering back outside he ordered the rescue crew to don masks. Wearing gas masks, Kilbride led Firemen Frank Clark, John Kistenberger, Walter Lamb and Joe Horacek inside the warehouse and began a search for the leak. Finding a cache of 14 large tanks labelled chlorine, Kilbride used an old trick. Wetting his hand, he swept around the tanks. When the escaping gas dried the water, he knew he had the right tank. The leaking tank was then carried outside to a vacant lot.

When Chief Smoky Joe Martin arrived, he decided the tank had to be moved from the highly populated neighborhood. Frank Clark and Charles Roggencamp used a wooden plug to stop the leak and then wrapped it in a rubber coat and placed it in Helm's chief's car.

As the members of Rescue 1 who'd worked inside the warehouse removed their masks, the fumes coming off their clothes gave them a bad dose of chlorine and brought them to their knees, wheezing and choking, barely able to breath. Doctor Archer and Honorary Chief Mainzer quickly moved in, stripped away their gas-soaked outer clothes and treated the men before driving them to the hospital.

The remaining members of Rescue 1 loaded the re-plugged

tank into the rescue truck and raced to the Canal Street pier. The tank was then tossed into the North River. (Sadly, a common practice in that era.)

Fireman Frank Clark and his three comrades were treated overnight for their exposure and inhalation of the chlorine gas. They were soon back to full duty.

On November 1, 1922, Frank C. Clark was promoted to lieutenant and transferred to Engine Company 76 on West 102nd Street (where he worked with my grandfather, Fireman Paul O. Hashagen). Lt. Clark spent the next six years in 76 Engine before retiring on April 5, 1928. He passed away on September 18, 1956.

James Smith

Born in New York City on September 2, 1880, James Smith joined the United States Navy in January of 1899. He was assigned to the USS *Newark* and was given the rank of landsman (at the time the lowest rank in the navy). His naval records indicate he served in the Spanish American War and then in the Philippine Insurrection. Most notable in his three-year enlistment was his service during the Boxer Rebellion in China.

During his time in China, James Smith was attached to the Seymour Expedition. This was an attempt to march on Beijing with a multinational force to relieve the Siege of the Legations and foreign nationals trapped in the city. Nine hundred soldiers, sailors, marines and civilians, mostly from Europe, Japan and the United States, and nearly 3,000 Chinese Christians took refuge in Peking's Legation Quarter after the Qing government sided with the Boxers.

The Boxer movement was an anti-foreign, anti-colonial, and anti-Christian uprising that took place in China between 1899 and 1901. The Society of the Righteous and Harmonious Fists, was an indigenous peasant movement, related to secret societies that flourished in China for centuries. The name "Boxer" most likely came from missionaries, who saw the acrobatic rituals, martial arts and twirling swords, reminded them of Western boxers.

Vice Admiral Edward Seymour, the commander of the British Navy's China Station, was placed in charge of the rescue mission. In just 24 hours, Seymour gathered a force of more than 2,000 sailors and marines from Japanese, European and American warships. He commandeered five trains and on June 10th set off for Beijing. On the second and third days of the trip the relief expedition encountered sabotaged tracks that were repaired while under attack by the Boxers. The closer they got to Beijing the more intense fighting they faced.

On June 18th they faced a large force that attacked at multiple points. This force of 5,000 included cavalry armed with modern rifles. Seymour's troops fought off the attack, killing hundreds of Chinese while only losing seven men and 57 wounded. Challenged with caring for the injured, diminishing supplies and facing additional attacks, Seymour and his officers decided to retreat. While retreating they came upon an unprotected arsenal stocked with weapons, ammunition and food. This allowed them to repel additional attacks.

On July 19, 1901, Landsman James Smith of New York City, was awarded the Medal of Honor for distinguished conduct in the presence of the enemy, in battles on the 13th, 20th, 21st, and 22nd, 1900, while with the relief expedition under Vice Admiral Seymour.

James Smith's enlistment ended on January 31, 1902, and he returned to New York City and got a job as an iron worker, until April 4, 1906, when he was appointed to the New York City Fire Department and was assigned to Engine Company 74 on 77th Street in Manhattan.

On July 7, 1916, Fireman James Smith transferred to Rescue Company 1. Early on the morning of July 30, 1918, Rescue 1 responded to the foot of Barclay Street where the lighter *Kingston* was docked. (Lighters were flat-bottomed barges used in loading or off-loading ships.) The firemen were faced with dangerous fumes and a missing captain. On board were 25 tons of chloride of lime, and some of the containers were leaking, giving off toxic fumes. (Chloride of lime was used for bleaching and was commonly referred to as bleaching powder.)

Members of Rescue 1 donned smoke helmets and searched the lighter looking for the missing captain. They found his clothes but no sign of the man. James Smith and the entire crew of Rescue 1 were placed on the Roll of Merit.

One of the most dangerous assignments Rescue 1 ever received was on the morning of October 5, 1918, when they responded to the Brooklyn Navy Yard for an explosion and fire onboard the U.S. Navy submarine *O-5*.

The Brooklyn Navy Yard was in full swing, its piers were crowded with ships of all types, most were laden with ammunition. One ship in particular, a submarine of the "O" class, one of the largest at that time, was moored at Pier 12 and preparing to go to sea. On board was its full complement of ordnance: eight torpedoes, quantities of guncotton, and ammunition. While trying the port engines on battery power, a vent in the battery room snapped closed and hydrogen gas began building up. When the officers became aware of the dangerous situation, they scrambled to prevent a catastrophic explosion.

Before any significant actions could be taken an explosion occurred in the aft battery compartment. This blast injured many, including the ship's captain, Lt. Commander Trever and killed Ensign Sharkey. The navy under the command of Admiral McDonald did what it could but realized they had to call the FDNY to extinguish the fire.

The first arriving units including Battalion Chief Kirk and Deputy Chief O'Hara sized up the fire and special-called Rescue 1 from Manhattan. Under the command of Lt. Blessing, Rescue 1 arrived and started their dangerous work. Blessing split the company into teams, and asked Fireman Smith to don a smoke helmet and together with a masked naval officer attempt to enter the submarine through the conning tower. They climbed down two connecting ladders and entered the central control room (CCR.) They found the various compartment doors shut tight, isolating the CCR, the ammunition room and the forward battery. They made several attempts to close the water-tight bulkhead door between the CCR and the aft battery but were unable due to the extreme heat and dense smoke.

Fireman Smith pushed himself a bit too far during this operation and was overcome. After a ten-minute rest he resumed work. The members of Rescue 1 were able to remove endangered ammunition, provide ventilation, recover the body and the missing ensign and eventually after two hours, control the fire. Fireman James Smith and all the members of Rescue 1 were placed on the Roll of Merit for extraordinary heroism.

On February 17, 1919, the FDNY responded to a fire in a four-story warehouse on East 48th Street in Manhattan. The former flour warehouse was currently being used by the United States government. When employees opened for business in the morning they were met by a wall of flames. The first floor was piled high with bales of jute. (Jute is a coarse fiber used in making sacks and ropes.) On the second floor, were bags of sulphur and on the floors above were other chemicals.

The blazing jute sent waves of super-heated gases across the ceiling heating the flooring and setting the sulphur aflame and causing dense clouds of noxious gas. First due units arrived and began fighting the fire. Hoses were stretched inside as members of the ladder companies worked on ventilation. Suddenly, an explosion occurred blowing the second-floor shutters from the building and sending flames high into the air. Several firemen working from ladders were thrown off or jumped to safety.

Inside conditions had become so dangerous that several men were overcome and slumped to the floor unconscious. Chief Kenlon called for Rescue 1, who arrived under the command of Acting Lieutenant John P. Ryan. Members of Rescue 1 donned smoke helmets and dragged several unconscious firemen to safety, then attempted to penetrate the dangerous second floor. Wearing a smoke helmet, Fireman James Smith was able to enter the second floor and battled the growing fire.

The interior battle lasted five hours with rescuemen taking turns on the attack lines. Even with the benefit of the smoke helmets, conditions were so extreme that Fireman James Smith was rendered unconscious and transported to the hospital. Thirty firemen, including James Smith were treated by Doctor Archer and Honorary Officer Mainzer who were later promoted for their heroic efforts to revive overcome firemen despite the overwhelming fumes that blanketed the neighborhood.

All the members of Rescue 1 were placed on the Roll of Merit for their heroic efforts.

This fire may have been the last straw for James Smith, who was transferred to Engine 57, the fireboat *New Yorker* for a respite. As it turned out James Smith would continue to respond to challenging and dangerous fire situations with the fireboat. On September 13, 1919, the *New Yorker* responded along with hundreds of units to the huge blaze at the Standard Oil yards on Newtown Creek in Greenpoint Brooklyn. Smith was among the more than 400 members of the department cited for heroism at this fire.

In 1922 James Smith was promoted to engineer of steamer and was assigned to Engine Company 245 in Brooklyn. Engineer Smith worked there until 1927, when he was transferred to Engine 78, the fireboat *George McClelland*, located at the foot of East 99th Street Harlem River. Smith worked there until 1927 when he was transferred to Engine 262 in Long Island City, Queens. In 1938 Smith was designated assistant supervising engineer. Now part of the headquarters staff, he was part of Fire Service Supervision Company 1. They responded to major fires to ensure pumpers and water supply were being utilized to their maximum.

James Smith retired on April 16, 1944, after 38 years of service in the New York City Fire Department. He died eight months later November 9, 1944.

Louis Tischler

Most firefighters gain notoriety by performing spectacular rescues. Their heroics, chronicled by local newspapers, remain as part of the historic record. The story of Louis Tischler followed suit, but with a most unusual twist, he got famous after he was fired.

The saga began when Tischler joined the FDNY on February 12, 1910, and was assigned to Engine Company 2. A few months later, after completing his probationary period, he was re-assigned to Hook & Ladder 11 on East Fifth Street in Manhattan. Tischler made several transfers and worked in Hook & Ladder 2, and Hook & Ladder 6, where he was detailed as a chauffeur in 1912. Tischler's named was mentioned on the Roll of Merit in 1915 and 1917 for actions taken while a member of Hook & Ladder 6.

In 1919 Tischler was operating at a building fire on Water Street, when Battalion Chief Walter Jones apparently criticized his work. An argument ensued and grew heated. According to reports Tischler then struck the officer and was quickly suspended. Apparently, a department trial was held without the suspended Tischler in attendance. A week later, on April 17, 1919, FDNY Special Order 79 was published and announced the dismissal Tischler to take place on April 30. In other words, he was fired.

Finding himself without a job, Tischler began working as a taxi driver in Manhattan. This new career continued without incident for more than a year, until the evening of August 15,

1920. While driving his cab on the lower east side of Manhattan, Tischler saw flames pouring from a five-story tenement building. Closer inspection revealed a group of screaming women and children, clinging to a wide window ledge on the fifth floor with flames closing in.

Louie Tischler did what most any firefighter would do—he sprang into action. Dashing into the adjacent tenement, he raced up five flights, broke into a top floor apartment and hurried to the front windows. Looking up he realized he was five feet below the trapped family and their dinner guests. He thought briefly of moving to the roof until it became apparent one of the children was about to fall from the ledge. Climbing out and standing on the windowsill, Tischler tried to calm the family as he stretched across toward their window. Flames were closing in and the trapped family were becoming frantic screaming for help. Tischler, now only feet away yelled "Shut Up!" The quieted group then listened as Tischler explained his plan. They moved back inside the window as the former smoke-eater stretched across the gap, shifting his weight from one leg to the other. With a desperate maneuver he was able to muscle himself across to reach their window, pulling himself onto the ledge.

Below, Captain Francis Roller and the men of Hook & Ladder 9 rolled to a stop and were raising their 75-foot wooden aerial toward the trapped family. With excited firemen scrambling up the ladder below him, Tischler stood on the windowsill cradling an infant, and was able to reach the extended ladder with his foot. While still holding the ledge he climbed onto the aerial ladder. As Firemen Kelly and Mivosky reached the ladder's tip, Tischler handed them the infant. Then using his broad back and shoulders as a bridge, Louis Tischler braced himself as one after the other, the trapped family members slid from the window across Tischler's back to the waiting arms of firemen.

The 200-pound mother followed her two daughters and lunged at Tischler grabbing him around the neck and nearly pulling him from his dangerous perch. She was finally persuaded to let go and was carefully transferred to other firemen. She was followed by two more women and the father. One by one they were safely passed to waiting firemen.

Still stretched between the windowsill and the top rounds of the aerial, Tischler feared a whipping action at the ladder's tip if he let go too soon. With flames pouring from the window overhead he waited until the civilians were clear, then let go. As the swaying ladder rocked back and forth the battered and exhausted hero started down to the cheers of the large crowd of spectators drawn to the spectacular fire. Tischler had personally saved the lives of eight people and they'd watched every thrilling second of it.

Reaching the ground Louis Tischler stood exhausted, his shoulders, arms and back muscles knotted in pain. His hands and arms bleeding from the grinding suffered against the unprotected concrete ledge. The cheering continued as, Assistant Chief Smoky Joe Martin recognized the former firefighter and shook his hand. "My boy, in 40 years of fire fighting I've seen a lot of rescues, but what you've done tonight beats any hero stuff I've ever seen. Martin further promised he would do everything in his power to have Tischler reinstated.

Refusing medical attention, the banged up Tischler climbed into his car and drove off as the cheering continued.

The city's newspapers took up his cause as the FDNY staff reviewed the case. This review showed that the battalion chief, who'd since retired, had instigated the original incident. With the full backing of the FDNY staff and at the mayor's direction, Louis Tischler would soon rejoin the department. On October 2, 1920, a year and a half after being fired, Fireman Louis Tischler again joined the FDNY and was assigned to Hook

& Ladder 18. He later returned to Hook & Ladder 6, before becoming a member of Rescue Company 1 on March 16, 1926. Tischler continued working in Rescue 1 until his retirement on New Year's Eve in 1932.

FDNY Special Order #205, dated December 14, 1948, stated: With regret the department announces the death of Louis Tischler formerly of Rescue Company 1, residing at the Hotel Lincoln, 44th Street and Eighth Avenue at 4:05 p.m. on December 11, 1948.

John C. Conners

Born in Illinois, on February 22, 1882, John Conners was an ironworker before his appointment to the FDNY on June 7, 1911. Assigned to Hook & Ladder 20 in the very heart of the dry goods district the six-foot-tall young fireman would start his career in one of the most difficult and dangerous parts of the city. After five years in the truck, Conners transferred to the FDNYs new unit Rescue Company 1 on Christmas Eve 1916.

Three alarms were transmitted for a fire in a warehouse at 345 West 36th Street. It was noon on January 16, 1918, when a member of Hook & Ladder 21 was passing by the address and noticed smoke coming from the building. He ran and transmitted the alarm box. Neighbors later stated they had been smelling smoke since eight o'clock that morning.

The six-story warehouse was being leased by a Broadway producer and was packed with highly flammable scenery, costumes and props. Engine 54 under the command of Lt. John Donaghey, and Acting Battalion Chief Thomas Murtagh, stretched a dry line deep inside with Fireman John Kocher on the nozzle. Conditions around them were severe and getting worse by the minute. Sadly, the company did not know that the long burning fire had eaten away the floor supports beneath them. As they advanced deeper into the room, and above the raging fire in the basement below them, their very weight was causing the floor to give way.

Suddenly, the floor began to collapse beneath them. The flooring began breaking and dropping in a "V" shape with

Fireman Kocher on the far side of the hole and flames belching up through the opening. "Go back! Go back, for God's sake, while you've got a chance. This floor is breaking up!" Kocher yelled to his comrades. Men clawed at the sloping floorboards trying to keep themselves from sliding into the blazing inferno beneath them. Scrambling to save their lives one burned and battered member reached a front window and called for help.

Assistant Chief Martin sent Rescue 1 in with their smoke helmets. Lt. Ben Parker and his men: Firemen John Conners, Frank Clark, and John Donohue, dove into the fire area and grabbed at the struggling members as the pitch of the collapsing floor increased. Frank Clark was able to pull Lt. Donaghy clear and remove him to safety.

A charged hose line was brought into position to protect the rescuers from the expanding flames. Under the cover of the hose stream Lt. Parker, with Conners and Donohue holding his legs, was able to stretch across the failing floorboards and grab Acting Battalion Chief Murtagh who was entangled in a section of the broken and burning floor. Showing great strength, the barrel-chested Parker lifted the officer from the blazing hole and dragged him to safety. The members of Rescue 1 regrouped and again, under the stream of water tried to reach the fallen nozzleman. The fire was now raging out of control and the men were forced to leave.

Young Kocher's body would not be recovered until the following day. The remaining members however would recover from their near-death ordeal. For their heroic efforts the members of Rescue 1 would be placed on the Roll of Merit. Lt. Parker received a Class I and was decorated with a medal the following year. Firemen John Conners and John Donohue were each awarded a Class II.

Four months later Firemen John Conners and John Donohue would team up for another rescue on April 11, 1918, aboard the USS *Frank H. Buck*, lying off Charles Street, in the North River. The ship's quartermaster and two other men were overcome by fumes while working in the hold of the vessel, in a compartment between the engine room and an oil tank. After the two workers who'd been lowered into the hold failed to return, the quartermaster entered the space to check on them. He was lowered by rope into the darkness of the hold and after a few minutes signaled to be pulled up. As he neared the top he slipped from the rope and disappeared back into the hold.

Rescue 1 was special-called and three members donned smoke helmets and entered the deadly hold. Firemen John Conners, John Donohue and John Ryan began their searches and were able to locate and remove the three missing men, who'd been killed by the fumes. Each was lifted by rope from the hold. The three rescue firemen were placed on the Roll of Merit with Class II awards.

John Conners and six other members of Rescue 1 were able to rescue several firemen overcome by noxious smoke at a blazing government warehouse on February 17, 1919. The five-story building was filled with hemp, sugar, flour, jute and sulphur. The smoke was so toxic that nozzle teams were ordered to work in seven-minute shifts and even with this limited exposure many were overcome. Six firemen were working on ladders when a chemical explosion inside the second floor of the burning building knocked them to the ground and blew the iron shutters right from the building. The overcome or injured members were treated at the scene by Doctor Archer, with several members sent to the hospital.

Official reports stated: Acting Lt. John Ryan, Firemen John Conners, John Donohue, William Dorritie, William Hutcheon, Thomas Kilbride, and James Smith, of Rescue Company 1, mask equipped operated under the most hazardous and trying conditions until weakened to a point of exhaustion, in stretching and operating lines in sulphur fumes; for a period of five hours and 30 minutes.

Rescue 1 was special-called to Bedford Avenue in Brooklyn when 18 workers were trapped inside a collapsed theatre November 29, 1921. Faced with unsupported sagging floors, and the remains of side walls hanging overhead, the rescue work commenced. As injured workers were removed over ladders 35 feet above the sidewalk, members of Rescue 1 including Fireman John Conners, entered voids to search and rescue entangled workers. All the members of Engines 209, 230, 211, Hook & Ladders 102, 104, 108 and 119, and Rescue 1 were placed on the Roll of Merit with Class A awards.

April 20, 1924, was Easter Sunday and five alarms were transmitted for Manhattan Box 55-433 for a fire involving factories and a lumber yard along the East River on the Lower East side. Strong winds carried flaming embers that ignited the adjacent structures. The high-pressure hydrant system ended at Houston and Lewis Streets so 1,500 feet of hose was stretched to augment the water supply. Several firemen overcome by the noxious smoke were rescued and treated by Doctor Archer. Fireman John Conners was also treated for burns of the face and hands.

The evening rush hour on February 19, 1929, became dangerous when a fire of blazing grease and oil stalled trains in the Hudson tube about 1,000 feet west of Christopher Street. The flames quickly reached the power lines, plunging the tunnel into total darkness and trapping 300 passengers. The FDNY responded to find other trains had also entered the dense smoke condition trapping an additional 600 passengers.

Arriving fire companies entered the thick smoke and began a difficult and dangerous evacuation. More than 250 people were treated at St. Vincent's Hospital, some were treated at first aid stations set up by the FDNY, others went to local drug stores (a common practice in the days before emergency rooms). All of the members of Rescue 1, including Fireman John Conners were placed on the Roll of Merit along with the members of Hook & Ladders 20, 5, and Engines 13, 18, 24, and 30.

It was 4 a.m., on September 14, 1930, when Manhattan fire companies responded to a fire in a 12-story loft building at 11 West 19th Street, a 200-foot-deep building that ran through to West 20th Street. Responding firemen arrived in a drenching rain to find heavy smoke pumping from the 11th floor. Teams were sent to vent the fire floor as a second alarm was transmitted. While operating on the fire floor, five men became separated in the smoke-filled darkness and tried to make their way to safety. Two men overcome by the smoke fell unconscious as others were able to reach the front windows.

In the street, the searchlight unit used its powerful light to illuminate Fireman Harry Williams of Hook & Ladder 3 who'd climbed out onto the window ledge. Surrounded by thick hot smoke and being pelted by the heavy rain, Williams swayed unsteadily as he fought to remain conscious, before slumping across the windowsill. Rescue 1 was ordered to the fire floor to initiate a rescue.

Battling a wall of flame and the biting smoke, the rescue men pressed forward searching for their downed comrades. A plan was devised where all the high-pressure streams on the floor were united to provide a safe lane for the removal of the trapped men. One by one the unconscious firemen were dragged to safety. All the members of Rescue 1 including John Conners were placed on the Roll of Merit with Class III awards.

John Conners responded to a reported building collapse on September 29, 1931, at 327 East 13th Street. Seven workers were trapped when two walls and the roof of a five-story building collapsed on them. Conners and the other members of Rescue 1 helped remove six of the trapped workers when the seventh and last worker was found by Fireman William Dorritie of Rescue 1. Dorritie dug and tunneled with Conners and the others helped with debris removal and shoring the unstable area.

For his heroic efforts Fireman Dorritie was awarded a Class II and later a medal. The remaining Rescue 1 members were also placed on the Roll of Merit with Class A awards.

A fire in a sub-basement paint locker inside the luxury 41-story Ritz Tower Hotel at 57th Street and Park Avenue, caused an explosion that killed five firemen and injured 30 more. It was 10:36 on the morning of August 1, 1932, when companies responded to Box 924 in Manhattan. On arrival firemen were informed of a small fire in the sub-basement paint shop. Believing they had a routine fire, 40 firemen entered the building and began their operations. Ladders were placed down into an airshaft and extinguishers were carried inside. Engine 8 began stretching a 2-1/2-inch line, as the trucks began to search and ventilate. Reaching the sub-basement level, they were met by thick, oily black smoke. The line was pulled forward, but the fire could not be located. (Unknown to the firemen the paint locker was a 7 X 7 foot cubical with terra-cotta walls and a metal ceiling. It was used for the storage of paints and contained lacquer type material made with a pyroxylin base and acetone solvent.) A ladder company was sent to the floor above to attempt ventilation. Reaching the location above the fire area they found the floor was 12-inches of concrete. Realizing the difficulty they faced, Rescue 1 was special-called for their special tools and smoke helmets.

Attempting to find alternative routes to the fire, members of Hook & Ladder 16 descended the ladder placed in a sidewalk shaft where another line was also stretched. Chief Ryan of the Eighth Battalion donned a mask from the chief's car and entered the smoke-filled subcellar hoping to locate the paint locker. Captain Ginty of Engine 8 donned an ammonia mask which was the property of the hotel and began his search for the locker. Fireman Thomas Finn of Engine 65 was left in the basement above the fire (apparently to show Rescue 1 where the officers wanted the hole).

Then the first devastating explosion occurred.

A sheet of flame erupted from the locker and roared over the heads of the firemen in the sub-basement as huge chunks of the concrete ceiling and walls collapsed down onto them. Lt. Hartnett and Fireman Finn were killed instantly as the lights went out and the sub-basement and basement filled with thick smoke.

Injured firemen, bleeding from their wounds and reeling from the blast struggled to search for their brothers. They were dragging the dead and dying back toward safety when a second, more violent explosion blasted through the subterranean chambers. Debris from the first blast became missiles, as jagged beams and chunks of concrete tore through the smoke as if blasted from a cannon.

Members of Rescue 1 donned masks and along with second alarm companies dove into the basement and sub-basement of the damaged structure. Despite suffocating smoke, extreme heat and the constant threat of additional explosions they searched for and rescued the more than 40 firemen injured by the explosions. A field hospital was set up and quickly filled with battered, burned and bloodied firemen, as the fire attack and rescue work commenced.

In all, eight firemen and officers were killed, a dozen were seriously injured and many received minor injuries. The heroic actions in response to the explosion and fire were noted, as 41 members including Fireman John Conners, were placed on the Roll of Merit.

Just after midnight on May 5, 1933, Manhattan fire companies responded to a reported fire in a five-story loft building at 316 Lafayette Street. Three alarms were transmitted at Box 341, for a spectacular fire that started on the fourth floor in a rag shop and was fanned by strong winds. Members of Hook & Ladder 6 were working on the roof of the fire building when the front and side walls collapsed without warning. The members operating on the roof plummeted three floors and were covered in debris.

Firefighters sprang into action climbing into the collapsed pile and digging to free the trapped men. John Conners and the members of Rescue 1 led the mission as one by one the trapped men were freed. Sadly, one man Fireman John Storch Jr. of Hook & Ladder 6 was killed, and three other members of his company were injured.

For their heroic efforts 81 members of the department, including Fireman John Conners were placed on the Roll of Merit.

On June 1, 1936, John C. Conners retired from the FDNY. His career spanned 25 years with 20 of those in Rescue Company 1. He responded to and worked at some of the most difficult and dangerous fires in the city. He helped pioneer modern rescue work as we now know it. He passed away on August 8, 1940, he was 58 years old.

John Kistenberger

Born on December 13, 1888, in Queens, New York, the son of German immigrants, John Kistenberger was a carpenter before joining the FDNY on July 1, 1913. He was assigned to Engine Company 225 on Liberty Avenue in Brooklyn.

In 1913 a special showcase under the auspices of the Military Athletic League, the National Guard and United States Military authorities showed the nation's military strength to the packed audience at Madison Square Garden. The week-long event featured parades, special drills by infantry companies, cavalry units, and demolitions experts.

Fireman John Kistenberger was a member of the FDNY Demonstration Team, consisting off 25 hand-picked members of the department. Under the direction of Battalion Chief Larkin, these members showed the capacity audience a demonstration of fire department life-saving and firefighting tools, and techniques including scaling ladders and rope rescues. On the floor of the auditorium the façade of a four-story house was erected and on cue the squad of firemen extinguished a simulated fire and rescued the "trapped" occupants.

The FDNY members each received gold medals from Colonel Nathaniel B. Thurston the commander of the 74th New York Infantry. Thurston was an honorary FDNY battalion chief and major supporter of the department. He had also served New York City as a deputy police commissioner.

In 1917 Kistenberger transferred to Hook & Ladder Company 124 on Himrod Street in Brooklyn. Then on June 16,

1919, Kistenberger transferred to Rescue Co. 1 on Great Jones Street in Manhattan. A few months after joining Rescue 1, he'd respond to one of the most difficult and dangerous fires ever battled in New York City: the Standard Oil Yard fire. It was September 13, 1919. The blaze involved huge tanks filled with flammable liquids that caught fire and began exploding. This fire required the transmission of two borough calls above a fifth alarm, plus special-calls for extra companies and for all off-duty members. Four hundred and nine members of the department were placed on the Roll of Merit for their heroic actions at this dangerous fire including Fireman John Kistenberger and the entire crew of Rescue 1.

Another dangerous call was the Thompson Warehouse fire on June 23, 1920. It was just after 11 at night when 200 families were driven from their homes by the greenish-yellow clouds of chlorine gas pumping from the Broome Street warehouse. The members of Rescue 1 entered the gas filled building. Wearing smoke helmets and filter masks Rescue 1 was able to locate 14 tanks labeled "chlorine." Lt. Kilbride was able to identify the leaking tank and remove it to a nearby vacant lot. Several members of Rescue 1 were overcome by the fumes clinging to their clothes including: John Kistenberger, Joe Horacek, Frank Clark and Walter Lamb. They were treated in St. Vincent's Hospital before being released. All the members of Rescue 1 were placed on the Roll of Merit for this dangerous operation.

On October 11, 1924 Rescue 1 was special-called to Bush Terminal in Brooklyn for a fire on the ocean liner *The President Polk*. Donning smoke helmets the members were able to locate the deep-seated fire below deck and extinguish the flames. They then conducted a search for a missing stevedore. They located his charred remains and completed the searches identifying additional hot spots and pockets of fire. For their efforts the members of Rescue 1 including John Kistenberger were placed on the Roll of Merit.

This ship fire was just another example of the need for additional rescue companies in the FDNY. So, in 1925 word went out within the FDNY seeking volunteers interested in becoming members of a new rescue company to be established in Brooklyn. There were 500 applicants. One of those chosen was John Kistenberger. Special Order No. 35 on February 27, 1925 established Rescue Company 2 to be placed in service on March 3, 1925. Named on the orders were Fireman John Kistenberger, and Lt. Peter Walsh from Rescue 1. They would join the other new members who would all be under the command of Captain Walter A. O'Leary (a former member of Rescue 1.)

Another connection was the rescue apparatus. Rescue 1 used a modified 1914 Cadillac touring car, which was replaced by a 1921 White. In 1924 Rescue 1 was assigned a new "Mack AC-10 Bulldog" freeing up the White rescue truck which was refurbished and fully stocked with tools when it was assigned to Rescue 2.

Unlike when Rescue 1 was established and the new members were taken off-line and received specialized training for over a month and a half. The members of Rescue Company 2 reported to quarters and their new boss, Captain O'Leary trained them in-house. Local newspapers reported that on Saturday, April 30th, the captain trained the men in the use of the cutting torch and the smoke helmets. It also stated the second day of training would begin on Sunday, March 1st, the very day the company went into service for fire and emergency duties.

Then on March 18, 1925, Rescue 2 responded to their first job, (again, according to the newspapers). The fire started on the first floor of a three-story loft building being used as a rag warehouse on Furman Street. This loft building stood at the foot of the cliff that separates the Brooklyn Heights residential section from the warehouse and pier district extending into Red Hook. The initial attack proved impossible due to clouds of thick acrid smoke being produced by the deep-seated fire. Firemen without breathing protection were driven back by the dense smoke. A second alarm was transmitted bringing Rescue 2 and other units to the scene.

Upon arrival Capt. O'Leary conferred with Battalion Chief Flaherty and Deputy Chief Davin who requested the Rescue enter the top floor and vent where possible. O'Leary, and Firemen William Dougherty, James Cummings, and Anthony Zurno donned filter masks and stretched a hose line up a 50-foot portable ladder and into a third-floor window. As the nozzle team pressed forward Fireman John Zoblotny perched himself on the top of the ladder and fed hose into the window as the line advanced.

Without warning a backdraft exploded across the top floor sending waves of debilitating smoke and heat violently across the area. On the tip of the ladder Zoblotny was instantly overcome by the noxious smoke. He would have fallen 50 feet from his position on the ladder if not for the quick and decisive actions taken by Fireman John Hederman who was a rung below. Hederman pinned Zablotny to the ladder while struggling to hold him fast. Gaining his balance he carried his unconscious brother safely to the ground.

Suddenly, the hose came flying out the window above, the nozzle shooting water wildly as it fell to the street. The members of Rescue 2 realized their comrades deep inside the top floor were in trouble. Donning gas masks John Kistenberger, William Barry and Hederman ran up the ladder and entered the thick smoke in search of their friends. They found the four men unconscious on the floor and dragged them back to the window.

They attempted to lift the unconscious men but were unable. Kistenberger rushed down to the street, grabbed a strong rope and returned to the top-floor. Another ladder was placed next to the first by members of Hook & Ladder 101 who helped in the rescue and removal operation. One by one, the rope was tied around each man and while Zoblotny, standing inside the top-floor window, lowered the rope, Kistenberger and Hederman held each unconscious man under the arms and guided them down. On the street below a crowd of several hundred people cheered their efforts. Fireman Dougherty and Captain O'Leary were taken to the hospital in serious condition. The others were revived at the scene and remained on duty.

For their heroic actions Firemen John Kistenberger, William Barry, John Hederman, and John Zoblotny of Rescue 2, and Firemen Taylor and Haugh of Hook & Ladder 101 were placed on the Roll of Merit with Class III awards.

Then on June 29, 1925, Rescue 2 responded to a spectacular blaze that enveloped a block of old buildings extending from 616 Franklin Avenue, and from 931 to 939 Bergen Street. Many of these buildings were more than 100 years old. The original fire started in 616 Franklin, a burlap bag manufacturing company.

Deputy Chief Thomas Langford quickly requested a second alarm, then later a third alarm calling out all the fire companies in the district. The growing crowd, now several thousand people, hampered the incoming response and operations so the police reserves had to be called in to gain control.

While battling the blaze Lt. Peter Walsh and Firemen Frank Anderson, James Boylan, Ray Fleming, Earl Cain, John Hederman and John Kistenberger, were trapped in an old hayloft at 616 Franklin Ave. Finding their normal escape routes blocked by flames the firefighters had to slide down a hoist wire to save themselves. They all required medical attention.

Two months later on September 1, 1925, John Kistenberger was promoted to Lieutenant and assigned to Engine Company 17 on Ludlow Street in Manhattan. The following April Kistenberger attended the FDNY Fire College. For the next four years he worked in Engine 17 until May 1, 1929, when Lt. Peter Walsh from Rescue 2 was promoted to captain and John Kistenberger was transferred back to Rescue 2.

Kistenberger was placed on the Roll of Merit two more times for his heroic actions. The first was on October 11, 1929, and again on June 20, 1930.

It was in the early morning hours of July 9, 1930, when Rescue Company 2, under the command of Lt. Kistenberger, responded to The House of St. Giles the Cripple, a hospital for handicapped children. Apparently, a new refrigeration system being installed in the hospital began leaking ammonia around midnight. While 40 young patients were sleeping nearby, Rescue 2 using a muffled bell arrived without waking the children. Donning masks they entered the basement and searched for the leak. Using hand-tools they were able to tighten several pipe joints in the refrigerating apparatus stopping the leak. They left as quietly as they arrived without disturbing a single child.

On February 3, 1932, John Kistenberger was promoted to captain and was assigned to Engine Company 66, the fireboat *William L. Strong*, berthed at the foot of Grand Street in the East River. He remained in command until his retirement on July 3, 1936.

Kistenberger's retirement was short lived with World War II looming. Due to his wide-ranging experience during his 23 years in the FDNY, John Kistenberger was named fire chief, Port Terminals, New York Port of Embarkation. He was entrusted with the protection of the many facilities in the great Port of New York. Brooklyn was the headquarters of the New York Port of Embarkation from which sailed half of all the troops sent to Europe and one third of all the supplies heading to the European Theater. The port facilities were scattered across 50 miles of New York waterfront and 40 miles inland. Included were installations in Manhattan, Staten Island, Queens, New Jersey, Pennsylvania and upstate New York. This included Warehouse B of the Brooklyn Army Base. This eight-story building (with a basement) was 300 feet wide and 980-feet-long, having 52 acres of floor space, making it the largest building in the world at this time (for floor space).

Chief Kistenberger even wrote an article in *Fire Engineering* magazine describing how best to prepare piers for battling fires beneath their structure.

John Kistenberger passed away on May 31, 1947, after a brilliant career in the FDNY and in his capacity as fire chief of the New York Port of Embarkation.

William A. Dorritie

Prior to joining the FDNY on May 1, 1913, Bill Dorritie worked as a stagehand. Born in New York City on May 10, 1885, Dorritie joined the FDNY on May 1, 1913, at the age of 28. He was assigned to Engine 39 on East 67th Street and attended the school of instruction from May 13, until June 19th. Dorritie also took part in a special duty during his first several months of service. He was part of the FDNY contingent at a large military athletic tournament held in Madison Square Garden. Dorritie was one of 25 hand-picked members of the department's demonstration team. They scaled the façade of a "four-story house" (specially constructed for this drill) using scaling ladders, slid down ropes, lowered people by rope and jumped into life nets (similar to the Life Saving Corps demonstrations years earlier).

So, a young Fireman Dorritie found himself on the third floor of headquarters, where the large meeting area was decorated for Christmas and converted into a reception hall for the day. The December 23, 1913, occasion was multi-faceted. The official department ceremony included the inauguration of the first fire department wireless communications system, allowing constant communications between commanders on the shore and the fireboat fleet in the city's rivers. Fire Commissioner Johnson used the new radio to speak with the fireboat *James Duane*, the first of the fleet to be fitted with a wireless communication system.

The commissioner was presented several gifts for his

service as Doctor Archer stepped in for the mayor and spoke of the commissioner's diligent work on behalf of the department. The commissioner then demonstrated the new fire alarm box designed by the fire department.

Then three firefighters who were retiring were presented. Battalion Chief John Howe, who'd led the FDNY companies sent to help in the great Baltimore fire in 1904. Howe had a long and amazing career having been placed on the Roll of Merit ten times. Then Captain Malachi Donohue, a hero of the Fifth Avenue Hotel fire, then Engineer of Steamer Moses Morgan, the oldest engineer in terms of service. All were cheered for their outstanding contributions to the department. A list of promotions was then read by the commissioner.

Finally, Colonel N.B. Thurston of the National Guard presented medals to Battalion Chief Larkin and 24 officers and firemen, including William Dorritie, who were winners of events in the Military Athletic Exhibition at Madison Square Garden.

On November 27, 1913, Fireman William Dorritie transferred to Hook & Ladder 16. Bill was still in the same firehouse but now worked in the ladder company where he could use all the specialized lifesaving training, he'd been given. Working in headquarters had both upsides and downsides. Headquarters contained Engine 39 and Hook & Ladder 16 on the ground floor with dormitories on the second floor. The third floor held the commissioner's offices and his staff, and a large board room that could be subdivided. The fourth floor held the Superintendent of Buildings and his staff. The fifth floor held the Bureau of Combustibles, the school of the Life Saving Corps, and the medical offices. On the top floor were the fire alarm telegraph system and the fire marshal's office. The training school utilized the rear windows and a large rear yard.

These two companies were constantly being observed by the fire commissioners, chief of department and his staff, by fire companies arriving for training and by the many visitors coming to headquarters. So, the brass quickly became familiar with those working there—great if you're a hard worker.

In 1915, Rescue 1 was organized. On July 15th Fireman William Dorritie, only a second-grade fireman became the first member to be added to the new company since the original eight firemen were chosen several months earlier. Two weeks after he reported to Great Jones Street, Dorritie responded to the foot of West 23rd Street where the British steamship SS *Cragside* was docked.

Flames broke out among 100,000 bags of sugar being stored in a hold and the FDNY was called. By the time the first due units arrived the interior of the ship was so hot and smoky firemen could not approach the openings leading below decks. Rescue 1 arrived, members donned smoke helmets and stretched a line deep into the ship's hold. Under extreme conditions they located the seat of the fire and were able to extinguish the flames. This was William Dorritie's first mention on the Roll of Merit.

A few weeks later Bill responded with Rescue 1 to a major ammonia leak at Ruppert's Brewery on East 92nd Street. It was 3:30 on the afternoon of August 15th, and the first arriving units found a large volume of gas escaping under great pressure, from what was said to be the largest ammonia installation in the country. The break was in a two-inch supply pipe above condensers on the first floor. A similar break had occurred before in the plant and had taken eight hours to be shut off.

Rescue 1 arrived and under the command of Captain McElligott donned their smoke helmets and went to work. They were able to control the leak in ten minutes. Ventilation of the entire plant, however, took an hour and a half.

The following month they responded to a leaking tank of sulphur chloride in the United States Rubber Company laboratory on West 58th Street. Despite the fact the atmosphere they entered was deadly, the members of Rescue 1 located the tank in the cellar, raised it to the street and transferred it to a new air-tight container.

Dorritie was again wearing a smoke helmet on September 11th as they battled a celluloid film fire in the Famous Players Film Studio on West 26th Street. Huge flames leapt 200 feet high as the debilitating smoke punished everyone in the neighborhood. Five alarms were transmitted and as Rescue 1 finished venting the roof and moved to safety the roof collapsed into the flaming building.

In his first three months in his new company William Dorritie worked four major jobs and was cited, as were the other members of Rescue 1, for bravery each time—and he wasn't even a first grade fireman yet! He had only two years and four months on the job yet was helping to set the standard for rescue companies to come.

A former flour warehouse now being used by the U.S. government on East 48th Street was the site of a suffocating smoke condition caused by the spontaneous ignition of bales of jute and spread to bags of sulphur stored on the second floor. It was February 17, 1919, and Bill Dorritie and the members of Rescue 1 worked for hours rescuing downed firemen and extinguishing the difficult fire.

Sometimes, even a vacation became more than you expected. In July of 1921, William Dorritie was enjoying some vacation time at Orange Lake in upstate New York when things became dangerous. It was a hot day and people were taking it easy and enjoying the cooling effect of the lake, when a fire broke out behind the general store. The owner, an older gentleman named John Hammond was able to escape and with the help of some neighbors attempted to put out the fire. The flames proved to be beyond their control and soon the two-story wood frame structure was blazing. At that point Hammond realized he wanted to save a valuable antique clock and re-entered the building despite the pleas of his neighbors.

Those outside quickly lost sight of their friend and began yelling for him to leave the burning building. Nearby, Dorritie heard the commotion, saw smoke and dashed over to see if he could help. After being informed of Hammond's plight, Dorritie dove into the blazing store and began a grueling search. Knowing full well there was no help coming (there was no fire department in the small town), Dorritie continued his search. While flat on his stomach, he inched forward and located the unconscious man behind a counter. Dorritie was able to drag the old man back across the floor with flames rolling overhead. Dorritie burst through the door and was pulled clear by neighbors just as the flaming building began to collapse into itself. Dorritie was able to revive the man before he returned to his cabin for a well-earned rest.

Another man-trapped situation occurred on October 11, 1924, but this time on board the ocean liner the *President Polk*, lying at Pier 6 at the foot of 42nd Street in Brooklyn. Responding units found an advanced fire situation with flames roaring through the ship's superstructure and reports of a stevedore missing. The smoke proved to be too noxious, so Rescue 1 was special-called.

After a difficult fire attack was commenced, a smoke-helmeted search was conducted for the missing man. Sadly, his charred remains were found by members of Rescue 1. William Dorritie and the members of Rescue 1 were again cited for heroism.

A gale force wind was sweeping across Manhattan on the afternoon of January 6, 1929. At 1:20 a.m. Box 164 was transmitted for a fire at 368 Broadway, a five-story commercial building.

Arriving first was Deputy Chief Heffernan, of the First Division. As they pulled up, the chief's aide Fireman Walter Hazrick of Engine Company 7, saw a man trapped on the top floor. As soon as a ladder was raised into position, Hazrick hurried up toward the man who proved to be a deaf mute. Seeing the man in an extremely agitated state Hazrick tied a rope around him to help calm him.

Below, Firemen William Dorritie of Rescue 1 and Harry Schnall of Hook & Ladder 8 moved in beneath Hazrick to help steady him. Just below them things became dangerous as flames were cutting off their descent. For the moment they were all trapped by the wind-driven flames.

A water tower was quickly positioned and used its powerful stream of water to protect the trio of firemen and the frantic man. With sheets of water cascading around them Hazrick handed down the man to Dorritie and Schnall who then carefully descended the swaying ladder to the street. All three men were cited for heroism with Fireman Hazrick receiving a Class I and later was awarded the Crimmins and Department medals. Dorritie and Schnall were awarded Class IIs.

The following month on February 19, 1929, 900 passengers on multiple New Jersey-bound trains were trapped when a fire filled the Hudson Tunnel with dense smoke. Responding fire companies were hard pressed to operate in the noxious smoke. Dozens of passengers were overcome and had to be carried long distances by exhausted fire crews. William Dorritie and the members of Rescue 1 joined in the search and removal. Two hundred and fifty people were seriously injured.

It was pouring rain at 4 a.m. on September 14, 1930, when William Dorritie and Rescue 1 responded to Manhattan Box 22-588, for a second alarm fire burning inside 11 West 19th Street, a 12-story loft building that ran 200 feet back to West 12th Street. Hoses were stretched from the high-pressure hydrants and the attack began as three members of Hook & Ladder 3 were sent to vent the 11th floor. While searching and venting, these members became separated from each other. Two of these firemen were overcome and dropped where they stood. When these men failed to return, a search party was sent to locate them.

Despite the rain, a huge crowd assembled to watch the fire. When a lone fireman became visible at an 11th-floor window the excited crowd shouted and pointed out his location. The searchlight unit swung its bright lights toward the trapped man. Meanwhile, those attempting to find the missing men were driven back by the dense smoke and building heat. Without breathing protection, they could not penetrate the smoke.

Acting Chief of Department McElligott ordered the hose lines to converge at a point around and above the window and Rescue 1, wearing their smoke helmets scrambled up the fire escape and plunged into the building under a protective waterfall. Inside they searched until each of the missing men was located and dragged back to the window and down to safety.

William Dorritie and the entire crew of Rescue 1 received Class II awards for the rescue of the three trapped firemen.

On September 29, 1931, two walls and the roof of a building under alteration collapsed trapping seven workers under 20 tons of debris. The fire department quickly responded to the building at 327 East 13th Street. Six workers were removed, when the moans of a seventh were heard. Fireman Christopher Walker of Engine 5 heard his moans and shouted out to the other firemen as he wriggled into the pile of debris. Fireman William Dorritie was right behind Walker as they worked their way to the trapped man. They found him buried with beams across his head, shoulders and arms, and bricks encasing his torso.

Together they carefully removed rubble and cut and

shored timbers to prevent further collapse. For two hours the duo worked stopping only long enough to allow a doctor to examine the patient and inject pain killers. They returned to their work and eventually were able to completely uncover the worker and remove him to safety.

For their heroic efforts Firemen Christopher Walker and William Dorritie found themselves on the steps of City Hall the following June. Mayor James Walker pinned the Prentice Medal on Dorritie and the Walter Scott Medal on Walker.

The Ritz Tower explosion and fire took place on August 1, 1932. William Dorritie and the members of Rescue 1 were all cited for their heroic efforts rescuing firemen trapped and injured in the sub-basement of the huge hotel.

In 1938, after more than 22 years in Rescue 1, Bill Dorritie took a detail to headquarters and was an aide to Battalion Chief David Oliver. He later worked at the World's Fair exhibit and in the probationary firemen's school before he passed away on October 6, 1941.

Richard J. Donovan

On November 1, 1922, Richard J. Donovan joined the FDNY and was assigned to Hook & Ladder 148 on Twelfth Avenue in Brooklyn. He spent the next five years there until he transferred to Rescue Company 2 on December 16, 1927. In 1927 Rescue 2 moved from Carlton Avenue and took possession of the old quarters of Ladder 118 on Jay Street. They would share these quarters with Searchlight 2 and Brooklyn's only water tower.

Flames were discovered in the Pratt branch of the Standard Oil Company on Kent Avenue. A tank containing 50,000 gallons of crude oil used to manufacture gasoline was ablaze. The flames soon spread to two other tanks holding similar amounts of crude oil and three alarms were transmitted.

Rescue 2 under the command of Lt. John Kistenberger utilized their foamite capabilities. Working with other companies while facing the constant possibility of an explosion, Firemen Donovan, Boutinger, Rosenson, Robin and Gillen produced the foam that was used in combination with steam and water to control the fire. All the members of Rescue 2, Engine 229 and Hook & Ladder 106 were placed on the Roll of Merit.

It was 1:20 on the morning of April 14, 1934, when Brooklyn units responded to an incendiary fire at 70 Cranberry Street, a four-story brownstone being used as a rooming house. Arriving at the scene before any ladder companies, Fireman Donovan could see a husband and wife trapped in their top-floor apartment. Dashing to the roof of the adjoining building, Donovan crossed over to the fire building and descended a wooden bulkhead ladder and found himself locked in a top-floor hall closet. He broke down the locked door, then crawled under flames until he found the apartment. Again, faced with a locked door, Donovan broke down the door and began his search despite the thick smoke. Reaching the front bedroom, he found the frantic couple near exhaustion and dizzy from the smoke.

Donovan leaned out the window and waved at the first due ladder truck as it rolled into the block, delayed after their response to another alarm. Finally, an aerial ladder was raised, and Donovan was able to hand the now unconscious couple out to waiting firemen.

Richard Donovan made another even more spectacular rescue on December 29, 1934, when Rescue 2 responded to a worker trapped up a flagpole on the roof of a building at 385 Jay Street. The worker had been placing a new rope into the pulley at the top of the flagpole on the roof of a theater when he slipped and ended up hanging upside down screaming for help. Rescue 2 arrived, and a ladder was placed on the slanted theatre roof and leaned into the pole. Donovan ascended the ladder carrying a length of rope. Reaching the inverted man, he tied the free end around the worker and supported his weight on the ladder as he cut the foot strap and righted the man. They both carefully climbed down the ladder to the roof.

The following June, Fireman Richard Donovan found himself on the steps of City Hall. Mayor Fiorello LaGuardia was about to make FDNY history that centered around Richard Donovan. The FDNY Board of Merit had conferred Class I awards to both of Donovan's rescues. For his flagpole rescue he was presented the Brooklyn Citizen's and Department medals for "the most deserving fireman in the Brooklyn Fire Department." For his fire rescue on Cranberry Street, he was presented the Kenny and Department medals. This was the first time in FDNY history a member had been awarded separate medals for multiple rescues in the same year. (In 1913, Fireman James G. Brown of Hook & Ladder 1, was awarded two separate Class I awards for his actions at the Equitable fire in 1912. He was presented the Bonner and Department medals with a footnote in the medal daybook about the second award.)

Rescue 2 responded to a reported crash of two empty IND (Independent Subway System) subway trains in the tunnel under Ninth Street just east of Fifth Avenue on February 17, 1936. It was 9:20 a.m. and both trains were travelling at high speeds. The force of the crash was so strong it rocked the buildings on the street above. The responding rescuers were faced with the motorman of the second train entangled in the wreckage.

Lt. William Barry and Fireman Richard Donovan had to crawl inside the telescoped train cars to reach the pinned man. Together they worked and hour and 20 minutes in a very cramped space using a variety of hand tools, jacks, wedges and a torch to cut the man free. A hose stream was used to extinguish their clothing during the torch operation. Sadly, the motorman died as a result of his injuries.

Richard J. Donovan was promoted to lieutenant on May 1, 1937, and was assigned to Hook & Ladder 131 located on Lorraine Street in Brooklyn. Both Donovan and Lt. Barry were placed on the Roll of Merit with Class I awards for their extremely dangerous rescue efforts at the train crash (Barry had also received a Class I award for a fire rescue the same year.) Both men were on the steps of City Hall on June 2, 1937, and were decorated by Mayor LaGuardia. Lt. Richard Donovan now wore five medals on his uniform.

On July 1, 1937, Lt. Donovan was transferred back to Rescue 2. He remained in Brooklyn until March 1, 1938, when he was transferred to Rescue 1 in Manhattan. Donovan transferred to Engine Company 250 on December 16, 1942, and worked there until he retired on February 2, 1943. He enjoyed nearly 40 years of retirement before he passed away on January 28, 1983.

Three Tough Months

The first weekend of 1958 started off with a frosty bang as the temperatures in New York City, driven by strong winds, plunged to 11 degrees on January 3rd. As the citizens huddled for warmth, FDNY firefighters were hard pressed as a series of difficult and dangerous fires began sweeping the city. Seven major fires, including a borough call, occurred in a five-hour period. The worst job was a seven-alarm fire in a large four-story building at Bedford and Halsey Streets in Brooklyn. This fire drove over 200 families out into the freezing cold.

There were also two second alarm and one fourth alarm fires in Manhattan, including a basement fire in a warehouse on East Second Street. The building's contents included paintings by American artists, being stored prior to their showing in a Madison Square Garden exhibit. A vacant building fire on Pearl Street would require four alarms to bring under control.

It was looking like a difficult year for the FDNY.

Alarm bells began ringing at 6:23 p.m. on Friday, February 14th for a blaze in a six-story loft building at 137 Wooster Street, in Hell's Hundred Acres. (The area of lower Manhattan above Chambers Street, the Bowery on the east, West Broadway on the west and West 8th Street on the north, acquired this nickname because of the horrible toll it took on firemen and civilians, in the days before breathing protection for firefighters and stricter fire laws and sprinklers were mandated.)

Three floors of the 80 x 100-foot, 100-year-old six-story loft building were being used as a warehouse by a paper and twine company. This occupancy contained not only heavy machinery, but large bales of paper and huge rolls of twine weighing 800 pounds a roll. The building was constructed with cast iron columns on the lower floors supporting heavy timber, wood columns and wood girders on the upper floors. Shortly after 6 p.m., employees went to investigate the sound of breaking glass. They discovered that flames from a fire on the first floor were extending up a shaft and spreading fire to every floor in the building. At 6:23 p.m. fire dispatchers received the alarm for Manhattan Box 334 and assigned Engine Companies 13, 30, 33, 55 and Ladder Companies 20, 9, Rescue Company 1 and Battalions 4 and 2, and Division 1. Fire Patrol 2 was also sent. (The Fire Patrol was created by the New York Board of Fire Underwriters and was tasked with loss prevention within the insured properties.)

Upon arrival, fire companies found flames on the upper floors with a very heavy smoke condition. Despite the biting cold and winds gusting over 20 mph, the firefighting commenced. Four members of Fire Patrol 2, under the command of Captain John Mullin, the first unit to arrive, entered the building and began operating on the fifth floor. Only moments later, FDNY members arrived. Captain Thomas McGrath of Ladder 20 had his aerial placed to the roof of the fire building, then he and his crew ascended to the roof with axes and began to ventilate. (Historical note: This was prior to Ladders 3 and other official FDNY SOPs. Individual companies had their own procedures for specific building types. This was also prior to the utilization of power saws and portable radios.)

Engine 13 arrived, took a hydrant and prepared to stretch a 2½-inch hose line to the fifth floor. Fire Patrol 1 also arrived and went to the fifth floor with tarps to back up Fire Patrol 2. The chief of the First Division, Deputy Chief Mitchitsch, arrived and special-called Ladder 1, then a minute later, at 6:35

p.m. transmitted a second alarm.

On the roof, Ladder 20's axes were swinging, and hooks were bashing as the vertical ventilation continued. Suddenly, a loud rumbling was heard, and the building began to collapse beneath their feet. Captain McGrath and another fireman dove for the windows of the eight-story building next door (Exposure 4.) McGrath managed to grab a window ledge and held on, as the roof vanished below him. He dangled there briefly until other firemen were able to pull him to safety. Two members, Fireman Second Grade Bernard Blumenthal of Ladder 20, three years on the job and married three weeks earlier, and Fireman William Schmid of Ladder 1, a 20-year veteran (detailed to Ladder 20 for the night tour), disappeared into the collapse.

Inside the building the sounds of the collapse grew. On the third floor Fire Patrolman Joseph Devine from Patrol 2 was throwing waterproof tarps when he heard the rumbling sounds above. He quickly moved to a sidewall as the floor above dropped down. He and a fireman were able to find a void and crawled ten feet to a stairway.

On the fifth floor, Sargent Michael McGee, and Fire Patrolmen Louis Brusati, James Devine, and Michael Tracy had nowhere to escape. The collapsing roof and floors plummeted downwards. The sounds of men screaming were added to the noise of the collapse.

At 8:36, DC Mitchitsch ordered a third alarm. Fourth and fifth alarms quickly followed.

The members were now faced with a major building collapse in danger of further collapse. The heavy front exterior wall was very unstable and the ice-encrusted water tank on the roof was sitting upon steel beams that rested on the rear and one of the side bearing walls. To compound the danger, a heavy smoke condition enshrouded the entire area, as flames broke through the three-story rubble pile. Despite the dangers firefighters began a feverish search, digging in the rubble, searching for their trapped comrades.

To complicate the situation further, temperatures were dropping into the single digits as snow and gusting winds buffeted the fire scene. By 8 p.m. ice was building and adding tremendous weight upon the already unstable exterior walls. Rescue teams were trimmed to small groups as chief officers assessed the potential for additional collapses. A thawing apparatus was special-called to help with the rescue effort. These special rigs, first placed in service in 1934, contained steam generators. Onboard water tanks fed the generator and live steam was delivered through special hoses.

Despite the work of the thawing apparatus, ice continued coating firemen and their apparatus. Fully aware of possible additional collapses, a collapse zone was set up around the exterior of the building. At 8:15, the rear wall collapsed further covering the area with chunks of flying brick and ice.

Two hundred firemen scoured the rubble pile trying to find any sign of life. Voids were entered and checked. The dangerous search continued until 11:55 when shouts echoed across the debris pile. A buried fireman had been found. A priest was rushed to the location as the digging continued. Fireman William Schmid was quickly and carefully removed from the hot debris and rushed to Bellevue Hospital where he was pronounced dead.

Three minutes later shouts again echoed as a second fireman was uncovered. A chaplain was again brought to the location. Fr. Bernard Blumenthal was removed and taken to St. Vincent's Hospital. Sadly, he only remained alive for a few minutes.

The searching and digging went on for hour after freezing hour. The on-duty firefighters had reached the limits of their endurance. Temperatures had tumbled into the single digits and nine inches of fresh snow covered the city. By 2:30 in the morning it was time to take a different course of action. For the first time in FDNY history Acting Chief of Department Arthur Massett and Fire Commissioner Edward Cavanagh put a call out on the department radio requesting volunteers to respond and help with the rescue work. Five hundred off-duty members responded to the scene.

A huge crane with a wrecking ball was positioned and the unstable front wall was removed. The search was renewed with vigor. Pavement breakers were used to breach a cellar wall as more rubble was removed by hand. This grueling search would continue for days.

About 24 hours after the Wooster Street alarm was received, another fire broke out in a storage shed behind 42 Avenue C. The alarm, received at 5:45, was blazing out of control as FDNY units pulled up. Flames driven by strong winds were rapidly extending from the shed to two tenements and a nearby loft building. The smoke and fire drove 150 tenants into the frigid snowy streets. Six people would require medical attention.

Arriving fire companies, most of whom had been operating at the Wooster Street fire and collapse, were greeted by heavy fire on the top two floors and through the roof of a six-story tenement at 308 East Fourth Street and a total of four-alarms would be transmitted. Exhausted firemen raised their aerial ladders and plucked people from windows as others were helped down the fire escapes.

Back at the Wooster Street job, conditions were becoming more dangerous by the minute as ice began to build up on the building and the rubble pile. Large bales of paper and twine, drenched by hose streams were solidifying into icebergs making the search even more treacherous. As firemen worked through the debris pile searching for the missing members of the Fire Patrol, 25 other firemen were battling the deep-seated fire in the basement of the building.

On Monday night, the bodies of Patrolman James Devine and Michael Tracy were recovered. The following day, Sargent Michael McGee and Patrolman Louis Brusati were located and removed.

Three blocks from the Wooster Street fire and collapse, stood a five-story loft building at 623 Broadway. The 77-year-old-building ran through to Mercer Street and housed a textile printing plant of the SGS Printing Company on the third floor. It was late on the afternoon of March 19, 1958, a chilly and dreary day in New York City. An intermittent rain was falling on Lower Broadway, as 66 persons were busy working inside the loft building. On the third floor a worker lit a textile drying oven. Used to cure the newly-printed designs on various fabrics, the 10-foot-high, 8-foot-wide and 10-foot-deep oven stood in the third-floor workroom.

Suddenly, flames roared from the oven and nearby workers quickly attempted to extinguish the fire as they had successfully done two months earlier when a similar fire occurred. As workers tried to douse the flames a tremendous explosion rocked the building plunging it into a smoke-filled darkness. Three employees on the third floor were able to escape as did those working on the floors below. Those working above however, were left in dire straits. On the fourth floor, 39 people were working at the Monarch Underwear Company, sewing, printing and operating drying machines. The open floor quickly filled with dense, hot smoke causing the workers to panic. Unable to find exits, many huddled under work benches, others tried to flee down the stairs. Several people were so frantic they hung from the windows to escape the searing heat and smoke.

Manhattan Box 341 was transmitted sending Engines 13, 30, and 33 along with Ladder Company 20 and 9. Also responding were Battalions 2 and 5 and Division 1. Ladder 20 arrived on scene first. Faced with jumpers down, and others screaming for help from the windows above, members quickly spread their life net and caught several jumpers. With the windows above obscured by heavy smoke, some jumpers missed the net and crashed onto the sidewalk below. As they carefully caught one young woman, another crashed down on top of her and toppled several firemen.

Upon arrival, Ladder 9, the second due ladder company, found heavy fire on the third floor of the loft building and thick clouds of smoke pumping from the upper floors. Lt. Kelley and Fr. Re started up the inside stairs to the third floor where they found an open door. Heavy fire was raging in the high-ceilinged room and was extending toward their position. They donned all-service masks (filter breathing masks) and attempted to close the door but could not completely close the jammed open door. Despite knowing the fire was extending toward them, they ascended the stairs and began a search of the fourth floor. During their search Fr. Re found a woman in a state of panic. He picked her up and headed back toward the stairs. In her excitement she tore the mask from his face. Undeterred he headed down the stairs. At the third floor, the hallway lit up, forcing Re to run with the woman past the flames. He carried her safely to the street.

While Re was negotiating the flames in the stairway, Lt Kelley found a second woman lying on the floor. He picked her up and then hearing the voices of other trapped civilians, he shouted to them to follow him to the street. With the woman on his shoulder, he held his flashlight pointing backwards on his other shoulder to guide the civilians. They were all brought safely to the street.

Both Lt. Kelley and Fr. Re were placed on the Roll of Merit with Class I awards. They would also receive medals for their heroic efforts. Six other members received Class III awards and a dozen received Class As.

When the flames were finally brought under control a secondary search was conducted. Ten people were found dead huddled beneath the worktables on the fourth floor. Sadly, in all, 24 persons were killed in this tragic fire. This fire, like the Triangle Fire in 1911, helped gain safety improvements for workers. Eight fire prevention laws were passed as a result of the fire.

Like the old loft building downtown, the more modern buildings being constructed in the city were also proving to be dangerous places to work when fires broke out. On April 15, 1958, a half-million-dollar project updating the building's air conditioning was underway in the Museum of Modern Art on West 53rd Street. Other teams of workers were painting and repairing nearby areas. Inside the museum were 60 workers, in addition to the 225 members of the MoMA staff. When the crews stopped for a smoke break, a drop cloth caught fire, igniting several open paint cans. A plasterer on his way to lunch saw the flames and together with a museum security guard attempted to fight the fire with extinguishers.

Heavy smoke pumping from the area quickly reached the stairs and began filling the upper floors with smoke. At 12:25 that afternoon the FDNY was called and responded to the scene. Inside the six-story white marble and glass building people were scrambling for their lives. People on the upper floors fled the smoke and took refuge on the roof of the museum. Others made their way to windows and shouted for help to the arriving firemen below.

With cries for help echoing in the street below, members placed an aerial ladder into position and were able to pluck two women from the sixth floor. Inside members of the Fire Patrol covered about 40 pieces of sculpture with tarps for protection. Engine company crews hustled in the street to feed the museum's standpipe system. Connections from hydrants to pumpers, and pumpers to the standpipe Siamese were made and water was pumped into the system. Unknown to the firefighting force, workers had disconnected large sections of the standpipe system to relocate some pipes. Thousands of gallons of water chugged from the open pipes on the sixth floor, cascaded across the floors and flowed down the stairs only adding more problems to the preservation and safeguarding of the valuable art inside the smoke-filled building.

Members of the hook and ladder companies began the difficult task of venting the smoke. Teams worked across the front of the building breaking windows to allow the smoke to escape. The museum featured five rows of large glass windows with a total of 31 panes on each row. In all firemen broke 62 panes of this glass.

Wave after wave of firemen entered the building, searching for the fire and trying to locate any victims of the noxious smoke. Despite using filter-masks, 28 firemen required medical aid, mostly for the debilitating effects of the smoke. Sixteen firemen were taken to Bellevue Hospital for additional treatment. Sadly, one worker, an electrician was found face down in six inches of water in the rear of the third floor. He had been killed by the dense smoke. Three women visiting the museum at the time of the fire also received treatment at the scene for smoke inhalation.

Amazingly only six paintings out of 11,000 art objects were destroyed or damaged. The two most severely damaged were water lily paintings by the French impressionist painter Claude Monet. Damages were estimated at just under $300,000.

During 1958 the number of alarms exceeded the number of fires by more than 23,000. This was a trend that would continue as false alarms were becoming an epidemic. Nine firemen lost their lives in the line of duty during the year. Four members of the Fire Patrol also lost their lives in the line of duty.

Fireground Medical Care

The New York City Fire Department has always utilized an aggressive interior attack as their primary firefighting tactic. This often took its toll on the firemen, who had no real breathing protection. The department did try various smoke helmets and breathing devices, but they proved unreliable or too complicated and expensive for widespread use within the department. (Rescue companies did utilized Draeger smoke helmets and a variety of different types of filter masks but even they mostly operated without breathing protection.) This of course would result in fire operations with numerous firemen overcome by noxious smoke or gases. My grandfather once told me you could tell how bad a fire was by how many firemen were unconscious on the sidewalk.

To put things into sharper perspective, modern emergency medicine can be traced back to the Civil War when a systematic approach to mass trauma was begun. The first public ambulance in New York City was begun in 1869 by Bellevue Hospital. This horse-drawn ambulance would arrive on scene equipped with a driver, an intern (typically a new doctor fresh out of school) and a quart of emergency brandy for each patient. The ambulance also carried two tourniquets, a half-dozen bandages, a half-dozen small sponges, splinting material, and pieces of old blankets for padding. There were two ambulances the first year, with five more added the following year.

The FDNY, in business since 1865, purchased their first ambulance in 1906. But it was for injured or sick horses! The first ambulance for injured firemen was purchased in 1923. (Some sources say an ambulance was bought in 1914 but I cannot find any evidence of its use in department records or newspaper accounts of the time.)

To fill the huge gap in medical care on the fireground Doctor Harry Archer, who'd attended Bellevue Medical College in 1894 and served as an ambulance surgeon, took matters into his own hands. Archer began his lifelong voluntary work with the FDNY after working on injured firemen from his Bellevue ambulance. He then began responding to fires and treating injured firemen and civilians on his off-hours. In 1907 Fire Commissioner Lantry appointed Archer an honorary medical officer for the boroughs of Manhattan and the Bronx, with the rank of battalion chief, without compensation.

In 1921 Archer purchased a bright red touring car and outfitted it for his specific needs. It looked like a pleasure car when it rolled by, but it was more like a hospital on wheels. The vehicle was divided into dust and moisture-proof compartments. Fully stocked with splints, surgical needles, and sutures for bad cuts and gashes. Cotton gauze, antiseptics, forceps, lancets and an oxygen machine. (The medical use of oxygen became common around 1917, but more on that later.)

According to a 1921 article about Doctor Archer and his automobile in *Popular Science Monthly* magazine,

> When oxygen was gaining prominence as a restorative agent in the treatment of partial suffocation, Dr. Archer found it successful. But he saw himself in a situation where the purest, freshest oxygen would be needed, and he realized that it might not be possible to get a tankful instantly.
>
> Forthwith the doctor provided himself with an oxygen generator and the chemical necessary to manufacture the gas. He had a special compartment fitted into the automobile, and in it stored his generator and the

chemical—sulphite of soda. Water poured on the sulphite of soda generates the oxygen.

At this time Dr. Archer was also using what was then a state-of-the-art medical technique of spraying melted paraffin wax on burns. This treatment began during World War I and gained some popularity. This machine was also stored in a compartment in his automobile. There was also a store of blankets, army cots, and a pulmotor for artificial resuscitation. (The pulmotor patent was awarded to Johann Heinrich Drager in 1907. This machine operated by pressurized oxygen provided alternating positive and negative pressure ventilation on a patient. This was the first portable resuscitation device accepted worldwide.)

Doctor Archer and the members of Rescue 1 were renowned for their effective use of the pulmotor in saving the lives of firefighters and civilians who'd been overcome by smoke and gases. This was long before the popular use of these devices by ambulance and hospital staffs.

In 1923, Honorary Chiefs William and Edward Kenny (their father had been an FDNY battalion chief) donated a new Cadillac ambulance to the FDNY. Designed in part by Doctor Archer, the rig designated as Ambulance 1, was housed in the quarters of Engine Company 56 on West 83rd Street. Ambulance 1 went into service on February 1, 1923.

It was 6:45 on the evening of February 29, 1924, when a police officer noticed smoke coming up through a cellar grate at 59 Reade Street. Closer inspection showed smoke inside the first-floor shoe store, so the officer ran to the corner fire alarm box and pulled the handle. Within minutes fire companies rolled in and went to work.

Leading the attack, Deputy Chief James Heffernan and his men crashed through the front doors and plunged into the thick smoke and descended into the cellar. The men had no sooner begun their work when a backdraft occurred, toppling the men and leaving several unconscious. These men were carried outside, and fresh men took their places. Within minutes these new men began to fall over unconscious. The chief realized at the rate the men were dropping he was woefully undermanned and ordered a second alarm. This brought Chief John Kenlon and numerous additional units. Fresh men moved in and found the flames extending to the first floor prompting Kenlon to send in a third alarm.

Meanwhile Doctor Archer responded from home to the quarters of Engine 56, where the new department ambulance was stationed. Archer and his department driver quickly covered the six-mile trip and arrived at the scene. At first Archer set up his usual sidewalk aid station, but quickly realized he was receiving too many patients. He told Kenlon he needed help, so requests were sent to hospitals at Broad Street, Beekman Street and Gouverneur Hospitals. Five ambulance doctors and several nurses arrived and reported to Archer.

As he was planning where to set up the new location of operations, the owner of the store next to the fire building stepped up and offered his store. Archer and his team moved in and set up shop. The floor was lined with blankets that were soon filled with unconscious firemen. Archer had his work cut out for him as he watched fireman after fireman get revived only to go back inside the smoke-filled fire building and get knocked out again. One man, Captain O'Toole of Engine Company 27 had been rendered unconscious three times, finally Archer ordered him to Beekman Hospital.

Conditions were becoming extreme, as the smoke continued to knock out man after man. Captain Walter Lamb of Rescue 1 had just carried out his eighth unconscious fireman when he too slumped to the ground. An ambulance doctor reported to Archer he thought Lamb's condition to be critical. Archer ordered that both Lamb and Battalion Chief Daniel Cavanagh (who'd been knocked out and revived four times already) be rushed to Gouverneur Hospital.

Meanwhile the subcellar was filling with water from the attack lines and had reached the waists of those working there. Now added to the danger of the smoke and gases was the real possibility of drowning. By 9:30 the fire was darkening down, and things were calming down in the make-shift field hospital.

In all, more than 40 firemen, including Chief Kenlon had been rendered unconscious at least once, several had been rendered unconscious multiple times. Six were taken to nearby hospitals for further treatment. The new ambulance and the equipment stocked by Doctor Archer proved to be invaluable. The idea of a field hospital was proving workable, at least for the time being. Firemen getting knocked out by the smoke was a problem as old as firefighting and would not become better until decades later when self-contained breathing gear worked its way into the fire service after World War II.

The addition of the new Cadillac ambulance had a special effect on one fireman in particular. Fireman John J. Delaney joined the FDNY on April 4, 1913, and was assigned to Engine 56. When the new ambulance was stationed at 56 Engine, Fireman Frank Boylan was detailed as chauffeur until August 1, 1924. From that date on Fireman John Delaney was detailed as chauffeur. He took this new position very seriously and made a study of all the facets of emergency medicine relating to firemen. This field was still growing, and Delaney quickly became an important part of the FDNY medical corps.

The Irish American fireman had what is called the "gift of gab." Working with Doctor Archer, Delaney became a resuscitation expert. A valued member of the International Association of Police and Fire Surgeons, Delaney became well known across the country for his knowledge and inventiveness. Doctor Archer said of Delaney just after he retired,

> Few laymen had a better practical knowledge of first aid. He knew all the antidotes that a fireman might need in the work of fire extinguishment. In resuscitation he could do as well as any doctor…He could write a report as well as any doctor for he had a thorough knowledge of medical terms. A splendid fellow has left us.

Delaney was known for his patient care and medical skills, but also for his inventions. He invented a lignum vitae jaw wedge (a wooden wedge apparently used to pry open an unconscious person's mouth) that was adopted by all inhalator manufacturers. Delaney also designed flexible body carrying splints that were used by many fire departments. He also modified the existing leg splint that had many advantages over the previous model.

After surviving a serious operation, John Delaney retired from the FDNY on August 9, 1939.

In 1937 the FDNY put on a "thrill show" at Madison Square Garden called the Midnight Alarm. Held on the nights of November 23rd and December 21st, the proceeds of the show were used to purchase a 1938 Cadillac ambulance. This new rig went into service on January 5, 1938, in the quarters of Rescue 2 at 365 Jay Street in Brooklyn. Department orders detailed three members of Rescue 2 to the ambulance and advised the three firemen they would work in accordance with the three-platoon system.

In 1948 the FDNY revamped their medical division to include: Medical Unit, Dental Unit, X-Ray Unit, Oxygen Therapy Unit, Office of Surgical Assistance Unit and Blood Donor Service. The Medical Bureau was located at 278 Spring Street, Manhattan.

January 26, 1948, saw the introduction of the FDNY Oxygen Therapy Unit, a 1948 International panel truck that was placed in service in the quarters of Engine Company 30. The following year the Uniformed Officers Association purchased a White Motor Company van that was modified in the department shops and became the new apparatus of the Oxygen Therapy Unit.

The idea of using oxygen to counteract the effects of smoke and gases is relatively new. Oxygen was first discovered in 1772, by a Swedish chemist named Carl Wilhelm Sheele who obtained the gas by heating substances like potassium nitrate or mercuric oxide. The English chemist Joseph Priestly independently discovered oxygen in 1774 using a different method. The first cylinders for storing oxygen were developed in 1868, and by 1885 oxygen was being used in acute care of patients.

By 1917 the medical use of oxygen became widespread as a hospital treatment. As mentioned earlier the invention of the pulmotor in 1907, was the first mechanical resuscitator used outside of a hospital setting. It was designed to automatically deliver gas (oxygen) or air at specific volumes. It was used to resuscitate victims of mine disasters, as well as victims of smoke inhalation, drowning and electrical shock.

New York, however, appeared to be slow in accepting the new device. In 1912, there was only one device in the entire city. It was at the Rockefeller Institute and was only used in research and was never seen in public. (Chicago police and fire departments already had three pulmotors.) A pulmotor arrived at the Grand Central Palace in New York City as a part of the United States government's exhibit in the electrical exposition and automobile show. (The Grand Central Palace was a 13-story Beaux-Arts style structure located on Lexington Avenue near Grand Central Station. It was the city's main exhibition hall from 1911 until 1953.) This year's event also featured a luncheon in honor of Thomas Edison, who inspected thousands of electrical appliances, most of which owed their origin to his genius. The pulmotor, billed as a new lifesaving device, was demonstrated at the show.

By November of 1912, the Consolidated Gas Company (which later became Con Edison), notified all the city hospitals that their emergency automobiles, equipped with pulmotors for resuscitating persons overcome by gases, smoke, or electrical shock, were available to any physicians who wished to use them. In 1914, the FDNY purchased and distributed pulmotors to select fire companies.

FDNY Special Order No. 10, dated January 18, 1915, stated: By direction of the Fire Commissioner Rescue Company No. 1, to consist of one captain, one lieutenant and eight men, is hereby organized, to be located at No. 42 Great Jones Street, Manhattan, equipped with the following apparatus: smoke helmets, oxygen tanks, pulmotors, lungmotors, lifelines, gun, etc. (The lungmotor was like the pulmotor but was manually pumped.)

It further stated they were to report for a period of instruction. This turned out to be 36 days of specialized training. Each man would learn how take apart and reassemble all their important tools, especially the smoke helmets and the pulmotors.

The introduction of the Rescue Company, coupled with the gas company's pulmotor squads, and many of the city's hospitals also being equipped with pulmotors, made the response to mass casualty incidents more effective. This was further expanded with the organization of Brooklyn's Rescue Company 2 in 1925 and the establishment of police emergency squads in 1928.

In 1929, the Department of Hospitals was created and unified New York City's municipal hospital systems. This meant there were 45 hospital-based ambulances now available in the city. Each of the hospitals had their own rules, and the patients were usually brought to the hospital where the ambulance was stationed. By the end of the 1930s city ambulance drivers only drove, they had no patient care responsibilities.

On February 1, 1938, the Department Orders included an amendment to the FDNY Official Action Guide regarding Ambulance 2.

> Section 8-1. Medical Officers assigned to Ambulance Duty with the Department Ambulance No. 2, shall keep themselves informed of all alarms and emergency calls for said ambulance. They shall promptly respond to such alarms and calls, take full command of said ambulance and assume full responsibility in connection therewith.
>
> Whenever any equipment or supplies of said ambulance are used, they shall see that all equipment is in proper order and that a sufficient amount of supplies are on hand for a subsequent call.

It is interesting to note that in 1938 New York City traffic regulations were adopted to provide emergency vehicles with the right-of-way. Fire apparatus, police department vehicles, public or private ambulances responding to or carrying injured or sick for treatment, prison vans, vehicles carrying the United States Mail, and only in cases of emergency vehicles of water, gas and electric public service corporations. Another interesting note is information contained in Department Special Oder No. 57 dated March 12, 1942:

> II. The attention of all Officers in command at fires or other emergency is directed to the fact that interns no longer respond to calls with ambulances from hospitals solely maintained by the City.
>
> This fact shall be carefully considered when sending for medical assistance. Where necessary, dispatcher shall

be requested to send for the nearest public ambulance, the department medical officer on duty with the medical service car, and where the need is apparent a special call for a department ambulance.

It also mentioned whenever the services of a physician could be obtained before a department ambulance arrived, to be guided by his advice regarding the need for hospitalization.

By 1948 public pressure forced the public hospitals to re-assign interns to the majority of ambulance calls. (This continued until 1962 when the cost of insurance for the responding doctors made the Department of Health replace the Interns with "ambulance attendants," who later were better trained and called ambulance technicians.)

In 1949, the FDNY received an ultra-modern ambulance. The 33-foot-long mobile hospital was built by the Flxible Coach Company of Louderville, Ohio. This company manufactured motorcycle sidecars, funeral cars, ambulances, intercity coaches and transit buses. This huge vehicle was the brainchild of Doctor Harry Archer, and contained features that he and members of the medical division knew from experience would be needed to give complete care and comfort to the injured.

The new ambulance was equipped with an independent electrical system. Powered by an onboard 110-volt generator that was driven by a 4-cylinder gasoline engine. The system could also be powered by any outside 110-volt source. This power system supplied current to lights, a sterilizer, a hot water generator, and heating pads. The ambulance was also warmed, when necessary, by a hot water heater hooked up to the unit's motor and by a gasoline heater.

It also contained four lower adjustable beds, with an oxygen outlet at each bed, and two upper litters. The oxygen system was designed by Fireman John Bresnan of Engine 56, who was also assigned to the unit. (He was the grandson of the famed battalion chief, who died in the line of duty in a building collapse in 1894. Chief Bresnan designed the distributor nozzle that bears his name.) The built-in system could supply 48 hours of continuous oxygen. In addition, 20 portable inhalators each with a 20-minute supply were also carried.

The ambulance also carried 28 cots, 6 stretchers and a supply of medications. The white baked enamel interior was kept hospital clean. Archer could now see a day when unconscious firemen wouldn't be lined up on the concrete sidewalk, but rather in a clean, hospital-like protected setting.

The new ambulance made its public debut on June 8, 1949, at the City Hall medal day ceremony. Mayor William O'Dwyer said the new ambulance was "the most modern and finest possessed by any fire department in the world." The new ambulance was purchased by the department's Honor Emergency Fund, for $16,000. Ambulance 1, now officially "in-service" responded from the ceremony to a third alarm at 131st Street and the Hudson River. Two firemen injured while operating at this blaze were Doctor Archer's first patients.

As the ambulance service improved, the methods employed by doctors, firemen and other responders did as well. Starting around 1910, the Shafer Method became popular. This "prone-pressure" method was accomplished when the patient was laid face down and compression applied to the middle of the back. This expelled air from the lungs, upon release of pressure, air would return to the lungs. The Silvester method was also used, and required the patient to be placed face up, with the shoulders elevated to allow the head to drop backwards. The rescuer then knelt at the victim's head and lifted the patient's arms and crossed them over the patient's lower chest.

Beginning in 1944, the Eve Method was used, this featured

a portable apparatus like a seesaw. The cot-like device was set up and the patient was placed face down on the board with their arms extended overhead (arms and legs are secured to prevent slipping). The board is placed over a metal horse (fulcrum) and gently rocked back and forth. About ten double rocks per minute were required. The idea was the weight of the abdominal organs would alternately push and pull the diaphragm up and down like a piston. Rescue 2 carried this apparatus for many years.

By 1957 the United States military had adopted mouth-to-mouth resuscitation. Three years later chest compressions were added, beginning what would become known as CPR. The American Heart Association formally endorsed CPR in 1963. New York City initiated the 9-1-1 emergency telephone system in 1968. (England started their 999 number for emergencies in London back in 1937!) In 1970 federal regulations formalized standards and requirements for Emergency Medical Technicians. In New York City, firemen began taking the classes on their own time at their own expense. By 1977 there were 1,000 members of the uniformed force responding to fires and emergencies who were certified EMTs.

The New York State legislature replaced the Department of Hospitals with a public service corporation and ambulance services then were coordinated by the newly-formed Division of Emergency Medical Services of the New York City Health and Hospital Corporation.

In 1975, the American Medical Association recognized the specialty of Emergency Medicine (for medical doctors). They also recognized the title of paramedic the same year.

Starting in 1994, engine companies in the 11th Division went on-line as Certified First Responders-Defibrillator. This started a city-wide program that took two and a half years to complete. Then on March 17, 1996, the Bureau of Emergency

Medical Service was established in the FDNY. This new bureau assumed the resources of the Emergency Medical Services previously operated by the New York Health and Hospitals Corporation. This transformed the mission of the FDNY that previously was almost solely dedicated to firefighting. It was now an agency that provided fire protection and emergency medical response around the clock for all New Yorkers. FDNY members now respond to 1.6 million medical emergencies and more than 300,000 fires and non-fire related emergencies per year.

In December of 2006, the U.S. Food & Drug Administration (FDA) approved the Cyanokit (hydroxocobalamin for injection), for the treatment of known or suspected cyanide poisoning. This was the first cyanide antidote to be approved in the United States in several decades. (The Cyanokit had been used in France for more than ten years prior in both pre-hospital and hospital settings to treat cyanide poisoning resulting from smoke inhalation.) Despite this use in Europe, recognition of cyanide exposure in the smoke generated in structure fires has only recently become widespread in the United States.

Fire smoke is a common source of cyanide (CN) exposure and can be produced by the incomplete combustion of any materials containing nitrogen, including common synthetic or plastic materials. It can also be produced by the burning of natural materials like wood, paper, wool or silk. In fires the toxic fumes are released in gaseous form and maybe inhaled by occupants or responding firefighters. In fact, CN poisoning and carbon monoxide (CO) poisoning most often occur together during a fire. These poisons have become recognized as the "Toxic Twins" of smoke inhalation. With the proliferation of plastics and synthetic polymer building materials, the risk of CN poisoning in victims of structural fires has increased.

Children, the elderly, people with cardiac or respiratory conditions and firefighters are at the greatest risk.

Even though CN poisoning in smoke inhalation has been known since the 1960s, the ability to measure it on scene has been lacking. Based in part by the protocols developed in France, the U.S. has adopted the protocol that CN poisoning should be considered in any patient removed from an enclosed-space fire scene who has soot in the nose, mouth or throat or sputum; or has any alteration in the levels of consciousness. Administration of a CN-antidote is indicated.

In fire smoke, HCN (hydrogen cyanide) can be up to 35 times more toxic than carbon monoxide. Studies proved CN was found at toxic to lethal levels in the blood of 33 to 87 percent of fire fatalities. First responders can no longer assume CO is the only toxicant requiring treatment. Times have changed.

On Sunday, January 9, 2022, Bronx FDNY units responded to a fire in a 19-story high-rise residential building on East 181 Street. The fire would expand to five-alarms, as members made rescue after rescue from the deadly smoke-filled building. Sparked by a space heater, the clouds of thick smoke filled the huge structure, spreading easily with the failure of several self-closing doors. The door to the fire apartment 3N remained open as did two third-floor stairwell doors. In all, 17 people were killed including eight children.

Amazingly, FDNY paramedics and EMTs treated 28 critical patients. Twenty of those patients received the Cyanokit treatment. Nine of those patients survived, including two who were initially in cardiac arrest.

The medical treatment provided to the members of the New York City Fire Department had come a long way since the beginning of the paid department in 1865. Injured members now received treatment or transport in modern heated or air-conditioned ambulances. Onboard telemetry now sends vital signs to emergency room doctors in real time. Every engine company is equipped and staffed to provide emergency medical care to medical patients, accident and fire victims, and their brother and sister firefighters. Members are trained as Certified First Responders-Defibrillator, now included as part of the FDNYs Probationary Firefighters training course. (On December 23, 1994, engine companies in Division 11 went online as CFR-D companies. This was the start of a city-wide program that took two and a half years to implement fully.)

Gone are the days when dozens of unconscious firemen were laid out on sidewalks. Pulmotors and bottles of milk as smoke inhalation treatment have given way to light-weight resuscitators and paramedics administering Cyanokits.

The job of the firefighter has always been dangerous.

Fire Departments still struggle to keep up with rapidly changing architecture, science, medicine and manufacturing. The peril faced by the improper storage of gasoline when autos were new in the early 1900s, has morphed into the volatile world of Lithium-ion battery fires in both commercial and residential buildings firefighters are facing today. Training, and situational awareness have always been key components of firefighting.

One bit of old-time wisdom still rings true — Stay Low!

Acknowledgments

The stories contained in this book are taken from documented sources such as of New York City Fire Department Medal Day Books, Minutes of the Board of Merit meetings, Department Orders, and other FDNY publications, as well as the many newspapers and magazines in print at the time. The Library of Congress online newspaper archives have opened the nation's reported history to anyone willing to dig through the years of information. Several books were also very useful for this and other projects: *Wheels of the Bravest*, by John A. Calderone and Jack Lerch published by Fire Apparatus Journal in 1984; *The Last Alarm*, by Michael Boucher, Gary Urbanowicz, and Fred Melahn, 2006; *Our Fireman*, by A.E. Costello, 1887.

The intention of the author is not to make it appear as if the only people who made rescues or performed heroic acts are the firefighters written about in this book. The work of those mentioned, was supported by many dedicated firefighters who never get specific mention.

I'd like to thank those who have helped me with my research:

First and foremost is the staff at the FDNY Mand Library. The late Honorary Chief of Department Jack Lerch. Jack was always a friend and a trusted resource. His knowledge and enthusiasm will be greatly missed.

Also from the library crew, Dan Maye, Fred Melahn and John Paulson have been very generous with their time, help and enthusiasm.

Working on various projects over the years has helped me build an impressive personal fire library of reports, stories, scrapbooks, books and photos. Those that have contributed information include, Herb Eysser FDNY Dispatcher 124 (retired), Jack Calderone (a true wealth of historical information and a guy who's been there, done that!), Bill Noonan, Gary Urbanowicz, Paul Wormsley, Paul Geidel, Ray Pfeifer, Dennis Whittan, Frank Sutphin, Tom Donnelly, David Handschuh, Bill Bennett, Fred Kopf, Danny Alfonso, Ed Pospisil, Ed Sere, Vincent Dunn and Peter Micheels. Special thanks to Lt. Nick Graziano, FDNY, Capt. Jack Cassidy FDNY Medal Desk, Captain John Cerillo Rescue Co. 1 and Lieutenant Justin Enzmann who help me stay current in the ever-changing world of firefighting.

Glossary

Backdraft—an explosion of the gaseous byproducts of incomplete combustion caused by the sudden introduction of oxygen.

Borough Call—signal transmitted after a fifth alarm to bring additional apparatus and manpower from one borough of the city to another.

Cockloft—the area above the ceiling on the top floor and the underside of the roof. Usually an open space that runs the entire length and width of the building.

Company Numbers—For identification purposes, fire companies have always been designated by number. Since both New York City and the City of Brooklyn had paid fire departments with similar numbers, when the cities merged and became the Greater City of New York in 1898, Brooklyn and Queens Engine Companies added 100 to their number designation, so Brooklyn Engine 1 became Engine 101. Ladder companies in Brooklyn and Queens added 50, so Brooklyn Ladder 7 became Ladder 57. A second reorganization happened again in January of 1913 and the same method was used again. This time Engine 101 became Engine 201, and Ladder 58 became Ladder 108. Those numbers have remained the same to this day.

Department Orders—directives sent from headquarters to all companies. They cover everything from transfers, alarm assignments, retirements, promotions, appointments, announcements of death, the decisions of the commissioner as it relates to charges against members, the Roll of Merit and medal recipients, and any other department business.

Engine—apparatus for pumping water through hoses; early models were pulled by hand and then pumped by hand by teams of men, next came steam powered engines pulled by horses, until modern diesel and gasoline powered engines replaced the horse. Engine is also the generic name for the company of men assigned to such a unit. High Pressure Engine Companies were not equipped with regular pumping engines, but rather with hose wagons. They operated with excellent success in areas of the city served by the high-pressure hydrant system. They could stretch and operate several hoses from a single high-pressure hydrant.

Exposure—a place considered to be threatened by flames. This could be the building next door, to the rear, or even areas of the building already on fire. The FDNY numerically designates exposures in a clockwise fashion. #1 is to the front of the building on fire (usually the street). #2 is the building to the left. #3 is the building to the rear. #4 is the building to the right. The term "auto-exposure" is when fire travels within the same building. For example: flames from a lower floor window lapping up and igniting the floor above. Or fire burning through from floor to floor.

Foreman—the rank of captain. The commander of a company. An Assistant foreman is the rank of lieutenant.

Engineer of Steamer—a rank above fireman but below a company officer. This firefighter operated the steam engine while pumping at fires.

Hose line—a series of connected sections of hose used to deliver water at fire operations. Also called "handlines." These hoses were "stretched" to the point of operations. ("Stretched" originally meant to pull tight to avoid kinks that restrict water flow.) "Take Up" is an order originally given to take the hose up out of the street; it now refers to any company's finishing their work, securing their equipment and leaving the scene.

Ladder Company—a company of men assigned to hook & ladder (aerial ladders; tractor-trailers with tiller, rear-mounted aerials or modern-day tower ladders.) Their basic assignment is to ladder the building, force entry and search for trapped occupants. Also called a "Truck Company."

Loft—a building with high ceilings originally used as a commercial structure, manufacturing and storage.

Medal Day—the day set aside for the annual presentation of FDNY medals for valor. In early years, with only one medal to award, it was often held every two years. The ceremony was held at various locations in past years; City Hall is now the proffered location weather permitting.

Nozzle—the business end of a hose line. On handlines it allows the control of water flow by opening and closing a built-in valve. Nozzles on large caliber streams shape the flow of water for better reach.

Rescue Company—a company of specially trained firefighters that are assigned a special apparatus that carries tools for major emergencies, building collapses, accident extrications, underwater search and rescue, etc.

Roll of Merit—three years after the start of the paid fire department in New York City a method of recording the heroic deeds of the members was begun with the following resolution on November 22, 1868:

> *Resolved, that the secretary be instructed to open and keep under his personal supervision, a book of record, which shall be called, "The Roll of Merit M.F.D.," in which shall be entered the names of such officers and members of the department as may have, in the judgment of the board of commissioners, distinguished themselves in the discharge of their duties, with a full record of the act by which they have become entitled to the honor of being there enrolled. Opposite each name shall be stated the action taken by this Board in making rewards in each case.*

(The department became municipally controlled in 1870 with the creation of the Fire Department of the City of New York. FDNY. The fire commissioner would now be appointed by the mayor rather than the governor.)

Scaling ladder—a ladder built with a single beam in the middle. The ladders steps were fastened to the beam. Very easily handled by one man. Effective but dangerous method of continuing beyond the reach of conventional ladders.

Transom Window—a window directly above a doorway used to allow passage of air and light between rooms even when doors were shut. They were very effective in buildings with long narrow floor plans and windows in the front and rear only. They did however have a dangerous downside, when they failed and allowed fire and or smoke to extend from hallways into rooms.

Water Tower—apparatus used to deliver large caliber streams of water to upper stories. A piped waterway delivered water up a raised mast. They ranged in size from the original 1879 fifty-foot version with one nozzle, to the sixty-foot versions with two nozzles. The last water tower was purchased in 1930. They were placed out of service in 1957.

About the Author

Paul Hashagen began fighting fires in 1976. In 2003, he retired from the FDNY after 25 years of service, with 20 of those years in Rescue Company 1. He is a former Chief of the Freeport Fire Department and is still a member of Excelsior Hook & Ladder Company No. 1. Paul was a contributing editor for Firehouse Magazine for more than twenty years, writing numerous feature articles and the monthly historical column *Rekindles*. Paul was also a contributing author at *FireRescue* magazine. He has written several books and numerous stories on the history of the fire service, including *The Bravest 1865-2002*, the official history of the FDNY.

Paul has appeared several times as a fire historian on the History Channel and the A&E Network. He was a lead instructor at the FDNY Special Operations Command Technical Rescue School for ten years and taught at the FDNY Probationary Firefighters School. Paul has lectured across the country on firefighter rescue, and historical topics.

Paul was inducted into the *Firehouse Magazine* Hall of Fame, Class of 2017.

Visit his website at www.paulhashagen.com or on Facebook at Paul Hashagen-author.

Paul and his wife Joanne, live in Massapequa, New York.